FORM & DECORATION

FORM &

PETER THORNTON

DECORATION

INNOVATION IN THE DECORATIVE ARTS

1470-1870

HARRY N. ABRAMS, INC., PUBLISHERS

For Lena, *ma compagne*

Library of Congress Cataloging-in-Publication Data

Thornton, Peter, 1925–

Form & decoration: innovation in the decorative arts,
1470–1870/ Peter Thornton.

p. cm.

Includes index.

ISBN 0-8109-3340-3 (clothbound)

1. Decorative arts—Europe.   I. Title.

NK925.T47   1998

745´.094—dc21   98-3411

First published in Great Britain in 1998
by Weidenfeld & Nicolson

Published in 1998 by Harry N. Abrams, Incorporated, New
York. All rights reserved. No part of the contents of this
book may be reproduced without the written permission of
the publisher

The publishers gratefully acknowledge permission to
reproduce illustrative material: copyright holders are
credited in the picture captions throughout the book.

Designed by Harry Green

Printed and bound in Italy

Harry N. Abrams, Inc.

100 Fifth Avenue

New York, N.Y. 10011

www.abramsbooks.com

CONTENTS

ACKNOWLEDGEMENTS

This book has no bibliography, but three works were always beside me while I was writing it. One is in English, one in French and one in German.

The English book, *The Penguin Dictionary of Design and Designers*, first appeared in 1984. It is written by Simon Jervis, who was a colleague of mine in the Department of Furniture and Woodwork at the Victoria and Albert Museum; we worked together for many years. I do not think I could have written this without having had the invaluable tool that that book constitutes ready to hand. It contains an enormous amount of information in a compact form, and my readers may like to acquire a copy (it is inexpensive) because it complements what I have written and it would, I believe, enrich their reading of my own work.

The second book that I used, in French, is a huge work in three volumes. It has numerous illustrations, many of them in colour and is costly in consequence. It was edited by Alain Gruber and bears the title *L'art décoratif en Europe*. The volumes were published between 1992 and 1994, and an English translation has since appeared. Organised as a series of essays by experts on what the compilers have decided are fundamental motifs, much of the latest information on the subject has been included – as have extensive bibliographies. This work will be found in large libraries. It also complements what I have written, if only because it contains so many more illustrations than I could hope to provide, each accompanied by a lengthy caption.

The third work that I continually consulted was a small volume by an industrious German scholar, Günter Irmscher, with the title *Kleine Kunstgeschichte des Europäischen Ornaments seit der Frühe Neuzeit, 1400–1900*. [A small art-history of European ornament from early modern times] which was published at Darmstadt in 1984. Not only is it written in German, which few English-speaking people can read; it is also couched in a rather convoluted form of academic German that does not make for easy reading. Nevertheless, it is the result of painstaking work. It includes many of the essential facts (notably, of course, about design in Germany, a country that looms large in the present work) and carried many acute observations that I found helpful. It also have numerous useful illustrations and, again, an extensive bibliography. But unless it has since been translated into English, this work will mostly be of use to students in Germany.

I am deeply indebted to the authors of these books that I found so indispensable. Their help and inspiration has been immense.

I have had the good fortune to spend most of my working life in the Victoria and Albert Museum which houses the largest collection of western decorative art in the world. I would certainly not have been able to write the present book if I had not enjoyed this experience over a long period, working alongside colleagues who in many cases were the greatest experts in their fields, and who were remarkably generous with advice and information in their respective realms – for which I am much in their debt. I have particularly appreciated the facilities made available to me by the Departments of Metalwork, Woodwork, Ceramics, and of Prints and Drawings, as well as by the superb National Art Library with its incomparable holdings. I was also helped by many scholars working in foreign museums to whom I am likewise much beholden. The names of those who gave me especial help are listed below.

To the owners of the various objects that are illustrated in this book I must also extend my gratitude for giving me permission to publish items that are in their possession or in their care. Their generosity in this respect is credited at the end of the relevant captions.

Michael Dover's team at Weidenfeld undertook the book's rather complex production, and I am enormously grateful to its editor Caroline Knight, its designer Harry Green, its copy-editor Celia Jones, its picture researcher Sara Elliott and its indexer Barbara Hird.

A very personal debt of gratitude goes to my daughter Dora who has always encouraged me in my work and has drawn my attention on numerous occasions to matters that she thought would be useful to me – and usually were. Moreover, now that she has married Jeremy Warren, a scholar with whom she shares so many interests, the flow of helpful information has continued unabated.

The lady to whom I have dedicated this book is my constant companion and has been intimately involved in its preparation, for which bounty it is difficult to express adequate gratitude.

PETER THORNTON

UNITED KINGDOM
Stephen Astley
Ariane Bankes
Clare Browne
Robert Charleston
Frances Collard
Martin Durant
Richard Edgecombe
Robert Elwell
Wendy Fish
Philippa Glanville
John Hardy
Eileen Harris
Robin Hildyard
Louise Hofmann
Peter Hughes
Alistair Laing
Susan Lambert
John Mallet
Sarah Medlam
Lisa Monnas
Anthony North
Andrew Patrick
Paul Quarrie
Alan Rubin
Caroline Sargentson
Michael Snodin
Anna Maria Stapleton
Ann Thornton
Gillian Varley
Clive Wainwright
Jan van der Wateren

Jon Whiteley
Michael Wright
James Yorke

ITALY
Marzia Cataldi Gallo
Maddelena Trionfi
Honorati
Graziano Manni
Alessandra Motola
Molfino
Marco Spallanzani

FRANCE
Daniel Alcouffe
Pierre Arizzoli-
Clémentel
Sophie Baratte
Antoinette Baraev
Anne Dion-Tenenbaum
Peter Fuhring
Alain Gruber
Bernard Jacqué
Odile Nouvel
Jacqueline du Pasquier

GERMANY
Dorothée Feldmann
Ernst Götz
Georg Himmelheber
Käthi Klappenbach
Hans Ottomeyer
Michael Stürmer

SWEDEN
Anki Dahlin
Elisabet Hidemark
Ove Hidemark
Bengt Kylsberg
Arne Losman
Karin Sherri
Bo Vahlne

THE NETHERLANDS
Reinier Baarsen
Willemijn Fock

AUSTRIA
Christian Witt-Döring

DENMARK
Mogens Bencard
Tove Clemmensen
Jørgen Hein
Charlotte Paludan
Vibeke Woldby

UNITED STATES
Janet Byrne
Elaine Dee
Kathryn Hiesinger
William Rieder
Marilyn Symmes
Gillian Wilson

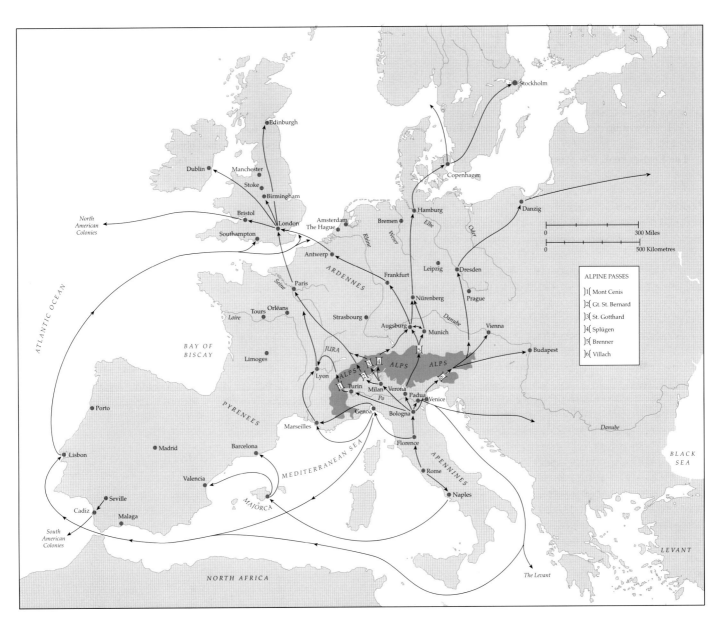

Stockholm

Edinburgh

Dublin   Manchester

Stoke

Birmingham

Bristol   London   Amsterdam
                                 The Hague
Southampton   Bremen   Hamburg   Danzig
                                 Antwerp   Leipzig
North
American   Paris   ARDENNES   Frankfurt   Dresden
Colonies   Prague
                    Seine   Nürenberg
          Tours   Orléans   Strasbourg   Augsburg   Vienna
          Loire   Munich
BAY OF   Danube
BISCAY   Limoges   JURA   Budapest
                                                      ALPS   ALPS   ALPS
                                         Lyon
                                              Turin   Milan Verona
                                                        Po   Padua
Porto   Genoa Bologna Venice
          PYRENEES   Marseilles
Madrid
          Barcelona   Florence   BLACK
                                                                                SEA
Lisbon   Rome
          MEDITERRANEAN SEA
          Valencia   APENNINES
                                                            Naples
Seville   MAJORCA
Cadiz
Malaga   Danube
South
American   LEVANT
Colonies
                    NORTH AFRICA   The Levant

ATLANTIC OCEAN

Copenhagen

Elbe   Weser   Rhine   Oder

0 ————————— 300 Miles
0 ————————— 500 Kilometres

ALPINE PASSES
)1(Mont Cenis
)2(Gt. St. Bernard
)3(St. Gotthard
)4(Splügen
)5(Brenner
)6(Villach

NOTE TO THE READER

I am grateful to my publisher for having provided a large number of illustrations to accompany my text. As I make points about specific designs, the reader will need to look closely at the relevant illustrations. It is very important that they should do so. Each reader will have a different way of analysing a design in order to understand how it is composed and to differentiate its composition elements, and it would be difficult to describe the process briefly, so I shall not try.

One feature of designs that does not generally receive sufficient attention, however, is that of their individual density, which can vary widely, from being open to being closely packed. Density varies greatly from one period to another, and even from one decade to the next. Students who are aware that density is an important criterion in analysing a design may consciously assess it whenever they are faced with a new one. They will look at the 'weight' of each element, the relevant tightness of scrollwork, the points at which curves have received their greatest emphases, and to what extent subsidiary decoration fills spaces between major features of the design. With practice the density of a design will impress itself on the eye almost subconsciously. In any case density needs to be taken into account when comparing the designs of one period with those of another.

I also want to draw attention to the way designers of printed patterns could offer alternative solutions in a single printed design by the expedient of illustrating the alternatives on either side of a vertical median or axis, making the resulting pattern look lop-sided, but it is of course nothing of the sort (e.g. Pl. 200). This was merely a device for offering two designs for the price of one. In rare cases four variations were offered by dividing the basic design into quarters and providing each with a variant pattern. This was most easily done where the basic design was within a roundel or a true square (e.g. Pl.58).

Measurements are given only where they are essential in order to comprehend the size of an object. They are first given in centimetres, then in inches. Distances are given in kilometres and then in miles.

The map above shows how the influence of Italian design spread across western Europe through the considerable barrier of the Alps and by long sea routes.

7

INTRODUCTION

This book is a straightforward account of how style developed in the decorative arts between 1470 and 1870. It is primarily written for students of design history, to remind them that the history of design is a long one, and to present examples from the vast repertoire of designs that this long history has generated. Anyone working in the field of design can, moreover, borrow examples from this enormous resource at will, either directly to use as models, or indirectly, as a source of inspiration, just as designers have so often done in the past. Because this book is essentially a primer in the subject, it has none of the trappings of scholarly writing, not even footnotes. Dates, on the other hand, loom large, although I have often been content to give the decade when an event took place rather than the precise year. I have also introduced a certain amount of geography into my narrative because I believe it matters.

In the field of design history, the period from about 1870 until our own time has been studied in depth most ably by Nicholas Pevsner and may others; in embarking on this volume I felt there was a need to provide a survey of earlier periods. However, although the history of design of course goes back much further, I thought four centuries would suffice for the present purposes. The year 1470 more or less marks the end of the Middle Ages and the start of the widespread adoption of *all'antico* ornament, derived from directly observed Antique Classical decoration, throughout the principal cities of Italy. The 1470s also saw the introduction of printing as a means of reproducing, among other things, illustrations of ornamental motifs on paper – a technological advance of extreme importance in the story I have to tell. Moreover, by this time Italians had acquired heightened expectations in the consumption of luxury goods. This ensured that there was a demand for goods of the type discussed in these pages.

It needs to be stressed that artistic innovation in the decorative arts takes place at the top end of the market. That is where discriminating people who have the wealth and leisure to exercise their taste and sense of what is fashionable are to be found in significant numbers. In this connection it is important to set aside any reluctance to admit that design and ornament filter downwards in the social structure, however unfashionable such a notion may seem at the moment; 'top people' (to use a phrase coined by the *The Times* in the 1960s) set fashions and others follow as best they can, if they so want.

Luxury goods tend to be made in cities of some size, often in the metropolis. In such large communities cultural and social stimulation are continually present. There are also likely to be banking and commercial facilities of many kinds, networks of family and trade relationships, and numerous interdependent systems of designers and artisans who have often worked together over long periods and who have learned to rely on each other. It is within such a framework that innovation can most easily take place; it never takes place in a vacuum. The solitary designer-hero, sitting on his own dreaming up new patterns, is nothing other than a fiction; there have been many great designers (many of them figure in our narrative) but all of them worked within a supportive system that nurtured, as well as benefited from, their talents – and usually paid them for their services. As conditions of the kind just outlined, conditions that are conducive to innovation in our field, are found in important cities, it seemed to me worth trying to organize the complex material that I want to present by focusing on the cities in which, during each phase in our historical and roughly chronological survey, significant innovation took place. This method has in some places been put under strain, but is probably no less satisfactory than any of the other acknowledged ways of imposing order on this complicated subject. A map (p. 7) is therefore provided to help the reader understand the relevant geography, as it is important to know where the chief cities lie, how far they are apart, how you reach them and what are the principal physical features of each, where this affects the issue.

It is unlikely that anyone, during the four centuries under review, has ever invented an entirely new design in any of the decorative arts, whether it be a shape or a decorative motif. Innovation invariably builds on what has gone before; it is therefore important to try and establish the date of designs in order to know which of several similar patterns came first. This is far from easy. There is, for a start, a great deal that we do not know about the past (for instance things that were taken for granted that a writer therefore did not think needed to be explained); and then of course the information that has come down to us is inevitably fragmentary because its survival has been so arbitrary.

The surviving information takes many forms. In our field there are the artefacts themselves, quite a few of which are dated or datable. The most prolific evidence, however, takes the form of drawings and prints on paper. Many of these are also dated. It is when they are not that difficulty creeps in. For example, we need to decide whether a certain drawing is an original project design or one made of an executed work afterwards and, if so, how long afterwards. An engraver may have produced the drawing in preparation for making a print on paper. There are many possibilities, and it gets even more complicated when one is dealing with actual prints. Not only were these often reissued; they were also copied, sometimes long after the original came off the press and sometimes even in a different city. However, the main thing that matters to us here is the date of the original design.

Many patterns were brought out to help other designers; it was a means of making money through sales (prints were not cheap) and could also be an advertisement for the designer who published them. In many cases, at any rate before 1800, he was a master-craftsman with his own business. By and large most prints are produced after the designer (or his employer, if he had one) had profited from the design; that is to say, prints were usually made some while after the design had first been executed – but how much later no doubt varied according to the circumstances. The idea was generally that the buyer of a print would derive inspiration from it, or might copy parts of it – certain motifs, for instance. '*Nem jeder draus was Ihn gefellt*', wrote Christoph Jamnizter in the preface to a pattern-book of designs he published at Nürnberg in 1610; 'let each take from it what appeals to him'. Objects or ornaments slavishly copied from a print in its entirety are really quite rare (they often turn out to be fakes, in fact); prints mostly served as guidance for producing details.

Unless a designer had a measure of financial control over a business that was to use or publish his designs, be it a craft workshop or a printselling establishment, he rarely had much say in what was manufactured or published. That decision rested with the business head of the firm who, as a result, could often exert a certain amount (sometimes a great deal) of influence on the course of the history of design through the commissions that he placed with a designer. He could stipulate that he wanted more designs of one sort rather than another, for instance, and the greater the number of prints of a given design that he issued, the more influence that design was likely to have.

There were many other classes of people who could influence the course of design history and I need not enumerate them all here. The client purchasing a unique individual object of course often had a considerable say in its appearance. Upholsterers and other contractors who were admitted to the houses of fashionable people and noticed what was new could often tell other house-owners about novel features, which might then be reproduced for the new client; such contractors acted as cross-fertilisers of fashionable taste and thus influenced the way things developed. Fashion, which thrives on innovation, moves in strange ways. Take, for instance, the case of Monsieur de Langlée who was the son of a lady's maid in the service of a Queen of France, Anne d'Autriche, who died in 1666. According to Madame de Maintenon, the mistress of Louis XIV, writing in 1707, this man grew rich from buying houses in Paris with money won at the gaming tables. He apparently became very influential at the French court late in the 17the century in matters of taste. He advised the elegant Madame de Montespan on her clothes and even sometimes had them made for her. Princes of the blood consulted him on how to furnish their houses, and even Madam de Maintenon indicates that she sought his advice. Was he really as influential as she makes him seem?

In my survey of the changing styles over four centuries, I have pointed out what I take to be the pre-eminent line of development.

There were of course subsidiary lines in use concurrently at various stages. I mention these where they seem of sufficient importance. One also has to take into account the matter of tradition and conservatism in design, which meant that patterns that had been fashionable, sometimes several decades earlier, continued in use alongside new fashions, even in the field of luxury wares. There is rarely any need to point this out in our present survey, but the effect of tradition and a resulting conservatism is to be seen here and there, and its underlying presence should always be borne in mind.

Other writers on ornament have spent much time analysing patterns and tracing their putative origins. I have adopted an altogether less precise method, finding that patterns evolve and often blend with others. Describing the result is too complicated so I urge my readers to use their eyes and look at the relevant illustrations; they are far more eloquent than any descriptions of mine can ever be. Design is after all a visual matter.

Finally, I would also like to urge the reader not to be too judgmental about the aesthetic merits of individual patterns. Tastes change, but I have learned from my long career in museums not to be surprised when they sometimes change from something I like into something I find ugly. One then has to say to oneself that people at the time must have liked it or no one would have invented it. After all, in studying the tastes of our forefathers it is their taste that matters, not ours.

PETER THORNTON
London, January 1996

CHAPTER 1

FLORENCE AND VENICE

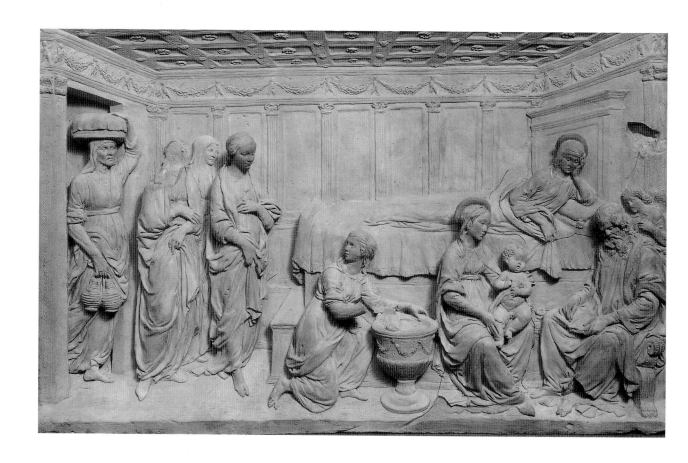

1470-1510

In almost every corner of Italy there are reminders of that country's Classical past. More or less intact Roman buildings still stand in several places; many more have been incorporated into later buildings and thus still serve a purpose. Impressive ruins are to be seen at every hand, and artefacts of all kinds, sometimes of great aesthetic merit, come to light as ploughmen till the soil and builders excavate foundations and lay drains. Roman civilisation was impressive in its day and has never gone unnoticed since the Roman Empire finally fell apart in the 5th century AD.

In the Middle Ages, while it was recognised that Roman civilisation had been remarkable in many ways, admiration for it was tempered by an awareness that the Empire had been a heathen society of which the Medieval Christian Church could not really approve. Even so, Medieval builders would sometimes record motifs to be seen on Classical monuments and such motifs quite often crept into the repertoire of Gothic artists.

Many factors combined to lead Italian artists to develop a style that was based on the observation of Classical ornament, adapted to modern purposes and with ingredients of their own time freely added to suit individual preferences. They spoke of this formula as being *all'antico*, in the Antique taste; we call it 'the Renaissance style'. It gradually replaced the style that

had previously found favour, the Gothic, which had come to be regarded as a foreign import and therefore un-Italian. By the 1460s a leading Florentine architect could advocate the rejection of this, as he called it, 'German style' which he suggested had been introduced into Italy by 'barbarians' in the distant past, and he urged that a style that was Classical in manner was far more appropriate and 'Italian'. Several important Italian artists (e.g. Donatello) had begun to introduce Classical forms and ornament into their creations in the early decades of the 15th century, but this practice did not become really widespread until the 1470s.

The chief assemblage of Roman ruins lay in the city of Rome itself; and fragments of architectural decoration, statues, coins and much else were continually coming to light, and with increasing frequency, as more people became interested in these relics of the Classical past. In the mid-15th century Rome was little more than a market town where the Pope lived; it had no industry and little commerce. But it was a place to which pilgrims flocked because it was a holy city.

Very different, on the other hand, was the city of Florence which lies some 300 kilometres (190 miles) to the north on the way to Bologna, Milan and Venice. Florence enjoyed the most flourishing economy of any Italian city during the 14th and 15th centuries. Its

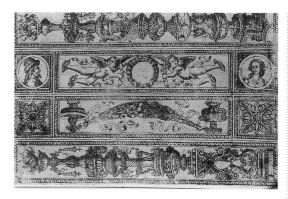

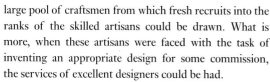

Pl. 3 A sheet of paper printed with characteristic Renaissance motifs intended to be cut out and pasted on to a wooden frame or some other object requiring such decoration. One of several sheets thought to have been produced in a Florentine workshop during the 1470s, perhaps that of Francesco Roselli; an early example of a mechanical process being used for series-production purposes. Several of the most characteristic Renaissance motifs are represented – the candelabrum, the wreath held up by flying cherubs, profile heads, rosettes and festoons. *Graphische Sammlung Albertina, Vienna.*

Pl. 4 Large tabernacle-frame forming part of the furnishings of the church of Santo Spirito planned in the 1480s. Note the candelabra ornament on the pilasters, the *rinceaux* 'scrolls' in the frieze, and the boldly projecting cornice. Gilded decoration on a blue ground. Made about 1510–12 in the workshops of Baccio d'Angolo, who fitted up many of the finest churches and best rooms in Florence at the time. *Santo Spirito, Florence*

Pl. 5 Early Italian print of ornament suitable for a circular object such as the back of a mirror-frame, the lid of a box or a pottery dish. The ornament is in the Renaissance style of the 1470s. Dia. 22 cm (8⅝in.) *Graphische Sammlung Albertina, Vienna*

exceptional commercial success was mainly built on its industries, and this success was to some extent shared by such nearby Tuscan cities as Siena and Prato. Tuscan merchants had close commercial links with most of Europe; not a few had offices or agents in Barcelona, Valencia, Marseilles, London, Bruges, Antwerp, Châlons and Rheims. In the wake of commercial enterprise, moreover, they offered banking facilities. And, quite often, along with Tuscan trade followed articles that possessed notable aesthetic qualities and were the produce of highly accomplished artisans. When Tuscan artists and artisans adopted the Classical manner, therefore, examples of work in this novel style were carried wherever Tuscan business was being done. So, although the original sources of inspiration of the new style could best be seen in Rome, it was in examples of Tuscan art that the new style principally manifested itself. Well before the 1470s Tuscan architects, goldsmiths, sculptors, painters and specialist workers in wood had become celebrated throughout Italy, and even further afield, and people of standing elsewhere often took pains to secure the services of a Tuscan to oversee important enterprises, particularly in the fields of architecture and interior decoration. The same people then tended to acquire furnishings and other works of decorative art from Florence for their new enterprises; this in turn reinforced the Tuscan message (Pls. 8 and 16).

Decades of prosperity had bred in Florence an elite that was not only wealthy and wished to display its wealth in a relatively discreet but telling manner, but also tended to be discerning, even highly discriminating, in cultural matters. The critical judgement this elite exercised acted as a powerful stimulus on artists and artisans who became increasingly skilful as the century wore on. Since Florence was an industrial city, there was also a large pool of craftsmen from which fresh recruits into the ranks of the skilled artisans could be drawn. What is more, when these artisans were faced with the task of inventing an appropriate design for some commission, the services of excellent designers could be had.

In the early Renaissance period the role of designer in the applied arts was often filled by goldsmiths, both in Italy and elsewhere. This was because silver and gold were expensive materials, the working of which could best be entrusted to men of exceptional skill, less likely than others to waste the precious material and commonly possessed of superior intelligence that made them better at mastering the intricate problems of design. Unfortunately, because very little Florentine secular silver of the 15th century has survived (it has almost all been melted down and refashioned by later generations, as of course often happened elsewhere), we really know very little about goldsmith-designers' works in their own materials. But we see the results of their intervention in many other works of art. Antonio Pollaiuolo was trained as a goldsmith, for instance, but was a designer of exquisite embroideries and splendid armour. He was also a painter and an accomplished sculptor, being invited to Rome to design and execute the bronze tomb-covers of Popes Sixtus IV (Pl. 16) and Innocent VII. The highly accomplished sculptor Benedetto da Maiano, who was himself trained as a woodworker and was a brilliant carver, ran one of the chief woodworking workshops in the city, where much of the panelling and furniture for the finest new rooms in Florence were made in the third quarter of the 15th century. Benedetto employed the goldsmith Tommaso Fineguerra as a designer of inlaid decoration, a role in which he was succeeded by Alessio Baldovinetti, a

Pl. 6 A Classical border pattern of paired stylized leaves, adapted for use on the broad rim of a *maiolica* plate of the 1470s. In the centre is an early and tentative attempt to introduce a pictorial subject as decoration. From Urbino, a major centre of *maiolica* production. *Reproduced by permission of the Trustees of the Wallace Collection, London*

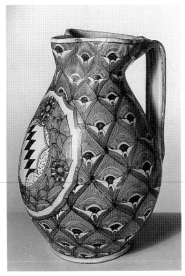

Pl. 7 *Maiolica* jug of the 1480s with a circular panel on its front, decorated with a family's coat-of-arms within a Classical wreath. Made at Caffaggiolo, a Medici family villa near Florence. Height 36 cm (14¹/₅in.) *Victoria and Albert Museum, London (Mus. no. 2602–1856)*

painter by training. The terracotta relief by Benedetto da Maiano illustrated in Pl. 1 shows how a room produced by his firm will have looked.

The other city that plays an important role in our story is Venice. Like Florence, Venice was a city where many industries flourished. It was also a rich city where patronage was assured, if rather conservative. During the early Renaissance, Venice was not a centre of major artistic innovation to anything like the same extent as Florence. The Venetian contribution to the dissemination of styles and information lay in its energetic exploitation of the new technique of printing texts and images on paper. Moreover, their exceptionally well-developed communications system enabled the Venetians to disseminate such sheets speedily and relatively cheaply across Europe.

The Venetian Republic was the only Italian state that had a colonial empire. It stretched down the Adriatic with a string of ports in Greece, reaching out to Crete and eventually, also to Cyprus. It had agents all over the Mediterranean, in Turkey and around the Black Sea. Much Venetian trade therefore travelled by sea; Venetian ships were excellent, and her sailors had extensive maritime experience. Bulk cargoes moved in heavy capacious vessels, and lightweight consignments were carried in swift galleys that made regular runs all over the Mediterranean and even out into the Atlantic on their way to Bruges, Antwerp, Southampton and London. Venetian trade also travelled by land – westwards across the Lombard plains to Milan and beyond; eastwards into Croatia and Slovenia; and northwards up through the Alpine passes into Germany. Long before 1470 Venice had grown rich, not so much from its own manufactures – it was noted particularly for woven silks, glassware and worked leather – as by imports from the East. Spices, dyes, and drugs came from the Far East (as did occasionally a piece of porcelain or some other curiosity); from the Near East came silks, cottons, rugs, glassware and fine metalwork. A high proportion of these goods remained in Venice, but much was carried onwards to other parts of Europe – along with Venetian goods, which could include books and other printed material, some of which were decorated, from towards the end of the 15th century, in the novel *all'antico* manner.

Although the printing of text and ornaments on paper was invented in Germany in the mid-15th century, it quickly spread south to Venice, where German printers were established by 1470. Ornament was sometimes added to printed pages, especially to title-pages. The decoration of bookbindings could also be a vehicle for transmitting novel patterns (Pls. 48, 51, 53). Printers in Florence and Rome were also active at this time (e.g. Pl. 3), but Venice was the chief centre of the book-trade in Europe: it was almost twice as productive as Paris, the next most important centre.

One of the most influential of all early printed books with engravings was the *Hypnerotomachia Polifili*, a romantic fantasy, set against a court background, which was published in Venice in 1499. Liberally illustrated with depictions of decorative art objects (Pl. 15), architecture and scenes in which Classical features abound, the book was a rich source of inspiration for those who got sight of a copy and were interested in such matters. The author's name was Francesco Colonna, and though he is usually equated with a Dominican friar of that name living in Venice, it has been suggested that he may in fact have been a member of the famous Roman princely family of the same name, a man who would presumably have been far more familiar with courtly settings – and the courtly literature from which this work springs – than would have been even the most worldly of friars.

Having sketchily set the scene against which the development of the Renaissance style took place, let us now look at some of the forms that early *all'antico* ornament took. A motif of Classical origin dear to Italian artists of the early Renaissance period was the candelabrum (plural, candelabra), which was derived from a

Pl. 8 Illuminated manuscript commissioned in Florence in 1488 by Matthias Corvinus, King of Hungary, for his splendid library at Buda on the Danube. Richly decorated with Renaissance ornament, this work attracted much attention among people of culture who had access to the royal library and its treasures; it was second only in importance to that in the Vatican. Before printing became widespread such illuminated pages were important vehicles for the transmission of ornamental styles. By Monte di Giovanni. *The Pierpont Morgan Library, New York (MS. 496. f. 32)*

form of candle-holder on a tall stand (Pl. 2). The motif is normally elongated and was therefore particularly well suited to the decoration of pilaster-panels (Pls. 4 and 10), but it was occasionally made squat so as to fit a square panel. It was always organised symmetrically, with scrolling arms, foliage or other projecting forms being rendered mirror-wise on either side of its vertical median. It was an infinitely variable form of ornament, as late 15th-century designers were quick to realise (Pls. 9 and 11). So useful was this formula to designers that several suites of engravings showing compositions of this kind were published very early in the 16th century (Pl. 13), while versions of it were reproduced as ornament in printed books three or four decades before that (Pl. 12).

The candelabrum was prominent among the forms that Florentine artists had begun to introduce into their sculptural reliefs and paintings by the middle of the century. The new manner of painting and the new form of sculpture evolved by Florentine artists at this time were of such exceptional interest to artists in other parts of Italy that decorative details of this kind were carefully noted wherever they appeared, and often imitated – thus spreading the style still further.

Foremost among those who were keen to learn more about fresh developments of this nature was the young Andrea Mantegna, who became one of the most brilliant painters of the Renaissance period. Mantegna was working in Padua when the already celebrated

Florentine sculptor Donatello was also in that city, engaged on an important commission in the principal church where those who were interested could easily have seen it. Donatello's work certainly cannot have gone unnoticed by Mantegna and the two men were probably acquainted. Donatello's art rested heavily on close observation of Antique sculpture, which also greatly interested Mantegna, and Donatello's example

clearly influenced the younger artists (admirers, followers, assistants) who in turn were quick to imitate his style, particularly the precise manner in which he represented Classical architectural ornament.

In 1466 Mantegna visited Florence from Milan, where he can hardly have avoided meeting Antonio Pollaiuolo, an extremely important character who, as a goldsmith, sculptor, painter and medallist, was involved in so many Florentine artistic enterprises. He was also fascinated by the new technique of printing on paper, and indeed he and Mantegna were the first artists to produce representations of their own paintings as images printed on paper. This enabled them to disseminate reproductions of their own work to a far wider public than would otherwise have been possible. While Mantegna was in Florence, Pollaiuolo was

Pl. 9 Miniature painted by Giovanni Francesco Maineri in the late 15th century, either in Ferrara or Mantua. Candelabra are prominent among the Renaissance ornaments. Shields with coats-of-arms are suspended on the walls near the bottom.
By permission of the British Library (Add. ms. 50002 folio 13r)

Pl. 10 Fine example of a candelabrum ornament on a pilaster in a painting of 1501 by Pinturicchio in a Tuscan church. A *maiolica* vase of high quality stands on the window-sill.
S. Maria Maggiore, Spello (detail)

Pl. 11 Bronze plaquette (height 6.9 cm [2³/₄in.]) of about 1505 with the Virgin and Child enthroned, flanked by Classical decoration including a flimsy variant of the candelabrum motif in the style of Nicoletto de Modena. Such plaquettes were mostly based on the carving to be seen on Antique gems; they were a favourite form of expression in the Classical taste among Renaissance sculptors and much prized by collectors at the time. By Moderno, a Veronese sculptor who also worked in Venice, Ferrara and Mantua, and may have spent some while in Rome.
Samuel H. Kress Collection, © 1996 Board of Trustees, National Gallery of Art (1957.14.288 (Sc))

may likewise be said to owe something to Florentine example, if only indirectly.

One of Mantegna's followers, Zoan Andrea, moved from Mantua to Milan in 1475 and there collaborated with the talented miniature-painter Giovanni Pietro da Birago, who had himself also once worked under Mantegna and was now in the service of the Duchess Bona Sforza, a member of the ruling family in Milan. Between 1505 and 1515 these two artists brought out a suite of delicately engraved candelabra designs of great complexity, which immediately became immensely influential (Pl. 13), particularly in France, with which country Milan had very close links. Nicoletto de Modena and Giovan Antonio da Brescia were two other followers of Mantegna who helped to spread information about his style, as we shall see in Chapter 2.

An early direct result of Florentine interest in the printing process is to be seen in Pl. 3. This is a sheet of ornaments that can be cut out and pasted on to objects, or around objects as frames. Few such sheets survive, but the practice may have been more common than is generally supposed. The application of cut-out prints, coloured before being pasted in place, has been a constant stand-by of Italian furniture makers, and in more recent times has been given the name of *arte povera* [inexpensive art]. Series production methods were in fact quite extensively used in Florentine industries during the 15th century, notably in the making of relief tabernacle images of the Virgin and Child or the

probably still refining the technique involved in this process and Mantegna may well have learned the printmaking techniques he adopted on his return to Mantua directly from the Florentine artist. Thus, the printed designs made by Mantegna's followers

Pl. 12 Decorated page from a late 15th-century book published by the brothers Giovanni and Gregorio de Gregoriis, prominent printers in Venice whose books were circulated widely, showing striking Renaissance motifs in white on a black ground, which will have impressed those into whose hands such a book came. The same decoration was used for other Gregoriis books in the 1490s.

Pl. 13 Candelabra motifs from a set of twelve published in Milan by Giovanni Pietro da Birago and his associate Zoan Andrea, between 1505 and 1515. Each unit offers a wealth of possibilities for designers to borrow and adapt elements to suit their own requirements.
The Metropolitan Museum, New York;
Harris Brisbane Dick Fund, 23.39.7

Pl. 14 Back-cloth of an embroidered throne-canopy, of room height, that probably belonged to Bona Sforza, who married the King of Poland in 1518. It is likely to be from a leading Milanese professional embroidery workshop. The style is close to that of Giovanni Pietro da Birago (see Pl. 13), and he is known to have worked for Bona Sforza. He, or a follower, could have designed this superb object. The arms are later.
The Royal Swedish Collections, The Royal Palace, Stockholm

Pl. 15 A tripod table-stand illustrated in the *Hypnerotomachia Polifili*, published in Venice in 1499, which contains several representations of high-class furnishings in the Classical taste. This tripod was made of ebony and supported a circular table-top (not shown). The book is a romantic fantasy of courtly life but there is no reason to suppose that the illustrations show objects that are totally imaginary.
By courtesy of the Trustees of Sir John Soane's Museum, London

Pl. 16 The bronze figure of Pope Sixtus IV on his tomb in St Peter's, Rome, which bears the proud inscription 'The work of the Florentine Antonio Pollaiuolo, famous in silver, gold, painting, bronze, 1493.' This versatile artist also designed embroidery, fine specimens of which are represented on the pillows. The rich woven silk material of the mattress-cover is also likely to have been a Florentine product.
St Peter's, Rome

Crucifixion for those who could not afford a stone relief. They were reproduced in terracotta, stucco or an early form of *papier mâché* from moulds and must have been a lucrative side-line in the larger sculpture work-shops.

Italian Renaissance designers also made great use of ornamental forms known to the French as *rinceaux* (the English have no single word for it), a linear arrangement of spiralling scrolls of foliage where the scrolls alternate from clockwise to anti-clockwise. The Florentine frame shown in Pl. 4 has candelabra ornaments on the pilasters and *rinceaux* along the top, below the massive cornice. Scrolling foliage was a common form of decoration in Classical times and was in turn eagerly chosen for use by Renaissance designers; it was never, in fact, out of fash-ion and can be found in both Romanesque and Gothic art. A charming *rinceau* pattern is to be seen in Pl. 5, a composition that would be suitable for goldsmiths fash-ioning the cover of a box for a lady's dressing-table, or a potter faced with decorating a dish. The back of a silver mirror made in Florence about 1490 for Queen Isabella

of Spain (who financed Columbus's transatlantic voyages) has a very similar pattern. Linear ornament can of course be taken round in a circle to form borders, as Pls. 5 and 6 show.

The term *maiolica* was given to a class of pottery (a tin-glazed earthenware), usually large and showy and often extremely handsome, that had been imported into Italy from Valencia, in the Spanish province of Aragon, since the early 15th century. It was costly and a great deal more refined than anything then being made in Italy. Wealthy Italians must frequently have displayed it in polite surroundings, for example on sideboards in rooms where they dined. The many large Spanish-made dishes of this ware often bear Italian coats-of-arms, which can only be seen to advantage when the vessels are displayed upright, standing on their rims, in the way silver dishes were also shown, as evidence of a family's social status. One could not introduce the products of Italian potteries into grand settings until the 1470s or

later because they were not sufficiently elegant or technically accomplished. By the end of the century, however, Italian potters had succeeded in emulating the refined body and stylish decoration of the Spanish wares, and discriminating Italians were beginning to buy the indigenous product; it was no longer something that was best confined to the kitchen.

The bold decoration of the early kinds of refined Italian *maiolica* was gradually adapted to suit the stan-dard forms that this pottery took. The rotund jug, for instance, such a common form in Italy in the second half of the 15th century, was often painted with a wreath or similar framing for a motif (a profile head, a symbol, a coat-of-arms) on the belly below the lip (Pl. 7). Likewise, dishes with wide rims lent themselves well to decoration with *rinceaux* or other formalised Renais-sance foliate ornament on the broad, circular flat sur-face (Pls. 6 and 19). Although the production of such refined wares only constituted a very small part of the total output of Italian potteries, well before the end of the century those that achieved such distinction were being decorated with fully assimilated Renaissance ornaments adapted to the relatively few shapes that came off the potters' wheels. Between the 1490s and the 1530s, pictorial subjects were depicted on some espe-cially fashionable pieces produced within the orbit of Florentine artistic creativity (at Siena, Urbino, Castel Durante, Gubbio, Pesaro, Faenza, Deruta and Florence itself), in painting techniques that had been developed to a very high level and could produce extremely subtle effects. The same subtlety could of course also be applied to the rendering of purely ornamental decora-tion and, by about 1500, immensely pleasing formally ornamented pottery was being produced; this has been unjustly overshadowed in modern estimation by the contemporary pictorial wares from the same workshops. A new range of pigments suitable for painting on *maiolica* was developed at this time and greatly added to the delightful effects created by these wares.

Another craft-technique that exacted a decorative repertoire of its own was that of weaving on a loom, and it is primarily the weaving of silk materials that con-cerns us here. This was a field in which Italian work-shops excelled; and they had been producing superb materials since the 14th century. A pattern devised in the Near East during the Middle Ages, and popular in its early forms in Europe during the Gothic period (both in Near Eastern and European weaves), was the so-called 'pomegranate pattern' (Pl. 17). It reached a high level of perfection during the second half of the 15th century and was by then being produced in such great quantities, with infinite minor variations, that it became the most characteristic pattern for grand silks of the Renaissance period. It was produced as a sumptuous velvet with two, or even three, heights of pile and the inclusion of much gold thread in its make-up; it was

Pl. 17 Woven silk material decorated with a 'pomegranate pattern', probably of Venetian origin, worn by the Virgin Mary in a painting by Carlo Crivelli dated 1482. Two other silks of similar character are used as a foot-cloth and for the hanging behind her.
Pinacoteca di Brera, Milan (detail)

Pl. 18 Calf-leather book-cover made in Nürnberg about 1495, the central panel decorated with a 'pomegranate pattern' inspired by those seen on Italian woven silks. Alongside are panels of Gothic ornament. Executed for the publisher Anton Koberger.
Courtesy of Sotheby's, London

Pl. 19 A delightful *maiolica* dish, made at Deruta, near Siena, about 1520, showing Classical *rinceaux* patterns on the rim and on the girl's stockings. The main *rinceaux* spring from bouquets of fruit, including small clusters of grapes.
Musée National Adrien-Dubouché, Limoges

also produced as a silk damask and as silks of less complex structure. Moreover, this basic formula was to remain a mainstay of European high-class weaving right through to the 19th century. In the 15th century such materials were chiefly produced in Venice, although other important weaving centres, for example Florence, also seem to have woven them. This pattern was also useful to other trades requiring ornament that could be applied to flat surfaces. The makers of gilt leather, who produced a material that was used for wall hangings to great decorative effect, adopted textile patterns for their product. At this period fine gilt leather suitable for making up into wall-hangings was still chiefly being made in Spain although some Italian cities could boast of gilt-leather production in the early 16th century – Bologna, Ferrara, probably Rome and presumably Venice. Another craft that found the pomegranate pattern useful was that of bookbinding (Pl. 18).

The loom imposes severe limitations on the kind of pattern that can be produced by weaving; the art of embroidery suffers from no such restriction. Indeed, one can execute with a needle almost anything that a draughtsman can produce with a pencil, if one has the skill, and people used to speak of 'painting with a needle'. Italian high-class embroidery, executed in professional workshops, was frequently exquisite both in design and execution especially that made in Florence in the late 15th century. But, around 1500, Milan began to overtake Florence as the chief centre for professional embroidery, and the back-cloth of a throne-canopy shown in Pl. 14 is a magnificent example of an exceptionally ambitious product of Milanese needlework dating from the first quarter of the 16th century. It was almost certainly made for the Duchess Bona Sforza, possibly on the occasion of her marriage to the King of Poland in 1518.

Conspicuous consumption distinguished Italy from other countries during the Renaissance, and it was consumption by an elite that lived in cities and whose lifestyle created a demand for luxury goods on an ever-increasing scale, both in terms of quantity and quality. Among these luxury goods were many that had been created as works of art, and these came in great variety – imposing furniture, superb silk materials suitable for clothes or room decoration, paintings that were generally an integral part of a furnishing scheme (notably in grand bedchambers), decorated books and small sculptures for the rich scholar's study, exquisite silver for sumptuous display on ceremonial occasions, striking jewellery and delightful objects to lie on a dressing-table.

New markets, new classes of goods, new techniques, much competition – all acted as a powerful stimulus on artists and artisans who became increasingly skilful and innovative. Of the two cities best able to meet these new demands, Florence and Venice, Florence was by far the most innovative centre, and she set a pattern in all branches of the visual arts that all Italy followed.

CHAPTER 2

ROME AND FLORENCE

Pl. 22 *Maiolica* plate of about 1510–20, made at Faenza, decorated on its broad rim with grotesques in the style of Pinturicchio, which may have been transmitted to the potteries at Faenza and Urbino by the painter Girolamo Genga who had assisted Pinturicchio in Siena and moved to Urbino at about this time. Dia. 26 cm (10¼ in.) *Victoria and Albert Museum, London* (Mus. no. C.2088–1910)

1510–1580

Pl. 20 Grotesque pattern engraved by Nicoletto da Modena (his name is on two labels at the top) published between 1500 and 1515, representing the first wave of such printed ornament. Its derivation from the candelabrum-formula is evident, and the crowded and somewhat incoherent character of early grotesque patterns is well exemplified here.
The British Museum, London

Pl. 21 The unreal character of grotesques is also well illustrated by this engraving attributed to Giovan Antonio da Brescia, probably dating from the early years of the 16th century. Only the right-hand side of what was clearly a symmetrical composition is shown. Note the strange beasts at the top, and the way a ram's head sprouts a trumpet-stand for a winged angel bearing a flaming torch on his head, and how a flaming grenade and a triangular altar swing from cords above.

We have seen that the candelabrum was the first obviously novel motif to be adopted by those who wanted to revive the Classical repertoire of ornament. The candelabrum did, however, have its limitations because it was really only suitable for decorating tall vertical panels, such as those on the fronts of pilasters (Pls. 2, 4 and 10). Related to the candelabrum in the Classical repertoire was a formula that could, on the other hand, be adapted endlessly to cover almost any space, shape or form – walls, ceilings or panels, plates, vessels or boxes. The formula was essentially a candelabrum spread out sideways so as to join up with the branches of a similar expanded candelabrum nearby (Pls. 21, 23 and 28) but the formula had many variants and the common origin of these patterns is not always immediately evident.

These expanded patterns are known as grotesques. Their name derives from the grottoes and caves (*grotte*, in Italian) in which these mainly painted patterns were found, among the ruins of ancient Rome. They must have been known throughout the Middle Ages, but they were not seen as worth copying for modern use until the last quarter of the 15th century. One of the first authorities on architecture and decoration to recommend the adoption of these lively but strange compositions was the celebrated Sienese architect Francesco di Giorgio,

who wrote a treatise on architecture in about 1480. It may be no coincidence that among the first generation of artists who sought to imitate Classical grotesque ornament most were Tuscans and many came from Siena.

One of the earliest depictions of grotesque ornament is in a fresco by Ghirlandaio in Santa Maria Novella in Florence, dating from the late 1480s, where such patterns are represented as being inlaid into the wood panelling – closely observed and probably an example of the work of Benedetto da Maiano's workshop (see p. 12). The important Sienese artist Pinturicchio was called to Rome by Pope Alexander VI (formerly Cardinal Rodrigo Borgia) to decorate the Sistine Chapel and the Pope's splendid apartment in the Vatican Palace. Some of the compositions he painted in the Borgia Apartment during the early 1490s betray an extensive knowledge of Antique Classical ornament. On his return to his native city, Pinturicchio decorated a library in the Cathedral for Cardinal Francesco Piccolomini in 1502, which was to be executed, as the contract for the work states, with designs 'which are today called grotesques'. The grotesques in Siena were quite like the Antique originals but the forms were more colourful, and were rounded out with shading '*chiaroscuro*' that made them more fleshy. The style of the Piccolomini grotesques was echoed on some *maiolica* vessels made at Faenza around 1510 (Pl. 22).

Pl. 23 Grotesque decoration carried out under Raphael's direction in the *loggetta* at the Vatican in 1516. Probably executed by Giovanni da Udine, who had made a close study of antique Classical mural decoration, notably some being excavated during the last years of the 15th century in the ruins of Nero's palace in Rome, to which the present composition on a white ground adheres closely.
The Vatican Museum, Rome

From 1485 to 1515 grotesque patterns were being devised by a number of artists throughout Italy, but the source of inspiration was principally to be found among the ruins of ancient Rome. From 1480 onwards, successive popes invited a shoal of distinguished artists to Rome in their efforts to make the Christian capital as magnificent as possible. These artists worked in the constant presence of the remains of the still famous Antique civilisation that they were in many ways trying to imitate, and it is not surprising that it was particularly through these men that an understanding of this striking and useful form of Classical ornament spread across Italy, although the availability of printed grotesque patterns from about 1505 onwards also helped the process. Two followers of Mantegna were influential in this last respect. Nicoletto da Modena had worked in Modena and Ferrara before moving to Rome, where he was established by 1507. Between 1500 and 1512 he published many engravings of Classical decora-

tions including candelabra designs (Pl. 20). Another artist from the Mantegna circle at Mantua who helped to spread *all'antico* patterns was Giovan Antonio da Brescia, who went to Rome in 1515, perhaps after having spent some while back in his native Brescia. He produced designs very like those composed by Zoan Andrea (and Giovanni Pietro da Birago), which is hardly surprising, since all three were pupils or followers of Mantegna (Pl. 21 and see Pl. 13).

As we can see from Pls. 20 and 21, the grotesques of this early stage were usually crowded and somewhat confused, and there was a tendency to accentuate the non-Classical elements and to make the fantasy world of this formula even more fantastic.

Alexander VI's two successors, Julius II and Leo X, were even more energetic patrons of innovation in the fields that concern us here. Julius invited Raphael to Rome in 1508 to decorate important rooms in the Vatican, a task that continued under Leo, who gave Raphael responsibility for the rebuilding of St Peter's (an enormous undertaking) after the death of the great architect Bramante in 1514. Furthermore, Raphael was appointed warden of the antiquities of Rome, reflecting an awareness in ruling circles of the vulnerability of these ancient monuments at a time of rapid expansion and the need to protect evidence of the city's former glory, which was invaluable as source material for architects and artists setting out to re-establish a magnificent city in emulation of the ancient Rome of the Caesars.

This much more serious attitude to the antiquities of Rome encouraged architects and scholars to record the monuments, often with considerable precision and, on many occasions, at considerable personal risk, as they measured details at the top of tall columns or deep in unstable buried ruins – the 'grottoes'. This intense interest in every detail was to have far-reaching consequences for the art of design in Europe.

One of the ancient monuments that generated particular excitement in Raphael's day was part of the ruined palace of the Roman emperor Nero which was being excavated from the 1480s onwards. The walls and ceilings of several important rooms were found to be decorated with a network of grotesque patterns that fired the imagination of the artists who saw them (several signed their names on the walls during their visit), and imitations – now rather careful ones – began to be painted on the interior walls and ceilings of important parts of new Roman buildings.

It was in a small cubicle in a new part of the Vatican, in a sauna made for a cardinal, that the 'new' form of grotesque ornament was first to be seen (1516–17). Leading to the sauna is a passageway, open to one side with a view towards St Peter's. This '*loggetta*' (or small *loggia*) was decorated, also in 1516, with grotesques painted on a white ground – in close imitation of some in Nero's palace – which were, in turn, to be much

Pl. 24 Grotesques in the style evolved under Raphael's direction, engraved by Agostino Veneziano in Rome in the late 1520s, although the fact that his initials on the small shield on the left are reversed suggests this impression is a later 16th-century copy. More clearly organized than the earliest Renaissance grotesques, Agostino's engravings were much in demand and extensively copied. *Graphische Sammlung Albertina, Vienna*

Pl. 25 A masterly engraving of a grotesque pattern dated 1532 which has been ascribed to Perino del Vaga. He was a celebrated exponent of this class of decoration which, as the poem states, had been provided by the grottoes of ancient Rome as examples to be used by skilful craftsmen. This print is now given to an anonymous designer although it was published in the year Perino returned to Rome. *The Metropolitan Museum of Art, New York; Harris Brisbane Dick Fund, 1953 (53.600.62)*

copied throughout the century (Pl. 23). This work was carried out by a team of exceptionally skilled artists under the direction of Raphael. Many of these artists were famous in their own right; indeed, never before, and perhaps never since, has such a galaxy of artistic talent been gathered to forward a single project – the creation of a magnificent new seat for the Papacy and its entourage. Raphael's great gift to posterity in the realm of decoration was to devise a less crowded form of grotesque ornament, more logically organized than the Antique originals, while still retaining the dominant elements of fantasy. This developed form of grotesque is to be seen in the adjacent, much larger Vatican *logge* (plural because there is more than one) of 1517–19, where the innovative decoration was striking also on account of the now faded brilliance of the colours.

After Raphael's death in 1520, his team went on to decorate with grotesques of this new formula, now incorporating white stucco reliefs, an imposing *loggia* in the villa of Cardinal Giulio de' Medici between 1520 and 1524 (subsequently called the Villa Madama after a later owner). This was an impressive attempt to re-create a great Roman villa of the Imperial period.

The principal financier to the popes at this time, Agostino Chigi, who came from Siena, invited a compatriot, the celebrated architect Peruzzi, to design a villa on the banks of the Tiber, today known as the Farnesina (built 1509). Although an independent architect, Peruzzi sometimes worked with Raphael's team, some of whom came to the Farnesina in 1517–18 to execute a *loggia* ceiling in *trompe l'oeil*. This is essentially a terrace fictively roofed by an openwork structure dressed with foliage and fruit, and supporting two large awnings, as if to shade from the sun the real people beneath enjoying the view from the terrace of the garden outside. The sky above is populated with mythological figures. Once again Raphael's team produced a model for decoration (this time, of a ceiling) that was to be imitated for many centuries.

But in Rome all this ended on 6 May 1527, when foreign troops occupied the city. For a whole week they sacked the city with peculiar brutality, leaving it gutted, devastated and impoverished. However, as a result of the Sack of Rome, Raphaelesque decorative formulae spread to other important Italian cities much more rapidly than might otherwise have been the case. Forced to disperse for lack of work, the most accomplished members of the Raphael 'team' soon found work elsewhere.

Giovanni da Udine, the extremely capable artist who seems to have drawn Raphael's attention to the potential of grotesques and who made the idiom his own chief *forte*, returned to his native city, Udine, in the northeastern province of Friuli, on the main route northwards from Venice to Vienna, Prague and Eastern Europe. He was later to find work in Venice, and in the

Pl. 27 Painted grotesques, coupled with relief ornament in white stucco, in the Casino of Pope Pius IV in the gardens of the Vatican, part of a scheme of decoration devised by the antiquarian Pirro Ligorio in the early 1560's, and executed by Frederico Zuccaro, Santi di Tito and Frederico Barocci – all celebrated artists of the time.
The Vatican Museum, Rome

Pl. 26 From a suite of 12 engravings by an unknown Italian artist who devised these insubstantial and highly mannered compositions in the 1530s, describing them as 'grotesques'. This impression is a copy of 1541 engraved (in reverse) by Enea Vico, who was working for the famous Roman print-seller Tomaso Barlacchi. They were much copied (e.g. by Ducerceau in Paris in 1550) and paraphrased.
The British Museum, London

1530s we find Giovanni executing grotesques on stained-glass windows in Florence. Perino del Vaga, a felicitous painter and a master of grotesque ornament prominent in the Vatican exercises, was later invited to Genoa by the powerful statesman Andrea Doria to decorate his villa and execute other important schemes, mostly involving grotesques confined within compartments. In 1532 Perino returned to Rome and executed influential schemes of grotesque decoration for Pope Paul III in the Castel Sant'Angelo and elsewhere; what may be an example of his style at that period is illustrated in Pl. 25.

Before leaving the subject of grotesque ornament, let us just consider the development of this idiom in 16th-century Italy. Several engravers belonging to Raphael's circle did much to popularize grotesque ornament (Pl. 24). Raphael's chief engraver, Marcantonio Raimondi, may perhaps have produced plates of grotesque ornament, but it is more probable that he left this kind of thing to his assistants, including Agostino Veneziano (Pl. 24) and Marco Denti. Enea Vico, who was not born until 1523, was to carry the torch much further, producing a large number of engravings of grotesque patterns, not necessarily all of his own invention, in the middle decades of the century (Pl. 26).

Grotesque ornament continued to be used for some of the foremost undertakings in Rome and its surroundings well into the second half of the century. The Casino of Pope Pius IV in the gardens of the Vatican was decorated in the 1560s by a distinguished team of painters and stuccoworkers under the direction of the antiquary Pirro Ligorio. There were further exercises involving grotesques at the Vatican in the 1570s under Gregory XIII and in the late 1580s under his successor, but the tough stance adopted by the Catholic Church in its efforts to counter the Protestant Reformation was sternly discouraging towards such expressions of light-heartedness. In 1582 the Archbishop of Bologna had published a book that inveighed against the use of grotesques, which he regarded as licentious and profane, having come from dark places among the ruins and dark places in the minds of their creators in Antiquity.

A word here needs to be said about 'strapwork'. In Pls. 20 and 24 a rod can be seen projecting horizontally from the central stem of a candelabrum. Such features gradually became more emphasized, often combining with the boldly framed label-like plaques that are also usually present in such compositions (Pl. 21). The result was that girder-like structures eventually evolved, around which the fantasy elements of grotesque compositions were assembled (Pl. 28). These bold forms were eagerly taken up by the French Fontainebleau School (see Chapter 4) but they had their origins in Italy. Today they are called strapwork. The chief Fontainebleau contribution was to make strapwork curl in three dimensions.

nTurning to Florence, which by the 1530s was entirely overshadowed, politically, by Papal Rome, we find Angelo Bronzino designing very fine tapestries decorated with grotesques for Duke Cosimo I de' Medici in 1549. At this time Cosimo was renovating the old-fashioned Palazzo

Pl. 28 Florentine bed-head painted with grotesques by Alessandro Allori, dated 1562. He spent some years in Rome in the 1550s and will have seen strapwork ornament like that around the central screen incorporated into grotesque compositions (see the stucco framing in Pl. 27), a formula he has used here.
Museo Nazionale, Bargello, Florence

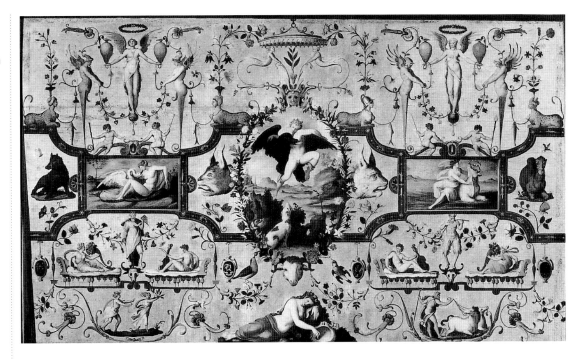

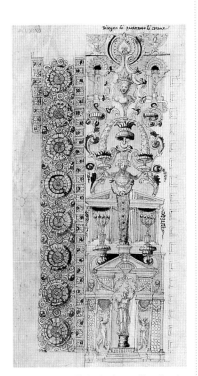

Pl. 29 Design for a wall hanging of gilt leather found in the Este archives and probably intended for one of that family's palaces at Ferrara. Pirro Ligorio (see Pl. 27), who worked for the family in the 1570s, may have been responsible for this meticulous composition.
Archivo Estense, Modena

Pl. 30 Tapestry designed by Giovanni Battista Castello about 1565. The grotesques resemble those he painted on many palace walls in Genoa in the 1560s. The central scene shows a splendid bed of the period. It is likely that this hanging was woven in the Netherlands.
Victoria and Albert Museum, London (Mus. no. 7.776–1950)

Vecchio to make it more suitable for the dukedom conferred upon him both by the Pope and the Holy Roman Emperor Charles V, the two chief figures on the Italian political stage. Cosimo also had to provide more modern and magnificent accommodation for his wife, the Spanish princess Eleanora of Toledo, who was used to rather grander surroundings than the old palace could offer. Bronzino was assisted by Alessandro Allori, who

tapestry-weaving enterprises in Italy were of of significance. So a common way for rich Italians to acquire tapestry hangings was to have designs made in Italy and to send them to be woven in the Netherlands. This procedure was adopted for tapestries designed by Raphael for the Sistine Chapel that were woven in Brussels (completed 1521). The tapestry illustrated in Pl. 30 was probably also woven in the Netherlands. The designer, Giovanni Battista Castello, who worked in Rome and in Genoa in the 1550s and 1560s, is thought to have been trained in Florence and Rome. In his figure subjects he was apparently influenced by Bronzino, and his border patterns are inspired by the grotesques that Perino del Vaga executed in Rome and in Genoa in the 1530s (see Pl. 25). Castello moved to Madrid in 1567, where he worked as painter and court architect to Philip II.

Grotesques were of course not the only form of

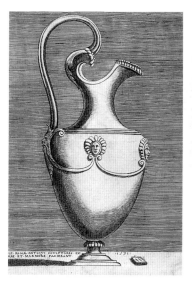

Pl. 32 Illustration dated 1531 of a ewer claimed to be of a kind made in ancient Rome of marble or bronze but quite possibly a fresh design in the Antique manner by a Renaissance artist. Engraved by Agostino Veneziano in Rome.
The British Museum, London

Pl. 31 Ceiling in a Florentine *palazzo* of the 1590s, presumably decorated by Bernadino Poccetti for the Gondi di Francia family, so-called because of their extremely close links with France.
Palazzo Orlandini, Florence

designed the grotesque borders of the above-mentioned tapestries (see also Pl. 28) and was later to decorate the galleries of the Uffizi with grotesques on a white ground (*c.* 1581), which derive directly from those of Raphael in the *logge* at the Vatican of more than half a century earlier. In the meantime Giorgio Vasari, who had studied the work of Raphael, Michelangelo and Peruzzi in Rome, and had executed important decorative schemes in that city, moved to Florence to become Cosimo's artistic impresario, in which role he replaced Bronzino in 1554. In both cities he painted grotesques, e.g. in the Palazzo della Cancelleria in Rome and the Palazzo Vecchio in Florence. Later in the century Bernadino Pocchetti covered large areas of walls and ceilings in the best houses in Florence with delightful grotesques (Pl. 31).

As we have seen, excellent tapestries were produced in Florence during the second half of the 16th century and others were woven at Mantua from the 1530s onwards; but production was not large and was geared to commissions emanating from the two ducal courts. And earlier

ornament used in High Renaissance Rome – or elsewhere in Italy. Pl. 34 shows a small room charmingly decorated by Baldassare Peruzzi in about 1511. Peruzzi, an architect and decorative painter, became an architect of St Peter's after Raphael's death in 1520, and returned to his native city Siena after the Sack. He was a skilful painter of grotesque ornament who had been influenced first by Pinturicchio and then by Giovanni da Udine and was therefore familiar with both the old and the new forms of this idiom. In Pl. 34 the walls are painted with fictive columns between which is a lattice of canes that holds back a cloth painted with emblems on shields. The frieze is decorated with grotesques among *rinceaux*. Peruzzi was perhaps also involved with the painting of the scene shown in Pl. 33, on the wall of Agostino Chigi's Villa Farnesina in Rome (see p. 21). Somewhat similar ornament is to be seen on the embroidered valance (pelmet) fixed beneath the tester.

Chigi and Peruzzi were from Siena and the artist who painted the fresco (Sodoma) was trained in that city.

Pl. 33 Illustration of about 1511 of a superb bed with posts, at that time a rather new class of furniture. Il Sodoma, who painted this fresco, is unlikely to have designed such a bed, which is depicted in accurate detail; an architect must have been involved. Peruzzi, who designed the villa where the fresco is to be seen, may possibly have been responsible. What we can be sure of is that beds like this were to be seen here and there in Rome by the 'teens of the century.
Palazzo della Farnesina, Rome (detail)

Pl. 34 Mural decoration in fresco by Baldassare Peruzzi, about 1511, an elaborate version of a once-common Gothic formula depending on lozenge-shaped patterns, which here serve as a reminder that by no means all wall decoration at this period consisted of grotesques or of large pictorial scenes. Small grotesques do, however, figure in the frieze above.
*Palazzo della Cancelleria, Rome
Photograph through the kindness of
Professor Simonetta Valtieri*

Pl. 33 is interesting also because it depicts a four-poster bed at the time when this was a novel piece of furniture, and we see it here for the first time in the form that such splendid beds were to take right through to the 18th century. It is quite possible that Peruzzi was responsible for devising this formula. A bed with a tester and hangings constituted a massive object in a room and, at an early stage in its development (which started around 1490), leading architects began to pay attention to this intrusive object in an attempt to make it harmonise with the bedchambers they were creating. If beds like this were being designed by Peruzzi in the 'teens of the 16th century, he has to be considered one of Europe's most important designers of furniture, because this formula for imposing beds was to be so widely adopted and remained in favour for so long.

The interest in Antique Classical forms was naturally not confined to those found in wall paintings. Classical articles of all kinds caught the imagination of people around 1500, and continued to do so until the 19th century. Tripod-stands and altars, candlesticks, ewers, the legs of couches and tables, armour, chair forms, vases, lamps and much else were studied and often drawn and even measured. Engravings of such objects were made and published in great quantity, and whole ranges of prints were produced purporting to be taken directly from original antiquities 'found in Rome', but actually the imaginative inventions of contemporary artists, although undoubtedly inspired by ancient Roman models (Pl. 32).

An artist who did much to forge the new Classical style of ornament and apply it to the forms that were required in up-to-date palatial settings was Giulio Romano. From 1524 until his death in 1546 he served the Gonzaga family at Mantua as both architect and designer-decorator – a talented and highly versatile man who designed whole rooms and everything in them, from beds and tapestries down to small silver vessels for sweetmeats, in many cases so as to present a unified and harmonious appearance within a decorative ensemble (Pls. 35 and 36). In this respect he followed Raphael, for whom he had worked in Rome.

Like Raphael also, Giulio headed a large team of highly capable artists and craftsmen well versed in the artistic repertoire of their master. Occasionally such assistants must have contributed to what now constitutes the *oeuvre* of Giulio Romano, because, although he exercised overall control over decorative projects, some of the designs drawn by his assistants must have included details of their own invention.

Giulio Romano was one of the founding fathers of Mannerism – that strange style which took up some of the more disagreeable parts of the language of ornament to be found in grotesques, often fantastic, not infrequently disquieting, but served up with brilliance. His example was eagerly followed at other centres, such as Florence, where Bronzino and Vasari in turn became leading exponents of the style that spread rapidly across Italy in the middle decades of the century. Another celebrated artist who followed the path indicated by Giulio

Romano was Francesco Salviati, who was not only a painter (mostly of enormous murals in Rome and Florence) but also a prolific designer of metalwork, probably chiefly for important Roman goldsmiths. The spread-eagled merfolk on the lid of a covered bowl attributed to him (Pl. 37) are characteristic of his style.

Much of the character of Roman ornament of the period can be gained from studying carved furniture of the grander kind, designed by architects and leading ornemanistes. Pl. 38 shows a fine chest of this class, made for a noble family in the middle of the century, probably to the design of Perino del Vaga. Italian furniture and other carved woodwork was at this stage mostly executed in walnut, which lends itself well to bold carving and was sometimes partly gilded. Pl. 39 illustrates a support for a table; such supports were

based on Antique originals – there was one at each end of such a table and, in this case, a third in the middle. The marble slabs such tables supported could be very heavy, so the supports needed to be exceptionally sturdy. This table was undoubtedly designed by an architect (possibly Jacopo da Vignola) and dates from 1565. The bearded terminal figures on the marble supports, with bats' wings pushing forward the central shields, are typical of Mannerist grotesqueness, thrusting an unsettling fearfulness at the viewer. Essentially a hangover from a nightmare quality found in much Gothic art, taken up with gusto and converted *all'antico* by Giulio Romano (in particular) and adopted widely, as here in mid century and with increasing frequency thereafter (Pls. 42 and 44), Mannerism was to be Rome's second great contribution to the repertoire of Western ornament. A powerful contribution to the spread of this highly mannered formula was made by engraved editions of the designs of Polidoro da Caravaggio, one-time member of Raphael's team at the Vatican, who seems to have died at Messina in the 1530s, having moved there after the Sack of Rome. Famous in his day for decorating the façades of Roman palaces, and especially for depicting some exuberant vases on the front of the Palazzo Milesi (greatly praised by Vasari), the forms of which were much imitated later, it was nevertheless through posthumous engravings of his designs by others that his name has become well-known. The earliest of these prints date from about 1540 and the contorted forms, which offer few concessions to practical purpose, inspired designers until the mid-19th century. A set was published by Cherubino Alberti in 1582 (Pl. 42) and another by Aegidius Sadeler appeared in 1605 when the latter was working at the court of Rudolf II in Prague, at that time an important centre for the dissemination of Mannerism.

An important technological development that took place in the 16th century was the refinement of the process of turning materials on a lathe – chiefly woods, but also ivory. This development may have been prompted by the need to make the bores of gun-barrels of regular diameter and smooth but, by the middle of the century, ornaments that had been turned on a lathe were common on small articles, such as wooden frames for mirrors and portraits (Pl. 43). The technique was also adopted for producing larger objects, such as the posts of beds (Pls. 33 and 161). Amazing ingenuity was applied to working lathes; perhaps most impressively to the tapering of spiralling columns. Such 'Salamonic columns' (so-called because King Solomon's temple at Jerusalem was supposed to have had such features) were to be a mainstay of Baroque architectural ornament.

This brings us to a consideration of the ornament of architectural form derived from Classical precedents. Different examples from the second half of the century are shown in Pls. 44 and 45. Images of a Classical

Pl. 38 Mid-16th-century carved walnut chest, probably made in Rome. The name of Perino del Vaga has been proposed as the designer but that of Bartolemeo Neroni is more plausible. The repertoire of ornament used by the leading designers at this time was common to all, and this chest is a good example of the current style in a grand manifestation.
The Henry H. Huntington Library and Art Gallery, San Marino, California (HEH 27.166)

Pl. 39 Table designed for the Palazzo Farnese in Rome, about 1565, probably by the celebrated architect Jacopo Barozzi da Vignola (1507–73). The magnificent slab, decorated with a design composed of rare marbles, was made in Rome.
The Metropolitan Museum of Art, New York; Harris Brisbane Dick Fund, 1958 (58.57a–d)

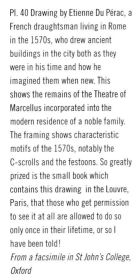

Pl. 40 Drawing by Etienne Du Pérac, a French draughtsman living in Rome in the 1570s, who drew ancient buildings in the city both as they were in his time and how he imagined them when new. This shows the remains of the Theatre of Marcellus incorporated into the modern residence of a noble family. The framing shows characteristic motifs of the 1570s, notably the C-scrolls and the festoons. So greatly prized is the small book which contains this drawing in the Louvre, Paris, that those who get permission to see it at all are allowed to do so only once in their lifetime, or so I have been told!
From a facsimile in St John's College, Oxford

doorway or triumphal arch were frequently adapted to the decoration of title-pages during the last two thirds of the 16th century, and the formula was to enjoy great favour for the next two centuries. That illustrated in Pl. 44 was probably designed by Salviati; the twisted figures are characteristic of the kind of Mannerism for which he was celebrated. A similar formula was used by the Roman architect Vignola in designing a chimney-piece for the principal bedchamber in the Palazzo Farnese (Pl. 45). This engraving first appeared in 1563 in Vignola's publication dealing with the Orders of Classical architecture (i.e. columns, with their capitals and bases).

An artist with an apt surname, Bernardo Buontalenti, was indeed talented as a designer. He served the Grand Duke of Tuscany, Francesco de' Medici, as architect, decorator and designer of a variety of objects including glassware, silver and porcelain. From 1574 until the late 1580s he decorated the presentation rooms on the principal floor of the Uffizi, the building occupied by the grand-ducal civil service and much used for official functions. Buontalenti was also responsible for the design of sumptuous vessels made of hardstone such as lapis lazuli (Pl. 46), which were mounted by goldsmiths of great skill, and set a pattern for vessels of this class. He also designed vessels that were made at a small Florentine workshop producing imitation porcelain, which had been set up by the Grand Duke in 1575. It was the only successful manufactory of this kind before soft-paste porcelains were produced in France very late in the 17th century. The shapes of the vessels produced by this short-lived Medici factory derive from silverware, or the contemporary products of *maiolica* factories at Urbino. Their decoration was invariably executed in blue on a white ground, usually in imitation of Chinese porcelain. Their patterns were also sometimes copied from Chinese vessels, but mostly they took the form of grotesques and a few were inspired by the lively decoration of fine pottery produced at this period at Isnik in Turkey (Pl. 47).

Rome was the powerhouse of inventiveness during the period that concerns us here, and Roman example in the field of decoration was spread speedily across Italy, not merely by published engravings, but directly by artists who had learned their business while working on important schemes in the Holy City and had then moved. Grotesque patterns suited to High Renaissance needs were the chief innovation derived from Rome at the beginning of the century and they

Pl. 41 Sturdy Florentine table of carved walnut, partly gilded, supporting a large slab of porphyry bought in Rome by the Grand Duke Cosimo I. Constructed between 1565 and 1574. Such vase-shaped baluster legs became a favourite form of support for furniture in the next century.
Museo degli Argenti, Pitti Palace, Florence

Pl. 43 A Tuscan mid-16th-century picture-frame of wood, partly gilded. Note the ornaments that have been turned on a lathe – an early use of this technique for such a purpose. The half-spindles must have been turned and then split down the middle to produce a pair of ornaments in relief.
Museo Comunale, Prato

Pl. 42 Design for a ewer by Polidoro da Caravaggio, who died in 1543. He is most famous for the engravings that were produced about 1540 of his bold, almost ferocious, highly mannered compositions. They were copied many times (this edition was published in Rome in 1582, by Cherubino Alberti) and remained popular with designers right into the 18th century. Pl. 157 shows another engraving after this artist.
Museum für Kunsthandwerk, Frankfurt am Main (Mus. no. LOZ 2476)

Pl. 44 Title-page of Antonio Labacco's treatise on architecture, published in Rome in 1559. Designed by Salviati with typically Mannerist features, notably the contorted female figures and the uncomfortably heavy swags of vegetation. Note the ruins of Classical Rome beyond.
By courtesy of the Trustees of Sir John Soane's Museum, London

continued to evolve until the end of the period. The unreality of most grotesque patterns, with their improbable juxtapositions, exaggerations and frequent inclusion of creatures of fabulous form, provided inspiration for artists working in a more conventional vein, who in turn developed what we today call Mannerism, which, with its disquieting undertones, clearly struck a chord with contemporary Italians. There was justification in plenty for feelings of unease among Italians during the 16th century – a century that saw the horrifying Sack of Rome which aborted

Pl. 45 Chimneypiece in the Palazzo Farnese in Rome, designed by Jacopo da Vignola and first illustrated in the 1563 edition of his celebrated and much-consulted book on the rules for drawing the Classical orders of architecture. This engraving was to influence later generations of architects profoundly, not merely in Italy.
The British Architectural Library, RIBA, London

Pl. 46 Vase of lapis lazuli dated 1583, with enamelled gold mounts, designed by Bernardo Buontalenti, the metalwork executed by the immigrant Flemish goldsmith Jacques Bilivert – a Medici commission.
Museo degli Argenti, Florence

cultural life in that city for a decade; the campaigns that swept so unremittingly through the countryside, often waged with lawless foreign troops; the rigorous measures adopted by the Church to counter Protestantism caused much distress and perplexity; and sudden epidemics that were still an ever-present menace. It was against this background that the great decorative achievements of the Italian High Renaissance were made and it is hardly surprising that some of the artistic expressions of this period display a strong measure of anguish.

Pl. 47 Flask made at a small factory in Florence set up by the Grand-Duke Francesco to produce imitation porcelain, 1575–87. It was supervised by the designer Bernardo Buontalenti, who adopted a shape based on silver flasks for this vessel. It is claimed that a Turkish potter from Isnik in Asia Minor was engaged at the Florentine factory; certainly the pattern in blue on the white ground is here inspired by Isnik wares. Chinese porcelain was in other instances the source of inspiration. Height 26.4 cm (10 1/8 in.) Width 20 cm (7 3/8 in.)
Collection of the J. Paul Getty Museum, Malibu, California (86. DE 630)

CHAPTER 3

VENICE

1510-1620

We discussed two important points about Venice in Chapter 1 – the enormous extent of her trade with the East, and the fact that the city was the principal centre of the book trade in Europe. The second factor led to her becoming the chief disseminator of information about new patterns, and the influence that this constant stream of pattern-books had on design throughout Europe, from the very early 16th century and far into the 17th, was immense. Nor was this influence solely brought about by books of designs; from the late 15th century the decorated title-pages of many Venetian publications, and subsequently the bindings of Venetian books, also often carried new patterns.

It seems that a group of humanist scholars at the University of Padua in the 1470s became interested in the patterns to be seen on imported Near Eastern book-bindings, which had presumably reached them through Venice which lies not far away. The Near Eastern formula for book-covers consisted of a central medallion or oblong panel, surrounded by a border within the four corners of which an ornament of triangular shape is inserted. The ornament in the corners at first took the form of 'knots'. These are interlaced formal patterns formed with flat bands which cross each other and either curve round so as to cross in a different direction or cross after having abruptly changed direction by

means of angular 'breaks'. Knot patterns of the first kind appeared on a number of bindings produced for Paduan humanists in the 1470s, but the less geometric second kind – those with breaks – quickly became the most popular and were soon used for general purposes (Pls. 55 and 57); we then see them forming the dominant pattern of European ornament in the Near Eastern taste. The subsidiary ornament within the knotted framing is of a type known at the time, and still today, as moresques. Knotted strapwork, or stylized vegetal stems, commonly formed the structure of the Near Eastern patterns that Europeans imitated, right through the 16th century, and are mostly combined with moresques (Pls. 56, 58 and 60). At first moresques play the role of a filling pattern (Pls. 48, 49 and 54), later they become fully integrated with the knotwork to form a single and very useful type of ornament that was quickly adopted in receptive centres all over Europe.

Moresques take their name from the Moors, Islamic peoples of North Africa and southern Spain, but such patterns are also sometimes called arabesques, Moors being Arabic peoples too. The term '*rabeschi*' occurs in 16th-century Italian inventories in reference to these patterns but is there used very loosely. 'Moresques' (and 'Mauresques') was a term more commonly used and it makes better sense to use it here for our present purposes.

At this period the terms 'Moorish' and 'Arabic' tend to refer to people at the western end of the wide area of Islamic domination around the southern shores of the Mediterranean. Ornament that can undoubtedly be called Moorish, because it was applied in Moorish, or recently Moorish, provinces of Spain (and often by Moorish craftsmen), reached Italy via Majorca or through Naples. Both places were ruled by an Aragonese dynasty (Naples from 1442) and therefore had direct and frequent contact with the Spanish province of Aragon, which had long since absorbed Catalonia with its important sea-port, Barcelona. Throughout the Middle Ages, Christian armies were steadily pushing back the Moors who, however, managed to hang on in the south until 1569–70 when they were finally defeated and then converted, deported or wiped out. In the 15th century, the important Moorish city of Malaga, in the south, was still capable of making and exporting fine pottery to Italy and other parts of Europe (Pl. 50); and potters from Malaga emigrated to Valencia in the middle years of that century and set up potteries there, as we have seen (p. 16). Tiles from Valencia of Moorish type were provided in the 1440s for the new castle being built at Naples by Alfonzo of Aragon, a clear reminder that one major route taken by Islamic influence on Italy was through the south of that country and came from Spain. But even more important was the route from the Near East to and through Venice. In the case of the introduction of gilding to the decoration of bookbindings (probably not long before 1470), however, the technique is likely to have taken both routes at about the same time.

The development of Venetian bookbinding patterns is summarily represented here by Pls. 48, 51 and 53, reflecting the adopting and adaptation of Islamic ornament in a craft that often served discriminating customers. Most books at the time were sold sewn into paper covers, and the purchaser could then have a book bound more substantially at his own expense. Venetian binders quite often bound books for important private libraries in Germany and France or for wealthy foreign patrons temporarily resident in Venice. By such means was a knowledge of Venetian design influenced by the Islamic Near East transmitted abroad. But the products of these countries at the eastern end of the Mediterranean were not given an omnibus label such as 'Moorish'. Distinctions were made and there was an awareness that items came from the Mameluk territories of Egypt, or from Persia, or the Turkish areas of Anatolia, or from Damascus in Syria. A class of silk material with a satin weave forming the ground, and the reverse of that weave forming the pattern, generally known as 'silk damask', owes its name to the Syrian city, although the weaving of silk damasks became an important industry in Europe from the mid-15th century onwards (it was still necessary in a Neapolitan official document of 1450 to explain that such materials were 'of the kind called *domasqui*').

Pl. 50 Bold moresque patterns on a dish made at Malaga during the 15th century. The patterns are rendered with a dark-blue pigment and the dark-brown golden metallic lustre so characteristic of these exotic Hispano-Moresque wares; part of the pattern is contrived by leaving the white tin-glazed ground unmasked by pigment or lustre. Such lustreware, called *maiolica* in Italy at the time, was greatly prized in many parts of Christian Europe.
Museo Arqueológico Nacional, Madrid

Pl. 51 A Venetian trade binding of 1512, from Aldus Manutius's publishing house. This is an example of a new book being finished with a binding in the workshop immediately after printing and before purchase by a customer.
Ex T. Kimball Brooker Collection, Chicago (present whereabouts unknown)

Linen damask (i.e. cloth woven in the same technique but of linen) was apparently being woven (probably in the Netherlands) already by the first decades of the century and was in Italy described as being *alla dameschina*. This all indicates that Italian links with the Levant were already strong by 1400, and we know they grew stronger still during the 15th and 16th centuries. Brassware inlaid with silver was a much prized import from the Near East, and so closely imitated in Venice that, even now, experts in the field are sometimes unsure as to their origin. Indeed, it has been suggested that Islamic crafts-men were brought to Venice in order to make these wares, or, alternatively, that Venetian craftsmen went to the Near East to study the techniques involved. In any case, these wares were all referred to as being *alla damaschina*, and the technique is still called damascening in England. In Venice the craftsmen executing this work were called *agemisti*. The Thomas Geminus who published in London a book on moresque patterns in 1548, under the title *Morysee and Damashin Renewed and Encreased very profitable for goldsmythes and Embroiderars*, must have had an Italian connection, for his surname must surely derive from *ageminus*. He is said

Pl. 52 Painting of about 1511–13 by Cima da Conegliano, depicting a magnificent throne canopy decorated with a handsome moresque design showing Turkish influence. Cima had links with the Venetian silk-weavers' guild and this could be one of their most ambitious products, but it may possibly be an embroidery.
Musée du Louvre, Paris

Pl. 53 Venetian binding of the second quarter of the 16th century. The commonest compositional formula for Western bookbinding design has here taken shape, although the influence of Near Eastern example is still very evident. Binding on a copy of Pliny the Younger's *Letters* of 1508 from the Aldo Manutius workshop.
Österreichisches Nationalbibliothek, Vienna

to have come from Lille, but his origins, or those of his father, must lie in Venice and a life spent in the realm of Venetian metalworking, where they were totally familiar with moresques and damascening.

Pattern-books of moresque designs began to appear in Venice in the 1520s. Pl. 49 shows a pattern from the publisher Giovanni Antonio Tagliente's *Essempio di recammi* [patterns for embroidery] of 1527. A publisher nicknamed Zoppino brought out another pattern-book for embroiderers in 1529 and at some point in the 1520s the 'Master *f*' (so-called because he signed his work thus, while his full identity is not known) produced a further book of elegant designs (Pl. 54). The latter's designs were copied and re-published, first in 1530 by Giovanni Andrea Vavassore, whose book was aimed at

Pl. 55 One of the elegant designs in Francesco Pellegrino's pattern-book of embroidery designs 'in the Arabic and Italic fashion', published in Paris in 1530. As his name indicates, Pellegrino was evidently Italian and he must have worked closely with the French court. It is here suggested that he may have been a professional embroiderer from Milan, a city at this time much celebrated for its embroidery (see Pl. 14).
Victoria and Albert Museum, London (from a facsimile copy, Mus. no. L.1637–1908)

Pl. 56 Ewer of damascened brass (i.e. inlaid with silver), probably made in Venice about 1560. The handle is a 19th-century replacement. The overall moresque patterns are striking. Vestigial knots may be seen around the neck and alongside the mouth. This work was executed by craftsmen called *ageministi*.
Victoria and Albert Museum, London (Mus. no. M.31–1946)

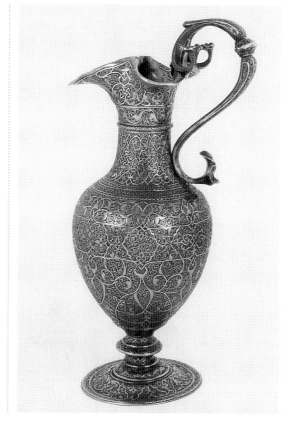

Pl. 57 Moresque decoration executed with inlaid wood (the geometric interlace) and gilding on black lacquer (the moresques) on a superb Venetian harpsichord of 1574 by one of the city's most celebrated makers, Giovanni Baffo.
Victoria and Albert Museum, London (Mus. no 6007–1859)

painters and goldsmiths as well as embroiderers, and by Heinrich Steyner in Augsburg only four years later (1534) – which shows how fast such patterns could be transmitted and that they were thought sufficiently useful for designers to make re-publication worthwhile. Tagliente incidentally described his innovatory patterns as being *groppi moreschi et arabeschi* [moresque and arabesque knots].

Pattern-books mostly reproduce designs of a kind that have been in use for some years and we see good evidence of this in Pl. 52, which shows a painting by Cima da Conegliano of about 1511–13, in which a silk

canopy decorated with handsome moresques figures prominently. But well before this, the Venetian printer Niclaus Jenson had produced a book-binding decorated with moresque border ornaments in much the same vein for Petrus Ugelheimer, a native of Frankfurt am Main, who had dealt with Jenson since 1483 and died in 1489. But both Jenson's moresques and those on Cima's canopy also resemble the pattern illustrated in Pl. 54 which was published in the 1520s.

The Italian lead in publishing designs for moresques continued strongly in the next two decades but one important Italian exercise was actually published in France. We shall deal with the Fontainebleau School of decoration in Chapter 4, but it was because this strange but potent manifestation of Italian art on French soil gave such strong encouragement to designers that this elegant suite of engravings appeared there – as early as 1530 (Pl. 55). Its author was Francesco Pellegrino, usually identified with a decorator of that name working under Rosso Fiorentino, the principal artist of the Fontainebleau School (see pp. 41 and 42). Pellegrino's publication bears the somewhat strange title *La fleur de la Science de Pourtraicture* (literally 'The Flower of the Science of Portraiture', a portrait being an image or likeness), but its subtitle puts us straight by telling us that the designs are for embroidery, '*Patrons de Broderie*', and that they are '*Façon arabique et ytalique*' [in the Arabic and Italian fashion]. A prominent family of professional embroiderers in Milan bore the name Pellegrino (one of them was commissioned to work the altar cloth for the cathedral there) and it seems rather more likely that our Francesco Pellegrino was an embroiderer from Milan, especially as he mentions only embroidery in his title. As we have seen, Milan was at this time the chief centre in Europe for high-class embroidery (Pl. 14).

The damascened ewer shown in Pl. 56 represents the state of development at which moresques had arrived by about 1560. The interlaced moresque pattern is set against a background of small scrolls, and knots may be seen on the neck and alongside the lip. The scrollwork is more carefully controlled in the decoration of an important Venetian harpsichord of 1574 (Pl. 57) which is overlaid with an inlaid network of geometric interlaced decoration.

Fine lacquerwork was made in Persia during the 16th century. It was commonly decorated with moresques executed in gold: this was done on relatively small items, such as folding book-rests, book-covers, containers for writing materials, etc. Such objects excited the admiration of Europeans whenever they saw them, and early imitations of this work embodying moresque decoration were made in Venice. The technique was deemed suitable for embellishing the covers of highly important government documents, so apparently carried no light-hearted or frivolous connotation in the

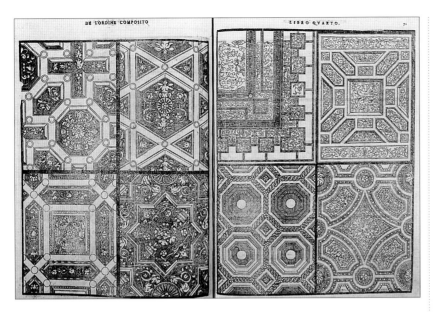

Pl. 58 Eight designs for the panels of suspended wooden ceilings of the sort installed in fashionable dining-parlours and bedchambers from the 1520s onwards; from the first published volume of Sebastiano Serlio's treatise on architecture – volume iv, of 1537. This immensely influential book bore fruit which can be found all over Europe. Note how the details of each small panel are usually different from its neighbour, even though they superficially look alike; this of course multiplies the number of motifs shown.
By courtesy of the Trustees of Sir John Soane's Museum, London

Pl. 59 Monument to a member of the Grimani family by Alessandro Vittoria and others; 1570s. This elegant architectural frame to an epitaphium represents the Classical tradition as expressed by a distinguished sculptor in an important Venetian church.
San Giuseppe di Castello, Venice

book appeared in 1615 but covers largely his own work in Venice and its surroundings executed in the late 16th century. Pl. 58 must suffice as an illustration of this new genre of engraved designs; it shows two plates providing eight patterns for panelled ceilings, several of them with alternative ornamentation within seemingly identical panels, and, incidentally, in some places embodying moresque ornament.

Serlio's illustrated treatise was very well received by the readership at which it was aimed, and works inspired by it were soon being published. One of these was Vignola's treatise on the Classical orders of architecture, published in Rome in 1562, which also quickly came to enjoy a high reputation. In the 1563 edition, Vignola illustrated a chimneypiece (Pl. 45), which became a model for architects faced with the problem of designing proportionately low, oblong features in the Classical taste. A monument in Venice to a member of the

way that imitations of Chinese artefacts were often to do later. Venetian lacquer was also used for making small objects, such as jewel caskets covered with moresques, although entirely occidental figure-subjects occasionally occupy panels within the imitation Islamic ornament. Sometimes the ground of the panels in such work was made of mother-of-pearl which reflects light back through the painted decoration applied on to it. A similar effect was contrived with a gold ground over which painted decoration was applied; the colours were often applied so as to form 'the ground', leaving the pattern itself unpainted (reserved, as it is called), a technique beautifully exemplified by Queen Elizabeth's virginals in the Victoria and Albert Museum, which is a Venetian instrument of about 1570. A superbly decorated harp, ordered for the private orchestra of Duke Alfonso II d'Este in 1581 and made in Rome, is decorated in a similar manner (Pl. 60). It will be seen that the panels have here assumed fanciful shapes, themselves 'Moorish' in detail but actually deriving from the multiple panels to be seen in much grotesque decoration from the 1560s onwards (e.g. Pl. 27), and which was well developed by 1590 (e.g. Pl. 31).

A number of architectural treatises were published in Venice during our period. Several of them were liberally illustrated and, as these publications were primarily aimed at the clients of architects rather than at architects themselves, information about architecture or architectural ornament, made doubly clear with the aid of pictures, became widely available among people who were mostly also patrons of craftsmen and designers of decorative art objects. This new class of publication was extremely influential, those of Sebastiano Serlio and Vincenzo Scamozzi playing particularly important roles in this direction. Serlio's work reflects the state of architecture in Rome, Bologna and Venice from the 1520s until the 1550s. Scamozzi's

Grimani family of about 1570 by the sculptor Alessandro Vittoria (Pl. 59) demonstrates this. It is composed within an extremely handsome and harmoniously proportioned architectural framing, that has affinities with Vignola's chimneypiece of a decade or so earlier. It is not suggested that Vittoria copied Vignola, but he will have been familiar with Vignola's illustration and may have known the original chimneypiece and its companions in Rome (in the Palazzo Farnese). What the resemblance shows, on the other hand, is that by the 1560s the broken-pediment formula had become established for compositions with a frontispiece-like character. The formula was to be long-lived. It was soon realised that the enclosed oblong could be either horizontal or upright.

The engraver Enea Vico has already been mentioned in connection with some early designs for grotesques that he executed for Tommaso Barlacchi, an important publisher in Rome (Pl. 26). Vico later worked for a

Pl. 61 From a suite of engraved portraits of the wives of Caesars [*Donne Auguste*] by Enea Vico, published in Venice in 1557. Each medallion portrait had an elaborate surround, often of architectural character, which reflects mid-century Venetian taste in decoration. Note the curling strapwork at the bottom and the cramped flanking figures – evidence of Vico's knowledge of contemporary developments in Paris and Antwerp (see pp. 71, 78, 100).

Pl. 60 Lacquered decoration of a harp, executed in Rome, commissioned in 1581 for the Duke Alfonso II's small private orchestra at his court at Ferrara. The Roman painter responsible was paid in 1587 for 'miniaturing a harp for his Highness', the term used being *miniare*. The panels have here assumed fanciful shapes, themselves 'Moorish' in detail, but actually deriving from the multiple panels to be seen in much grotesque decoration from the 1560s onwards. *Galleria Estense, Modena*

while in Florence and then in Venice where, in 1557, he published a series of portraits of the wives of twelve Caesars based on ancient Roman coins. The portraits (he later did the Caesars as well) served as a useful source for those wishing to produce medallion-head ornaments ('Romayne heads', as they were sometimes called in England in the 16th century) but far more important for our purposes are the fanciful surrounds that Vico provided for each medallion. Mostly architectural in character, they exemplify elegant Venetian taste in ornament in the middle decades of the century (e.g. Pl. 61). They betray an intimate knowledge of contemporary French and Flemish ornamental patterns (with which we deal in the next two chapters), particularly with regard to scrolling strapwork which begins to become an important feature of Venetian carved ornament in the second half of the century. For example, the scrolls at the bottom of Vico's composition have much in common with those on the Venetian picture-

frame shown in Pl. 63, while another Vico pattern (not illustrated here) has scrolls forming an openwork surround reminiscent of those on a page from a Bolognese illuminated manuscript of 1580 shown in Pl. 62, which is strongly influenced by Venetian taste.

The picture-frame is an early specimen of the kind that it today often called a Sansovino frame, after the celebrated Venetian sculptor and architect Jacopo Sansovino (he was actually from Tuscany), although it seems highly improbable that he ever designed frames. Pls. 62 and 64 show pages from documents in the Bologna city archives bearing representations of frames couched in a similar vein. This Venetian style spread right across Italy, as a carved and partly gilded frame made in Siena in 1591 shows (Pl. 65).

Characteristic of this style are eyebrow-like scrolls which, in the case of the Sienese frame, form a broken pediment at the centre of which is a shield with a coat-of-arms. A far more refined example of such work, of great elaboration, is the ceiling of the Senate Chamber in the Doge's Palace in Venice. The design for it, drawn in 1578, is shown in Pl. 66. The 'eyebrow-scrolls' are now combined to form framed compartments that were to house paintings by Tintoretto and others.

We saw that pattern-books for embroiderers were among the first illustrated manuals to be published, and that the earliest were all, with one exception (published in Augsburg in 1524), brought out in Venice. This class

Pl. 64 A leaf dated 1584 from the same collection as that shown in Pl. 62, showing a bolder version of the style. If executed in wood (normally walnut) high points would often be gilded (see Pl. 65).
Archivio di Stato, Bologna (Insignia collection)

Pl. 62 Manuscript leaf of the year 1580 concerning appointments held by Bolognese noblemen, with the representation of a carved openwork frame conforming closely to Venetian taste of the time. The fancily shaped panels within the frame have elaborate scrolled edges.
Archivio di Stato, Bologna (Insignia collection)

Pl. 63 Venetian carved frame of the second half of the 16th century, with gilding and black details characteristic of its period. The arms are those of the Cavalli family of Verona.
Musei Civici, Padua

of handbook continued to be produced there throughout the 16th century. The genre was aimed at 'noble ladies' (as many of the titles of these books proclaim), because ladies at that time had plenty of servants to do menial tasks, tending to leave them with time on their hands. As it was thought wise to keep such hands occupied, especially if the hands were those of young women, what could be better than to set them to work on making something both beautiful and useful – clothing, a tablecloth, purses and all kinds of trimmings?

In the second half of the century a new sub-division of such work became popular with this clientele; this was the making of various types of lace. Lace is mostly made of linen (which is white, and this led to such patterns being printed with a black ground so as to leave the design white) but could also be made of gold or silver thread, or of coloured silks. The patterns devised specially for lacemaking became very sophisticated towards the end of the century; Cesare Veccellio, a

Pl. 65 Framed notice-board of carved and partly gilded walnut, made for a bank in Siena in 1591, embodying features seen earlier on Venetian work. The names of those officials on duty were written on this board. *Banca Monte dei Paschi di Siena. SpA Collection*

Pl. 66 Contract drawing, signed by the two celebrated craftsmen who were to execute the design, for the ceiling in the Senate Chamber in the Doge's Palace, Venice, drawn in 1578 by Cristoforo Sorte. The ceiling survives and represents the high point of Venetian design in this vein. *Victoria and Albert Museum, London* (Mus. no. 509–1937)

former pupil of Titian's, designed such patterns, and his pattern-books became the most widely known of all (his designs began to appear in 1591), while some excellent compositions by a Venetian needlework designer, Federico Vinciolo, were published in Paris in 1587 (Pl. 67). Catherine de' Medici, the Italian-born widow of King Henri II, must have called him to Paris, where he was given the monopoly for producing the enormous starched linen collars, trimmed with lace, that the Queen had made fashionable at the French court.

Dentilated edgings (i.e. with pointed tongues or rounded lappets) had been developed in the 15th century but the delicate patterns that were made at the end of the 16th century were novel and remained in favour for both men and women's dress far into the 17th century. Many women working on their embroideries in their homes managed to produce excellent needlework displaying great skill, but their productions were of a different character from those executed in professional workshops such as that which produced the elaborate throne canopy shown in Pl. 14. Professional embroiderers can have had little or no need for the kind of pattern-books we have been discussing, which is not to say that the work of the most dextrous 'domestic' needlewomen was in any way amateurish.

Glass-making was, and still is, a major industry in Venice and was already well established by 1500. Pl. 69 shows a drinking glass decorated with a pattern executed in coloured glass by the enamelling technique which had begun to go out of fashion by 1540. The vessel already has the conical bowl that was to be the

Pl. 67 Pattern for needlepoint lace border published in 1587, by Federico Vinciolo, a distinguished Venetian lacemaker working in Paris. Such a pattern was particularly suitable for starched collars and cuffs. *Kunstindustrimuseet, Copenhagen*

Pl. 68 A Venetian woman having her hair dressed, holding a small dressing-mirror. A stool serves as her dressing-table. Her chair has members that were turned on a lathe, and is of a type that was furnished with a rush seat. From Giacomo Franco's *Habite delle donne venetiane* [Venetian women's costume] of 1610, although the style of her dress and hair indicate an earlier date for this illustration – more like 1580. *Victoria and Albert Museum, London*

Pl. 69 Venetian 16th-century goblet of soda glass with enamel decoration. An eminently practical yet decorative model, a far cry from the exceptionally delicate tall-stemmed glasses so characteristic of many later high-class Venetian products. Height 14 cm (5½ in.) *Collection of the J. Paul Getty Museum, Malibu, California*

standard form for drinking glasses until the mid-18th century but it still has no stem. The making of mirrors of glass speedily became an important branch of the industry after 1492, when a French glassmaker came to Murano (the island in the Venetian lagoon noted for glassmaking), evidently in possession of fresh know-how, and when in 1502 two Italians acquired the privilege of making 'crystalline glass, a valuable and singular material'. By the end of the century Venice had attained the dominant position in this branch of manufacture, providing the whole of Europe with high-class plates of looking-glass, which she continued to do until the end of the 17th century.

Mirrors as pieces of furniture became highly fashionable articles of room-decoration from the late 15th century until about the middle of the 16th century in Venice, and great pains and much money were expended on the frames into which these items were fitted, rich carving and gilding being by no means rare forms of decoration. The authorities thundered against such 'vain and superfluous expense' and introduced sumptuary laws to try to curb what they believed constituted a drain on the state's finances. The first of such laws was enacted in 1489; it also applied to mirrors with plates of polished steel, which was the more common form before about 1520. No picture of such an elaborate mirror is included here but Pl. 68 shows a Venetian woman holding a dressing-glass as her maid dresses her hair.

Venice played the role of disseminator, first of Eastern goods and styles through trade, and secondly of styles through printed publications. She also had her own luxury industries, of which glass-making was the principal. There were also thriving *maiolica* factories and some of the best musical instruments made in Europe were produced in this city (Pl. 57).

CHAPTER 4

PARIS

1530-1580

That area of France centred on Paris, where the French royal court spent its time and the chief courtiers resided, can for our purposes be regarded virtually as a province of Italy during this period. The princely courts of Italy were relatively small and not all that powerful; when one of them wanted to take action against another, it was usual to seek allies among the other Italian courts – and, often, to try to acquire France as an ally as well. Generally speaking, a royal court is likely to be more powerful than a princely one because its revenues from taxes and other incomes are larger. Power of this kind not only strengthens a country's hand in political negotiation and in times of war; it also makes the court, and particularly the king, more able to play the role of patron in the cultural field, not least in the arts. The French kings of the period that concern us here played this role to the full, surrounding themselves with a magnificence that overshadowed all other courts except that of the Holy Roman Emperors (in Austria and in Spain) and which was considerably more innovative, stylistically, than any other.

Such munificent patronage acted as a powerful lure to artists, especially Italians, who flocked to France throughout the 16th century (Leonardo da Vinci was appointed Painter and Engineer to the French king in 1506 and died in France in 1516 in a château presented to him by the king). The Sack of Rome in 1527 (see p. 21) provided additional stimulus to artists whose livelihood had been curtailed by this disastrous event, and among the artistic superstars who went to France in the years after the Sack were Rosso Fiorentino, Francesco Primaticcio and Sebastiano Serlio. It should be added that it was not only the French monarchs who built magnificent new residences for themselves; many leading members of the nobility followed the royal example. Many of them had spent long periods in Italy during the successive campaigns between 1494 and 1555, when French armies were fighting in, or occupying parts of, that country, and they were all greatly impressed by the splendour, the comforts and the way of life that was enjoyed at the Italian courts. The result of this French experience of Italy was that numerous fine residences were erected in France at this period which required decorating or filling with contents. French architects, and artisans working in the luxury trades, flourished as never before; and their efforts were supplemented by those of the immigrant Italians.

Rosso Fiorentino, whose name has just been mentioned, had already made a considerable name for himself as a painter in Italy before going to France in 1530 to work for François I (1515–47). However, the embellishment of the Gallery in the royal palace at Fontainebleau was his chief contribution to the history of decorative art. Building began in 1528 and this enormously long room was more or less ready to receive decoration by the time Rosso arrived on the scene. What Rosso and his (mainly Italian) assistants created may still be seen today. Each of 14 compartments flanked by windows is differently ornamented, but nevertheless forms part of a visually unified whole. Large frescoed scenes on the upper part of the walls are surrounded by exceptionally bold stucco decoration consisting of figures, in many cases greatly elongated, amid aggressively scrolled strapwork that looks like heavy metalwork. Pl. 70 shows a tapestry that reproduces the central panel of the Gallery very closely. Rosso's decoration was a remarkable innovation, although it had its roots in Italian stuccowork and carving of the 1520s. Michelangelo's entirely painted ceiling in the Sistine Chapel of 1508–12, with its scenes in framed compartments and many figures seeming to be made of white stucco, foreshadows the Fontainebleau formula of fresco painting combined with real stucco in virtually free-standing relief. Rosso had tried out mural decoration on such lines in Rome in 1524, it seems, and would also have been familiar with the grotesques of the early 1520s (see p. 21) embodying stucco reliefs such as those at the Villa Madama. But he had also spent some time in Venice before moving to France, and it is likely that he there came across north Italian work, which has a richer plasticity than anything he had hitherto seen, and would seem strongly to have influenced his later work.

Rosso died in 1540 and his chief collaborator Primaticcio took over the direction of work at Fontainebleau, where he was responsible for creating a bedchamber for the king's mistress (the Duchesse d'Etampes), using a refined version of the Gallery's decoration. The room was later incorporated into a staircase, but the fine chimneypiece survives. Primaticcio had worked under Giulio Romano at Mantua (see p. 25) before moving to France in 1532, so was familiar with the early Mannerist style of that great architect and master of decoration.

The important factor in our story now is the dissemination of the Fontainebleau style by lesser artists who had been involved in projects at the palace, or elsewhere for members of the court. This was effected in part by their own work, but more effectively by their publication of engravings based on the decoration of the Gallery and the Etampes Bedchamber from the 1540s to the 1560s. Although these engravings were enormously influential in the Netherlands, their chief influence was on Italian artists working in their own country. Salviati and Vasari, for instance, were much influenced by what they thus learned about the Fontainebleau style, which had a powerful effect on their work in Rome and Florence during the 1550s and 1560s.

Antonio Fantuzzi who, like Primaticcio, came from Bologna, was promoted in the works hierarchy at Fontainebleau by the latter after Rosso's death. Fantuzzi ran a workshop there between 1542 and 1548 from which he published many engravings based on the Gallery's decoration that were often hurried, even summary, but nevertheless conveyed the spirit of the originals. He was inventive and played fairly freely with the Gallery formula. Léonard Thiry, a Flemish painter who had worked at Fontainebleau under both Rosso and Primaticcio, surrounded scenes of his own invention with variations on the Gallery's decorative formula. His work was reproduced by Pierre Milan, a prominent Parisian engraver, and later by René Boyvin, a goldsmith and pupil of Milan. Both seem to have been well able to devise variants of Fontainebleau patterns. The composition shown in Pl. 70, with a modified central scene, was apparently composed by Milan and Boyvin and published in 1554, while a sequence, designed by Thiry and engraved by Boyvin, showing the story of Jason and the Golden Fleece, also with characteristic Fontainebleau-style frames, came out in Paris in 1563. A very sensitive rendering of the Etampes chimneyp-

iece was produced in 1544 by Jean Mignon, another Parisian engraver. To this list we should add the anonymous engraver of Pl. 71.

The title-page illustrated in Pl. 78, in a book that had a wide readership at the time, also carried an impression of the Fontainebleau style with its close-packed character, its metal-like scrolls, massed fruit and vulnerably naked figures crammed into inches that are too low for them as they look nervously (or lasciviously) over their shoulders at each other. Such niches are to be seen in Pl. 70 although they are there crammed with fruit. Those who feel uncomfortable when faced with such awkwardness, which sometimes borders on the sadistic,

an assistant; it looks a little heavy-handed although it clearly derives from the example set at Fontainebleau. Dell'Abbate must also have worked at Montmorency's château at Ecouen, north of Paris, where some splendid painted chimneypieces embody vigorous strapwork ornament of great virtuosity (Pl. 74).

François I, who commissioned the work at Fontainebleau and brought over many of the Italian artists who were to work on this project, died in 1547. He was succeeded by Henri II, who reigned for twelve years. His Italian consort, Catherine de' Medici, who has already been mentioned for inviting a leading Venetian lace-designer to Paris (p. 38), was doubtless responsible for bringing other Italian artists and practices to France.

Several court entertainments arranged for Queen Catherine were designed by another painter from the Fontainebleau project, the Frenchman Antoine Carron, who became a noted tapestry designer and succeeded dell'Abbate (d. 1571) as chief designer at the French court. His reputation was considerable and his influence is likely to have been great. Do we see his style in the drawing reproduced in Pl. 73, the design for which must surely be related to that of the fine embroidery shown in Pl. 75 that is believed to have been made at a workshop established in Paris by Henry II in 1551? Or are we looking at the work of Jean Cousin, no less celebrated as a designer and draughtsman, who was responsible for the amazing title-page illustrated in Pl. 76? The figures at the bottom have much in common with those in the drawing and on the embroidery. But this is a reminder that a style may be adopted by a number of people, all working within a relatively small circle in the same city, so there is reason enough for their work to have many resemblances. It is therefore not surprising that the work of Etienne Delaune should be couched in the same vein, as he was a talented engraver and goldsmith who seems to have enjoyed a measure of royal favour under Henri II (1547–59). Delaune was a very capable designer of jewellery and other small items (e.g. hand-mirrors, Pl. 81) whose work is also couched in a delicate and refined version of the Fontainebleau style, although it was claimed of an artist named Guido, who must have been Italian and presumably worked within the orbit of the Fontainebleau circle of artists, that he and Jean Cousin had designed 'almost all of the work of Etienne [Delaune]' (see Pl. 79). No doubt an exaggeration, this does suggest Etienne had a number of assistants.

Because of their ability to draw, goldsmiths have often become involved in the process of design (as noted before; see p. 12), and this was very much the case in 16th-century Paris. When designing a vessel, a goldsmith would often adopt a motif from a print – a mask, for instance – but it seems to have been rare for an

have to remember that people at the time admired this manner, and that a considerable number of them were happy to spend large sums of money to have their rooms, and objects in them, decorated in this way.

Among the Italians working at Fontainebleau was the painter Niccolo dell'Abbate, who became chief designer to the French court. The illumination of a book of hours made in about 1549 for the powerful statesman Anne de Montmorency (Pl. 72) was presumably dell'Abbate's work, although the framework may be by

entire design to be copied. Goldsmiths often owned lead or plaster casts of ornamental details, from which moulds could be taken and then applied to their work (see Pl. 80). These, and the engravings in the goldsmiths' possession, were sometimes called 'portraits' [*pourtraicts*] in contemporary documents, an indication that they were 'a likeness' of the real thing. The presence of moulds or casts indicates that a certain amount of series-production was already then well established

Pl. 74 Chimneypiece in Anne de Montmorency's château at Écouen, painted with brilliant *trompe-l'oeil* decoration in the Fontainebleau style in the manner of dell'Abbate (see Pl. 72), in the mid-1550s. The interlaced strapwork is striking. *Musée National de la Renaissance, Château d'Écouen*

in Parisian workshops, as we know it also was at Nürnberg and no doubt in other major centres of the trade.

Very little Parisian goldsmiths' work of the period survives and it is now difficult to envisage what their products were like. A silver-gilt reliquary with a rock-crystal bowl (Pl. 80) made for François I in a court workshop in the 1530s probably reflects current taste in ceremonial drinking vessels. Its design relies very much on scrolled brackets linking the components, as does the elaborate pottery made at a small royal factory in Paris (Pl. 82), which was clearly based on silver models.

At the time of his death the court goldsmith Richard Toutin (d. 1570) owned a large and handsomely bound scrap-book of prints and drawings as well as nine engraved copper plates 'suitable for making likenesses', i.e. he produced engravings, presumably of his own designs. Another Parisian, Hierosme [Jérôme] de Gormont, who must also have been a goldsmith, judging by the title of a book he published in 1546 telling us that it was in the first place useful for members of that trade, was very likely something of a designer; his moresque patterns were copied from Pellegrino, who had published his original work in 1530, citing embroiderers as the principal potential users of his work (see p. 34 and Pl. 55). Jérôme de Gormont should not be confused with Jean Gourment, who also designed moresques – very fine ones of greater originality – in about 1545. Etienne Delaune, although apparently trained as a goldsmith, never became a master and was later taught engraving by Pierre Milan; he was subsequently the producer of a great many designs suitable primarily for workers in metal (Pl. 79).

One of the most important designers active in France during the mid-16th century, Jacques Androuet Du Cerceau, engraver and architect with a royal appointment, published from a workshop in Orléans an enormous number of prints of architecture and ornament from 1549

and into the 1570s, including designs for silver vessels. He
was sufficiently well informed about goldsmiths' work to
be able to draw a ewer 'in the Italian fashion' and a standing cup 'in the German taste', both of which typify the
favoured styles of those two nations at the time. Du
Cerceau seems to have been more a publicizer of the current style of his time – a fusion of the Fontainebleau
manner with Netherlandish Mannerism (see Chapter 5)
and with a dash of direct Italian input – than a great inno-
vator, but his publications were so numerous and sold so
widely that he had a marked influence on design in general during the second half of the century.

Although Du Cerceau may have moved to Paris after
1575, he spent most of his life working from Orléans, a

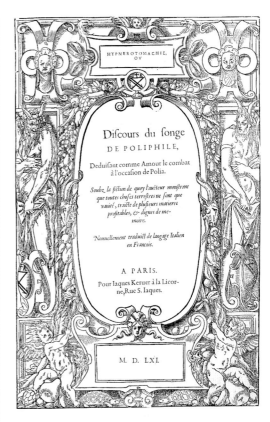

established there; a high proportion were involved in the importing of Italian silks (at this time the best in Europe), but Italians occupied positions of importance in other Lyonnais industries, notably that of book-selling, with its associated trades of printing and publishing. Sebastien Gryphius, the most prolific printer in Lyons, had learned his business in Italy, as had the publisher Guillaume Rouillé who wrote Italian fluently. Some 75 books in Italian were published in Lyons during the 16th century, including excellent imitations of the productions of Aldus (see pp. 48 and 51), to the extent that he complained about this plagiarism in 1503. These reproductions were produced by Balthazar de Gabiano, an important citizen of Italian extraction who at the time headed the family business. However, the most interesting Lyonnais publisher of the time was Jean de Tournes, who, with Rouillé, was the chief printer of illustrated books at Lyons in the middle of the century and employed a fine designer of ornament, Bernard Salomon, to decorate his works

Pl. 80 Silver-gilt reliquary in the form of a standing-cup, with a rock-crystal bowl; set with rubies and pearls. Made in Paris for François I in the 1530s.
Musée du Louvre, Paris

Pl. 81 Design for a hand-mirror by Etienne Delaune in a manner derived from the Fontainebleau School, but miniaturized. From a suite of engravings published in Paris in 1561. Such small mirrors were worn hanging by a chain round the neck as an item of female adornment.
Rijksprentenkabinet, Rijksmuseum, Amsterdam.

Pl. 82 Candlestick of so-called 'Saint-Porchaire' pottery; made for Anne de Montmorency in the mid-16th century at a royal factory on the site of the Tuileries Palace, adjacent to the Louvre. The design is evidently based on contemporary French goldsmiths' work, and the moresque and interlace patterns clearly derive from engraved ornament published in Paris at the time.
Ville de Paris, Musée du Petit Palais, Paris (Mus. no. O.Dut.1126)

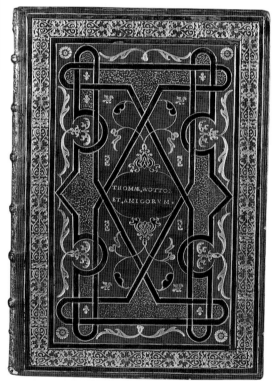

Pl. 83 Parisian bookbinding believed to have been commissioned by an erudite English traveller in about 1548. Thomas Wotton, whose name is stamped on the front cover, was the owner of a great library and the first Englishman to commission gold-tooled bindings in any number.
Reproduced by permission of the Provost and Fellows of Eton College Library, Windsor

city that had long enjoyed royal associations, lying rather more than 100 kilometres south of Paris, well within reach of a great many seats of the nobility. A city that played an even greater part in the development of styles in France at this period, however, was Lyons, which lies on one of the main routes from Italy into Northern France, and was the site of a great annual fair at which an enormous amount of business was conducted. Lyons had long been a city with strong Italian connections, and many Italian merchants were

Pl. 84 Parisian bookbinding of the so-called 'Grolier' type made in 1550 for Anne de Montmorency (see Pl. 74). The brown calf is tooled and gilded; the strapwork is painted with coloured waxes. A closely similar binding was made for Catherine de' Medici in the same year. The pattern is inspired by one of Pellegrino's designs of 1530, re-issued in 1545 by Jérôme de Gormont (see p. 44). *Bibliothèque Mazarine, Paris (Res. 4955 A)*

Pl. 85 Door-panel of carved walnut, partly gilded, from a house at Clermont-Ferrand bearing the date 1557 and the emblems of Henri II and Catherine de' Medici. The interlaced patterns and cartouches correspond to Parisian bookbinding ornament of the same date. *Musée du Louvre, Paris*

A particularly exciting development of the current French style took place in the field of bookbinding. It is not quite obvious why this should have happened in a field that tends normally to be conservative and not all that closely associated with fashionable taste in other crafts, but in mid-16th-century France a quite exceptional degree of innovation entered this field and was not to be matched again until the second half of the 18th century.

Perhaps one reason was that now books were more readily available, private libraries could be formed, and such a mass of volumes now began to loom large in an interior. Their covers had, in effect, to fit in with the

(Pls. 88 and 91). Salomon produced the 179 illustrations for a French edition of Ovid's *Metamorphoses*, published in 1557, which reached an extensive audience; each scene had a wide border of moresques often combined with strapwork, and some printed patterns of moresques in much the same style are now attributed to Salomon. He was clearly a highly inventive artist whose influence was enormous. In a book containing illustrations and ornaments by him, published in the year he had died, he was described as 'a painter as excellent as any in our hemisphere'.

The Lyons book-trade suffered badly as a result of the intermittent but ferocious wars of religion that caused much misery in France from 1562 until 1589 (with the accession of Henry IV), as Huguenots fought Catholics. Many Huguenots (Protestants) fled the country; they included many printers from Lyons who mostly went to Geneva. It was not only religious persecution that drove capable artisans and artists away, however; France at the time also suffered from severe economic depression which must have made the pastures of less turbulent nations look greener to men with skills to offer. Among the French designers who left France at this time was Etienne Delaune, who went first to Strassburg (after the St Bartholomew's Eve Massacre of 1572), and then to Augsburg where he was eagerly welcomed and was able most effectively to spread the style that he himself had espoused in Paris. He eventually returned to Paris.

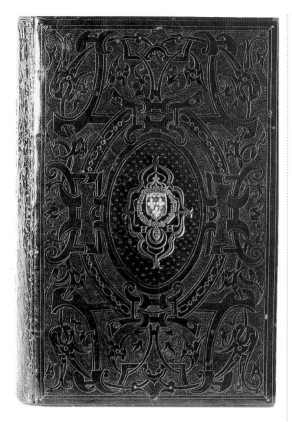

Pl. 86 Bookbinding from the Fontainebleau Library bearing the arms of Henri II on a book published in 1554. The exuberant strapwork takes the Fontainebleau style on to a new, lighter and more elegant plane (a development of that shown in Pl. 74). The central medallion with the royal arms echoes Venetian practice (cf. Pl. 53). Probably the work of the binder to the Crown, Gommart Estienne. *Bibliothèque Nationale, Paris (Res. Vit. 9 Loc.)*

Pl. 87 Bookbinding made in Paris about 1531 stamped with a pattern (engraved on a single plate), with gold tooling; designed by the publisher and engraver Geofroy Tory. Based on Italian models, his moresque patterns are larger and more formal so that they become a wiry form of *rinceaux* (see p. 16). The border is still in the Gothic taste. *Victoria and Albert Museum, London (Mus. no. L. 1402–1931)*

Pl. 88 Title-page for a New Testament published by Jean de Tournes at Lyons in 1559 with a fine framing of 'enlarged moresques' (see Pl. 87) that now include 'breaks'. Designed by Bernard Salomon in the previous year for a complete Bible, it continued in use by de Tournes for a number of title-pages into the 1560s.

decor, and not simply protect the contents or give pleasure when held in the hand. Now they had to look good from a distance when displayed on a shelf or a table. Another reason is said to have been the availability of high quality morocco leather as a result of a mid-century Franco-Turkish alliance. This leather lent itself well to tooling and gilding, and the best Parisian binderies proved adept at transferring elaborate interlacing patterns and moresques from contemporary pattern-books and adapting them for application to book-covers faced with this receptive material.

Pls. 83, 84 and 86 show brilliant variations of this elegant style which lifted the art of bookbinding on to a quite new plane, where it could vie with the finest kinds of decoration in other media. Pl. 83 shows a binding probably commissioned in Paris in 1547 by an Englishman and indicates that the purchaser was fully aware of recent developments in the production of fine books in that city. Its cover epitomises the new taste admirably, with interlaced strapwork surrounded with foliate scrolls and a border of moresque ornament forming a candelabrum pattern, all executed with gold tooling. The binding made for Anne de Montmorency in 1550 (Pl. 84) is almost exactly like one made for Catherine de' Medici in the same year; and incidentally the central strapwork motif of two triangles within a circle was adopted for the decoration of an enamelled silver cup made in Paris for the same queen and her husband Henri II. Characteristic of the style is the way the interlaced straps suddenly change direction,

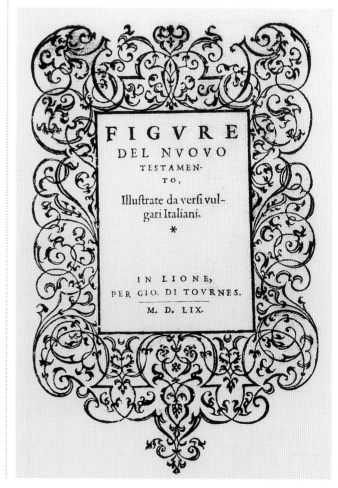

FIGVRE DEL NVOVO TESTAMENTO,

Illuftrate da verfi vulgari Italiani.

*

IN LIONE,
PER GIO. DI TOVRNES.
M. D. LIX.

spread to Italy whence its distant origins must paradoxically be sought.

A different idiom, which is well exemplified in the bookbinding by Geofroy Tory, is based on the old candelabrum formula with large scrolls organised symmetrically around a vertical median (Pl. 87). It presumably derives from Italy but seems, in France, to have been developed to something rather more imposing than the related patterns on earlier Italian bindings of the 1520s and the 1530s. We are here really dealing with a development of moresque patterns, carried out on a large scale. By about 1550, covers with designs that seem to have been inspired by Tory's formula were being produced in Italy, so, once again, an Italian formula apparently was 'returned' to Italy, where it was re-adopted in revised form. The Tory style also seems to have influenced book-design in Switzerland and Germany (see Pl. 123) and was further developed by Bernard Salomon at Lyons in the 1550s (Pl. 88).

forming a sharp angle which in some cases is acute. These 'breaks' were to become an important feature of much European decoration in the second half of the century, and continued in favour during the Baroque period.

This style in high-class bookbinding reached its apogee in the 1550s, apparently in the workshop of the royal binder Gommart (Gommar) Estienne, who held the appointment from 1550 until 1559 (Pls. 86 and 90). We do not know who provided the designs for Gommart's bindings, but he was clearly an artist of considerable brilliance; someone who had worked in the orbit of Niccolo dell'Abbate may well have been responsible (compare Pl. 74 and Pl. 86).

The gaiety of these designs, which depend on elaborate strapwork on to which coloured wax has been applied with a paintbrush, aroused widespread admiration and the group as a whole is usually referred to as being in the Grolier style (Pl. 84). Jean Grolier was from a Lyonnais family of Italian origin who entered the royal service and was appointed treasurer of the Duchy of Milan in 1509, a post he held until 1520. He settled in Paris about 1525 and became one of the treasurers of France in 1532, which lucrative post he occupied until 1555. He was a great collector of books and had them specially bound by first-class binders, first in Italy and later in Paris, until his death in 1565 (Pl. 89 which is, however, not characteristic of the 'Grolier style'). His example was quickly followed by others, and eventually the style

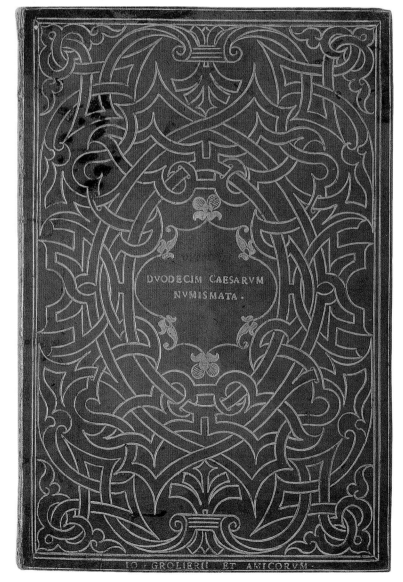

PI. 91 Strapwork framing of a figure representing the month of April. Designed by Bernard Salomon for a book published at Lyons in 1560 by Jean de Tournes. Note the 'breaks' in the strapwork.
Victoria and Albert Museum, London (from a facsimile, Mus. no. PP20E)

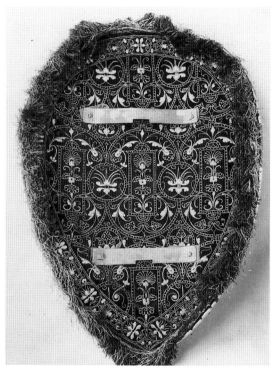

PI. 92 Reverse of a buckler (small shield) made for Charles IX of France (1560–74), decorated with a pattern executed with silk cord couched (onlaid) on silk velvet. This type of decoration resembles the equally tight and formal patterns to be seen on a class of late 16th-century French book-bindings of a type very different to those in the Grolier style. A late example of these so-called 'fanfare bindings' is illustrated in PI. 179.
Musée du Louvre, Paris

The work of Gommart Estienne in the 1550s becomes even cleverer, as he interlaces strapwork in ever more complicated patterns, with numerous breaks (Pl. 90), which again find echoes in Bernard Salomon's work of about 1560 (Pl. 91). A royal buckler (small ceremonial shield) of embroidered crimson velvet displays a somewhat more formal pattern (Pl. 92) and is of a kind that returns in bookbinding with the so-called 'fanfare' patterns which consist of tight little scrolls, often interlaced, frequently with breaks, all amid scattered foliage (Pl. 179). These patterns are much admired for their virtuosity but they are dull and repetitive compared with what had gone before and, by 1600, French bookbinding had settled back into being just a skilled trade. Gone (for a long while) were the days when binders were up there among the great artist of their time.

The well-carved table in Pl. 93 is in the style of Jacques Androuet Du Cerceau, whose Renaissance ornament has already been mentioned (p. 44). Du Cerceau published a suite of designs for this class of table in about 1560, many of them shown with the double-leafed top which indicates that they are designs for draw-leaf tables (i.e. where the lower leaves pull outwards and the upper leaf drops to the lower level to form the central section of a tri-partite table-top). This useful and clever invention must have originated either in France or in the Netherlands. It was not taken up in Italy until much later. Du Cerceau also published (among much else) designs for cabinets and what he called '*dressoirs*', small buffets or sideboards for use in the, by then, highly fashionable dining-parlours, relatively small-sized rooms where the owner and his family could dine in private rather than taking their meals in a large hall.

Last but not least should be mentioned Philibert de l'Orme, who had been Chief Architect to the Crown under Henri II in the 1550s when he had done important work at Fontainebleau. In the mid-1560s Catherine de' Medici commissioned him to build the Tuileries Palace in Paris, close to the Louvre. De l'Orme dedicated to the Queen the first part of his excellent treatise on architecture (in nine volumes) which was well illustrated and widely read. He designed the plates himself, including the title-page (Pl. 94), and these were an important source of inspiration, providing patterns for architectural features in a sober Classical manner.

Netherlandish influence on the decorative arts in France was very considerable, and there were a number of immigrant designers, engravers and craftsmen – the last often bringing the secrets of new techniques, notably in the art of setting jewels and cutting diamonds which was to place Paris in the technological lead. The immigrants from Antwerp came to Paris because the Flemish economy had collapsed (see p. 54)

and some, who were Protestants, came because of religious persecution.

Paris, with its satellite at Fontainebleau, took an Italian style, exaggerated some of its features, thus turning it into what was essentially something new, and then played it back to the Italians exuberantly transformed and ready to inspire Italian designers to make their own thing out of this fresh example. Paris also inspired northern Europeans with this revamped Italian style, as we shall see in the next two chapters. From being an Italian province, artistically speaking, France with Paris at its heart became a major centre of inspiration for the whole Renaissance in northern Europe.

Pl. 93 Draw-leaf table of walnut in the style publicised by Jacques Androuet Du Cerceau, the most prolific disseminator of French Renaissance decorative formulae of the mid-16th century. This table has three baluster legs rising from the cross-piece that links the end-supports, one of which can be seen here.
The Metropolitan Museum of Art, New York; The Michael Friedsam Collection, Bequest of Michael Friedsam, 1931 (32.100.329)

Pl. 94 Title-page of Philibert de l'Orme's famous treatise on architecture, published in Paris in 1567, a work dedicated to his patron, Queen Catherine de' Medici. He designed all the plates himself and the book forms a rich repertoire of French ornament in the Classical taste of the time.
By permission of the Houghton Library, Harvard University, Cambridge, Massachusetts

CHAPTER 5

ANTWERP

Pl. 95 Painting in the Cornelis Floris
style on stained glass from a
building in Antwerp, presumably
about 1550. The heavy metal
character of strapwork is here very
evident but a strong humorous streak
often pervades such compositions,
counterbalancing the otherwise
brutal concept of naked flesh
hemmed in by unyielding ironwork.
Museum Vleeshuis, Antwerp

PI. 97 The Cornelis Floris style was long-lived and remained fashionable even after 1600. Here the letter K has been turned into an elaborate initial with all the standard features of the style. From an alphabet composed in 1595 by Theodor de Bry, engraver and publisher of Frankfurt am Main, but here seen in an edition issued in Cologne in 1613 by Johann Bussemacher with a title suggesting the designs are new.
Museum für Kunsthandwerk, Frankfurt am Main (Mus. no. LOZ 1358)

1530-1620

PI. 96 Drawn initial dated 1543, in a new style in a book recording the names of new masters and apprentices of the Artists' Guild at Antwerp; believed to be the work of Cornelis Floris. The strapwork, with its lobed lugs and holes seemingly pierced to hold screws or bolts, has the appearance of steel. This is a very early manifestation of Netherlandish strapwork grotesque ornament. The style spread quickly among Antwerp artists, notably Cornelis Bos.
Royal Academy of Fine Arts, Antwerp, Archive

Brussels was the capital of the Spanish Netherlands during the 16th century and became the seat of the governor's court. But it was Antwerp that was the principal city of the province, the most important centre of commerce and banking enterprise in northern Europe at the time. Its deep-water port at the mouth of the River Scheldt, which provided access to the North Sea and thence to the Baltic and the Mediterranean, made it a focal point of maritime trade, while the overland trade-routes that converge on the city ensured its dominant position until the end of the century. In the summer months, when the Atlantic permitted their passage, fleets of cargo-carrying galleys (lightweight and swift-moving vessels suitable for the transport of luxury goods) from Venice and Genoa were to be seen moored in rows in the roads outside Antwerp's harbour, while ships of greater burthen unloaded bulk goods at her quays.

The presence of many rich and often discriminating burghers in the city, and of a powerful fashion-conscious court nearby, provided an assured market for trades involved in the production of luxury wares, an industry that increased enormously in size as the century wore on and as foreigners became aware of the great skills that Antwerp craftsmen had acquired against this stimulating background.

Superb silver, beautiful jewellery, splendid faience, first-class musical instruments, striking stained glass, handsomely printed books and numerous sheets of printed ornamental patterns were produced in the city, and much was exported. Add to this the goods made in other Flemish cities and shipped abroad through Antwerp – tapestries and a wide range of other furnishing fabrics, brass goods such as chandeliers and fire-dogs, gilt leather for the cladding of walls to brilliant effect, lace for clothes and trimming furnishings, glassware that was often of great elegance – and one can appreciate the enormous influence the city had on the decorative arts of Europe at this period.

Moreover, while the most skilled craftsmen remained in Antwerp, those of the second rank often went abroad to seek their fortunes in major foreign cities, where they sometimes rose to leading positions in their professions. Flemish artisans were to be found all over Europe by the mid-16th century, exercising their skills and spreading advanced techniques as well as novel design features into the countries where they took up residence. The most skilled goldsmiths in London in the middle of the century were Flemish and the same was evidently the case in other trades, if we can believe the assertion made in 1531 that, when an Englishman wanted 'anything well paynted, kerved or embrawdred', he was obliged 'to abandonne our owne countrymen and resorte to

Pl. 98 Page from 14 sheets of cartouche designs by Cornelis Floris and described as new inventions for sepulchral monuments in the Antique taste; published at Antwerp by Hieronymus Cock in 1557. A first suite was issued the year before. The imprisoned figures here tend to dominate the strapwork.
Museum für Kunsthandwerk, Frankfurt am Main (Mus. no. LOZ 2048)

Pl. 99 Bold strapwork cartouche on the title-page to a suite of 20 designs for silver vessels (of extreme Mannerist character) by Cornelis Floris, published by Hieronymus Cock at Antwerp in 1548.
Rijksprentenkabinet, Rijksmuseum, Amsterdam

Pl. 100 From a suite of decorated cartouches by Jakob Floris, brother of Cornelis and primarily a painter on glass; issued by Hans Liefrinck, a prominent Antwerp publisher, in 1564. Note the way the vigorous scrolls now encompass a plain inner frame.
Rijksprentenkabinet, Rijksmuseum, Amsterdam

forced to work covertly for a master who was a native of the city. But their creations, albeit accredited to their master, nevertheless often influenced taste and techniques.

Antwerp's fortunes declined from the middle of the century onwards although, even in the 17th century, she remained an important artistic centre (see Chapter 9). The River Scheldt began to silt up making the approach from the sea less easy, but it was the Dutch of the northern provinces of the Netherlands who, having gradually established independence from the Spanish-dominated south, administered the final *coup de grâce* to Antwerp's maritime trade by exercising an increasingly effective naval stranglehold on the passage between the sea and the city. The stress imposed on the city by the civil and religious strife of the time undermined its commercial and industrial prosperity, and many citizens emigrated – by no means all on account of their religion but through the general pressure of a diminishing economy which tended to affect artisans in the luxury trades first. A particularly horrifying event indirectly arising

from the wars was the Sack of Antwerp in 1576 when Spanish troops, whose wages had not been paid on time, vented their wrath on the prosperous citizens, killing thousands and burning down their houses. But, as with the Sack of Rome in 1527, this had the effect of spreading the unfortunate city's culture, and not least its artistic culture and skills. However, those artists and artisans who remained in the city soon found themselves greatly in demand, so prosperity at this particular moment only suffered a temporary setback. The overall decline due to quite other factors was more serious.

Antwerp's flourishing publishing trade acted as a great disseminator of western culture, freely re-publishing foreign books, often in translation. It also re-published suites of foreign ornament prints, sometimes mixing them in with other suites, and frequently omitting to acknowledge the sources. To such assemblages might also be added patterns composed by Flemish designers. One of the principal publishers of such compendia was Hieronymus Cock, whose shop at the sign 'Aux Quatre Vents' [The Four Winds] had an extensive export network for its publications in Italy,

straungers'. Much the same could be said of many other cities of Europe; powerful local guilds tended to make every effort to exclude foreign craftsmen, and even highly skilled immigrant craftsmen were prevented from practising their trade openly and were therefore often

Pl. 101 Silver-gilt casting-bottle for scent with chased and embossed strapwork ornament in the Floris style, made in London (probably by a Flemish goldsmith) in 1563–4. Height 15 cm (6 in.)
Victoria and Albert Museum, London (Mus. no. M.13–1986)

Pl. 102 Handsome faience vessel of Germanic form but produced with techniques introduced from *maiolica* factories in Italy; made at Antwerp in 1562 at the workshop of Jan Bogaert. The decoration is based on designs of 1554 by Cornelis Floris.
Musées Royaux d'Art et d'Histoire, Brussels (Mus. no. 5931)

Pl. 103 Painted decoration in the Floris manner inside the lid of a harpsichord. This was made in 1579 by the celebrated Antwerp maker of keyboard instruments Lodewijk Theewes in London, where he worked for several years. The normally symmetrical disposition of such patterns has here been skilfully adapted to fit the shape of the instrument's lid.
Victoria and Albert Museum, London (Mus. no. 125–1890)

France and Germany. A well-known book on moresque patterns that Cock published in the early 1540s, a direct copy of an Italian work, had his name and address on the title-page and a long descriptive title in French, Italian, German and Latin – an indication of the range of the sales he anticipated.

The links between Paris and Antwerp were especially strong in the middle decades of the century and Flemish designers seem to have been well aware of the nature of what was being created at Fontainebleau soon after it was devised in the years around 1540, in the first place most probably through the medium of Fantuzzi's prints (see p. 42). A more personal link was provided by Léonard Thiry, a skilled Flemish painter who actually himself played an important role in the decoration of the Fontainebleau Gallery (see p. 42). He returned to the Netherlands in the 1540s and died at Antwerp in 1550. Before leaving Paris he had designed 25 scenes depicting the story of Jason and the Golden Fleece, surrounded with Fontainebleau-type framing which René Boyvin apparently began to engrave about 1545 (at which point it becomes possible, at least in theory, for individual printed sheets to go on sale) although the complete suite was not published until 1563 – in Paris. The heavy strapwork, to be seen in the framing of several decorative panels at Fontainebleau, looking as if cut from massive iron plates, sometimes curves forward and partly envelops human or semi-human figures. The chronology at this point is confusing but it is conceivable that, where this particular feature is present, Flemish influence has been at work, although it is more likely that the influence came from France to Antwerp soon after 1540. Whatever the case, an Antwerp sculptor named Cornelis Floris drew some crazy but quite graceful figures in the Register of the artist's guild at Antwerp. They depict naked human figures held captive by strapwork that is seemingly of iron. These figures, and their successors through the next few decades, can have much charm but their unmistakable sadistic character makes one feel uneasy – for cold metal clasping bare flesh is by no means a comfortable combination. The earliest figure of this type in the Register dates from 1543 (Pl. 96) and the style was quickly taken up by other Antwerp artists, notable by Cornelis Bos, who in 1546 published a group of crowded and not very attractive designs with 'imprisoned beings'. Bos may have had a somewhat warped view of life, as he belonged to an extremist religious sect that was suppressed in the southern Netherlands and he had to flee Antwerp in 1544. Before his exile Bos brought out a book of moresque patterns based on those Pellegrino had published in Paris in 1530 (see p. 34 and Pl. 55); no copy of this work is known but it was copied in Paris by Jérôme de Gormont in 1546; its title-page is one of the earliest fully developed examples of Flemish strapwork grotesque decoration and is entirely different from the

Pl. 105 The cabinet of drawers enclosed by a hinged front that, when open, dropped to form a writing-surface was originally a practical piece of furniture that had been developed in Spain around 1500. By the 1590s, when this elaborate specimen of ebony and ivory was made in Naples (which still had strong links with Spain), it had become a highly decorative object, in its finer qualities, although purely utilitarian models continued to be made. The maker of this piece was apparently Flemish, although the artist who executed the delicate ivory work was Italian. The design he executed betrays a knowledge of those designs the Floris brothers had devised in the middle of the century in Antwerp.
Philadelphia Museum of Art; Foule Collection (Mus. no. '30–1–188)

book's contents. Bos also issued prints with rather faithful representations of some of the mural decorations in the Vatican *Loggetta* and *Logge* (Pl. 23) which had never previously been properly recorded and indeed were not to be fully recorded and published until late in the 18th century. As they are in what was at that time a rather private part of the Vatican, they were celebrated largely by repute. The architect Sebastiano Serlio (see p. 35) had recommended in 1542 that artists would benefit from close study of these works and it is quite likely that these engravings by Bos, some of which are dated 1548, were commissioned to help those wishing to follow Serlio's advice. Bos's Roman work was apparently published in that city but the designs he produced on his return to the north were published in Antwerp despite his being a refugee.

It seems, however, that Cornelis Floris, rather than Cornelis Bos, was the inventor of the 'imprisoned beings' style and he was undoubtedly a better artist; even when complicated, his designs possess clarity and even his most spooky compositions tend to be elegant. The designs of these two artists were to be much copied all over Europe, particularly in the north, where they were the first distinctive flowers of Netherlandish Mannerism, but also in Italy (e.g. a north Italian spinet of 1568 in the Victoria and Albert Museum bears painted decoration incorporating elements from a Bos engraving of about 1550).

The patterns we have been discussing were based on the Italian grotesque formula (see Chapter 2) by means

Pl. 106 Plate from a volume commemorating the triumphal entry of the future King Philip II into Antwerp in 1549, published the year after, for which Cornelis Floris is believed to have provided many designs. This temporary structure set up on the processional route displays the dentilated cresting that became the hallmark of Northern Mannerist architecture and ornament generally.
From Cornelis Graphaeus, Le Triumphe d'Anvers, *1550*

of which broad surfaces could be covered; but an equally important development that took place in the Netherlands at this time was the evolution of the cartouche. This shield-like motif, useful to decorators in so many ways, evolved rapidly between 1540 and 1640. Floris took up the Fontainebleau-style 'heavy iron' strapwork and turned it into an enframing shield for the title-page of a book of his own designs for strange silver vessels, issued in 1548 (Pl. 99); and his brother, Jakob, a prominent painter of stained-glass windows, can be seen taking the development a step further in Pl. 100 of 1564. One can see how such designs could be used from a glance at the small silver-gilt scent-bottle, made in London (probably by a Flemish craftsman), shown in Pl. 101. By combining such cartouches with the related grotesques, overall schemes punctuated by framed scenes could be contrived to great effect. We see this in Pls. 102 and 103. The characteristic holes, often set in protruding lugs, are very much present in Cornelis Floris's compositions of the 1550s but may be seen in rudimentary form in his work of a decade earlier. But it was Hans Vredeman de Vries who took up this formula with gusto in the 1560s and included it in his designs for strapwork grotesques, and architectural ornament derived therefrom (Pl. 107), and established this as the dominant style in northern and central Europe for the next few decades. Novel Antwerp cartouches of the

Pl. 109 Detail of the back of a gable, or tine, on the gold and enamelled crown made for the coronation of King Christian IV of Denmark in 1596 by an immigrant goldsmith who was thoroughly familiar with recent developments in the field of design in the Netherlands and Germany. 'Strengthened joints', here very evident, were developed shortly before 1600, and feature in several suites of engravings for jewellery at about this time (see Pls. 137 and 163).
The Royal Danish Collections, Rosenborg Castle, Copenhagen

Pl. 107 The Northern Mannerist decorated gable or dormer formula, as foreshadowed in Pl. 106, is here fully developed. Published by Hieronymus Cock at Antwerp in 1565 after designs by the prolific Hans Vredeman de Vries.
Rijksprentenkabinet, Rijksmuseum, Amsterdam

Pl. 108 Design for a pendant jewel set with pearls and presumably to be of gold with colourful enamelled details, drawn by the highly competent Antwerp designer of jewellery, Hans Collaert the Elder. Here we see the Northern Mannerist style applied to a small object, but the general principles of the composition echo those used in contemporary Netherlandish architecture.
Musée du Louvre, Paris

PI. 110 A pendant in the late Northern Mannerist style drawn by the anonymous Netherlandish designer signing himself 'P.R.K.' from a suite dated 1609. The sweeping scrolls, strengthened joints and halberd-like forms of this now much lighter style are well illustrated here. These features were rapidly disseminated throughout Northern Europe, appearing in work in Paris, Amsterdam, Stuttgart, Copenhagen and Augsburg.
Museum für Kunsthandwerk, Frankfurt am Main (Mus. no. LOZ 2835)

PI. 111 The Jacobean Hall at Audley End, Essex, shortly before it was altered in about 1820. The fine screen, with its strapwork superstructure in the Netherlandish style of about 1600, was probably designed by Bernart Janssen. He started to build Audley End in 1603 for Thomas Howard, who became Lord Treasurer the following year. *Present whereabouts unknown*

1560s had a framing that is distinctly separated into inner and outer components, the latter being of great complexity, tending to overpower the central enframed subject.

Designs such as that shown in Pl. 107 derive from structures erected in Antwerp in 1549 to welcome the young Philip II (Pl. 106). They had been devised by the artist Pieter Coecke van Aelst, who had overall direction of the arrangements for the prince's triumphal procession through the city and were engraved the year after. The building here illustrated has a superstructure with a dormer-like centrepiece not unlike those in de Vries's design of 1565. This is not surprising if we note that de Vries was a member of Coecke's team in 1549 and probably was trained by Floris. Strapwork rising to a peak was a motif much used by architects working in the Netherlandish Mannerist taste (Pl. 111), but could also be employed on a small scale (e.g. Pls. 109 and 110) and variants of it were in great favour during the decades around 1600.

The importance of Hans Vredeman de Vries can hardly be exaggerated. He owed much to the example of Du Cerceau (see pp. 44 and 51) and, like him, issued numerous suites of engravings for a wide range of objects, from architecture to furniture, from silverware to books on perspective. He settled in Antwerp in about 1561, fled to Aachen in the early 1570s but returned in 1575. Ten years later he was forced to flee for good – settling first at Frankfurt, then at Wolfenbüttel, and subsequently at Hamburg, Danzig, Prague, Amsterdam, ending up at The Hague – and at each of these places inevitably ensuring that the style of which he was the chief protagonist became familiar to the indigenous artisans. During this period, probably at Wolfenbüttel in about 1588, he issued the first furniture pattern-book, his *Differents Pourtraicts de Menuiserie*.

De Vries's son Paul worked closely with him, publishing a further work on architecture in 1607 after his father's death, and a pattern-book of furniture in 1630 which adheres so closely to his father's that one could be forgiven for imagining it was executed decades earlier.

The sweeping shapes of French and Netherlandish decorative work (the Germans call it *Schweifwerk*, from *schweifen*, to sweep) are commonly joined to each other by straight, sometimes paired bars which developed into right-angled 'breaks' in otherwise uninterrupted stretches of strapwork (Pls. 97, 103 and 110), a feature originally inspired by the strapwork of Islamic moresque patterns (Pl. 55). These 'breaks' were to become notable features of 17th-century grotesque ornament (Pls. 182 and 240). Shortly before 1600 designers began to strengthen the joints in strapwork by adding 'metal' to either side of the crossing-points, usually with a halberd-like profile. One can see these strengthenings in Pls. 109 and 110. A further development is to be seen in the designs of Hans Collaert, a prolific designer of jewellery active at Antwerp from the 1550s until his death about 1581 (Pl. 108). A striking feature of many of his patterns are the C-scrolls ending in fat volutes, often with raised edges or rims – a motif that becomes very common during the first third of the 17th century, notably in Germany (Pls. 137 and 145).

Flemish 16th-century ornament of the types we have been studying springs from fertile, some might say overheated, fantasies and sometimes displays an almost burlesque character. Patterns are often heavy, crowded and confusing; no heed has been taken of the cool constraints of Classicism. Conservative Netherlandish artists – and there were many – regarded these bizarre expressions of their compatriots with derision. One of them, Karel van Mander, who wrote a book about painting (published in 1604), spoke of such ornament as being 'a heap of craziness' and maintained that 'such lameness' was 'very disgusting to see'. Classicism was of course admired in intellectual circles in the Netherlands, and a number of celebrated painters and architects worked in this formal tradition but, even in the work of such people, awkward and uncomfortable elements may be found, such as the sphinxes (?) in Pl. 113. Interest in Antiquity was strong in many quarters and most important artists had visited Italy. But while the conservatives adhered by and large to the principles of Classical theory, a great many others indulged their fantasies. It has to be admitted that what they created,

Netherlandish Mannerist contribution was to be of very considerable importance to the future development of decorative art in Europe.

While ornament was one of Antwerp's principal products, in the form of prints and drawn designs, the actual creation there of objects by skilled artisans was no less important for the history of design in Europe. Once again Italian forms, mainly Mannerist, were a potent source of inspiration, but Antwerp artists developed characteristic three-dimensional forms of their own during the middle decades of the century (Pl. 114).

Diamond-cutting and setting was an important trade at Antwerp, as was the setting of jewels generally. Besides gold, large quantities of precious stones and pearls came to Antwerp from the Spanish Americas, and were skilfully incorporated into silverware and jewellery, while, at the same time, the art of enamelling such wares was carried to a high degree of perfection (Pl. 109).

Italian *maiolica* workers were tempted to come

Pl. 112 Title-page to an English book of music using a design copied directly from one used at the Plantin press in Antwerp from 1566. It was adopted by the London publishers for about ten books between 1600 and 1618. The style is essentially Classical and owes little to Northern Mannerism, except in the framing of the oval in the cresting and the dated panel in the base.
By permission of the British Library, London (Pressmark K.8.h.5)

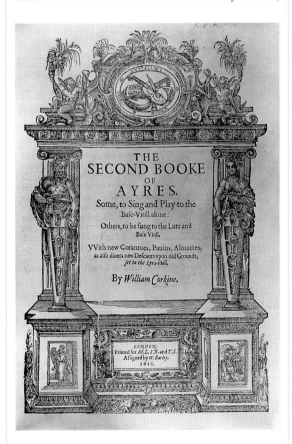

Pl. 113 Portrait by Hendrik Goltzius, dating from 1593, in which he was strongly influenced by contemporary Italian forms of decoration (Goltzius was in Italy in 1590/91). The advanced taste of the design heralds the italianate Baroque, with only the plumpness of the figures betraying the composition's Netherlandish origin.
Courtesy of Sotheby's, London

inspired directly from Italy or from Italy via France and there given a twist before being sent out across Europe, possessed a freshness and vigour that many people found exciting in the second half of the century. Such designs were soon to be seen in the applied arts everywhere north of the Alps, even in many parts of France, and occasionally also in Italy. As the centre of artistic creativity was beginning to move northwards, away from Italy (even though she still had much to offer), the

north and practise their craft, usually under indigenous management; their wares could be of high quality, as Pl. 102 shows. Much the same happened in glassmaking; Flemish glasshouses adopted Italian techniques and forms but eventually developed shapes of their own. The painters of stained glass were already well established at Antwerp by 1500 and were celebrated all over Europe during the 16th century. While many copied printed designs, quite a few

Pl. 114 A splendid silver-gilt tazza-like standing-cup made at Antwerp in 1541–2; maker unknown. An exceptionally fine example of Antwerp goldsmiths' work, displaying most of the characteristic features of their best mid-century products, including a marked horizontal tendency, even in objects that one might suppose would be essentially vertical. *Reproduced by permission of the Master, Fellows and Scholars of Emmanuel College, Cambridge*

Pl. 115 Painting by Jan Brueghel the Younger of about 1600 showing a handsome silver-gilt tazza in the Antwerp taste as well as a superb pendant lying with other jewellery on the table. *Musée Royaux des Beaux-Arts de Belgique, Brussels (Mus. no. 5013)*

were highly competent painters in their own right, fully capable of devising their own compositions (Pl. 95) and some, such as Jakob Floris, even issued prints of their own designs for publication (Pl. 100).

A branch of Antwerp publishing that became important towards the end of the 16th century was that of printed music. The Netherlands produced many internationally celebrated composers during the century, and the making of music was an important activity in Flemish cities. This in turn stimulated the makers of musical instruments, particularly keyboard instruments, whose work was sought by discriminating clients wanting to acquire the robust and reliable products for which the city became famed in the later decades of the century (Pl. 116), a fame that lasted right through the 17th century and until the 18th century. Keyboard instruments differed in quality and price, and an expensive and richly embellished one was a decorative object in its own right.

The Antwerp makers of keyboard instruments often made use of strips of paper printed with patterns which could be pasted on to their productions as a relatively inexpensive form of decoration. Some strips were of thick paper gilded on one face; this was then pressed in moulds so as to impart ornament in relief to the gilt strip, which thus acquired the appearance of gilt gesso decoration. Such embellishment could be reproduced in quantity and quite speedily at no great cost, once the moulds had been made. Large sheets of paper bearing simulations of grained wood could likewise be pasted on to the inside of harpsichord lids, often then trimmed with a border of moresques printed in black. Wood-grained papers were also made for pasting on to panelled ceilings, while gilded-relief strips were suitable for decorating boxes, frames and other small objects. Such 'mass-produced' ornament became something of an Antwerp speciality in the 17th century and shows how the city's industries developed ways of cutting the cost of its manufactures. Indeed, Antwerp should be seen as a centre where modern industrial practices, especially series production and the use of less costly materials that nonetheless produced telling effects, were adopted at an early date.

By far the most important industry in the south-western part of the Netherlands (the area to the west of Brussels with Tournai at its centre) and the adjacent territory across the French border around Lille was that of textile manufacture. An enormously wide range of materials was woven and exported to other European countries, the Near East, across to the Americas and round Africa to the Far East. Woollen materials (including worsteds) were the chief products, but materials made of linen came a close second, the linen damasks of Courtrai being particularly famous. Lace was also produced, as were cords and trimmings of all kinds. Among the woollens and worsteds were materials suitable for clothing in wide variety, and splendidly

Pl. 116 A fine Flemish spinet of 1581 sent by Philip II of Spain to Peru as a present to the Marchesa d'Oropesa. Made by the most celebrated Antwerp instrument maker of the time, Hans Ruckers. It has a smaller keyboard instrument (an *ottavino*) tucked into a receptacle on the left, which can be removed for playing separately. The main keyboard surround is decorated with moresques. To reach Peru this instrument had a long crossing of the Atlantic and the Caribbean, a land-crossing of the isthmus of Panama, a further sea-journey down the Pacific coast of South America to Peru, after which it had to be carried up-country to its destination, presumably on mule-back. It then suffered the usual vicissitudes to which old instruments are subjected, before being brought to New York in 1929. This testifies to the robustness of such Flemish instruments.
The Metropolitan Museum of Art, New York; Gift of B. H. Homan, 1929 (29·90)

showy materials specially suited to the furnishing and decorating of houses. We all know about tapestry (chiefly, at this date, coming from Brussels), but little attention has so far been paid to the woven materials with bold repeating patterns that could be used on walls, or for bed-hangings or chair-coverings. They could be very rich, with details woven in coloured silks and even with gold thread, although most were of wool with linen warps. This large class of materials (it came in several qualities with large patterns for hangings, and lighter weights with small patterns suitable for cushions and table-covers) was known by the term *hautelisse* at Tournai and other centres, and in English the material went by the name of Dornick, which derives from the Flemish name for Tournai. It is often illustrated in paintings, is mentioned frequently in inventories and was clearly to be seen in the best households, but its importance as textile decoration has largely been forgotten. It deserves serious study as the product of a major industry.

Attention must here be drawn to the book by Peter Paul Rubens on the great patrician palaces of Genoa, the first part of which was published in 1622, with the second appearing in 1626. It was extremely influential

among architects and their patrons in northern Europe. The organization of the façades had an influence on much Netherlandish building in the Classical vein during the 17th century, the ornaments on the buildings were much copied and their plans (included for each building) greatly inspired northerners, so that the distribution of rooms in important houses was soon greatly improved. Rubens's draughtsmen did not include the dimensions of any of these buildings because he hoped the plans and elevations would be helpful to those in the North who were erecting 'ordinary buildings', as he put it, and it can indeed be seen how the proportions of grand 16th-century Genoese town houses, through the exemplars that Rubens published, offered a pattern for more modest buildings of a respectable sort, first in the Netherlands, then in 17th-century England and eventually in the English colonies in America. Thus Rubens can be said to have had an influence on the creation of what in architecture is called 'the Georgian style'.

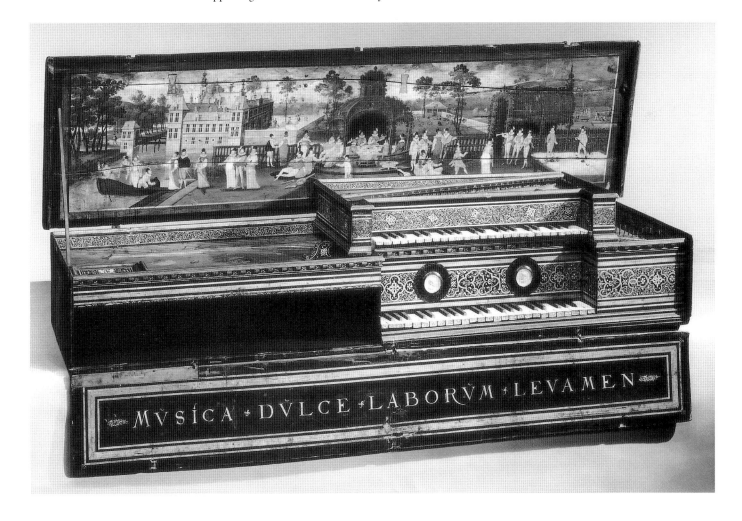

CHAPTER 6

AUGSBURG AND NÜRNBERG

PI. 118 Title-plate for the service of the German Mass devised by Martin Luther, published at Wittenberg in 1526. From the workshop of Lucas Cranach the Elder, who worked closely with Luther at this period. Luther also collaborated with the Elector of Saxony's Kapellmeister, Conrad Rupff, on the music he wanted sung during the service, the notation for which is included in the volume.
By permission of the British Library, London (Press mark K.3.C.10)

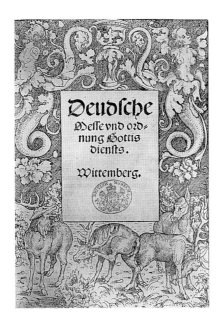

1510–1640

PI. 117 Etched portrait of Charles V by Daniel Hopfer of Augsburg (d. 1536), presumably executed in 1520 when the young Emperor came to Germany from Spain to preside over the Reichstag Assembly (or Diet) at Worms. The clear-cut profile of the Emperor is based on a knowledge of contemporary portrait medallions, while the embellishment of the frame is clearly Raphaelesque, but is here crowded into the available spaces in a cheerful Gothic manner. The small figures amid vegetal scrollwork in the surrounding frame established a form of decoration that remained greatly in favour in Germany until the middle of the century.
The Metropolitan Museum of Art, New York, Gift of J. S. Morgan (Mus. no. 19.52.19)

Augsburg and Nürnberg lie on the main routes north from Italy into the heart of Germany. If you cross the Alps through the Brenner Pass, coming up from Verona or Venice, you first reach Innsbruck and then Munich, the capital of Bavaria. Some 60 kilometres west of Munich lies Augsburg, while northward, at about twice that distance, lies Nürnberg. While Munich was the seat of a court (a factor that usually promoted a certain degree of conservatism), Augsburg and Nürnberg enjoyed special privileges as 'free cities' of the Holy Roman Empire, giving them enormous commercial advantages and the incentive to break fresh ground in all sorts of ways – including that of design in the decorative arts. Thus, as a result of both location and circumstance, the two cities were especially receptive to stylistic innovation coming from Italy, either as imported artefacts or sheets of printed ornament.

Other free cities within Germany enjoyed similar advantages but their importance for our story never quite matched that of Augsburg and Nürnberg at this period. Frankfurt am Main, to the west, was the next most important centre, together with Strassburg on the French border, while Cologne, dominating the upper Rhine Valley adjacent to the Netherlands, was of only slightly less significance. In the north, on rivers flowing into the North Sea and Baltic, lay the free cities of

Bremen, Hamburg and Lübeck. To the east the most important centre was Dresden, the seat of the Saxon court. Berlin was at that time of no great consequence. The reason that no single centre within Germany was dominant at this period (unlike Paris in France) lay in the fact that Germany was politically fragmented, with some 300 states and free cities making up a whole in which people felt themselves to be 'German', to be sure, even though their principal allegiance was to the state or city in which they lived.

The fashioning of wood had become a German speciality already by the early 1400s, and Germany had a reputation for producing both skilful joiners and brilliant carvers, and inlaid work of great delicacy. Most people know that many important cabinet-makers in 18th century Paris were Germans (see Chapters 13 and 14), but fewer know that skilled German workers in wood were being given privileged positions at discriminating Italian courts long before this. A notable instance is provided by the court at Ferrara where, in 1450, three Germans (Leonardo, Simone and Augustino *de Alemagna*) were working on an important commission alongside an Italian, Arduino da Baiso, who directed the court workshops and whose works in carved wood and inlay were at that time widely celebrated. Delicate work in wood can of course only be achieved with good tools,

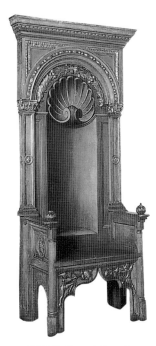

PI. 119 The Emperor's Throne from the City Hall at Nürnberg, provided in 1520–21. The tall canopy takes the form of a tabernacle in the Renaissance style, while the seat remains stubbornly Gothic in shape and decoration. Its grey paintwork is intended as a reminder of the most venerable of all such imperial thrones, that of Charlemagne in the Minster at Aachen.
The Altstadtmuseum, Fembohaus, Nürnberg

and the making of woodworking tools was for the most part the province of metalworkers. Moreover, much woodwork (furniture, carriages and doors, for instance) embodies metalwork in its make-up, so that woodworking trades generated a related group of craftsmen skilled in working metal for locks and hinges, hasps and bolts, and eventually for elaborate mechanisms such as mechanical music players. Thus the Germans also became famed throughout Europe for their skill and ingenuity as mechanics and engineers.

Their metalworking talents were also applied to a wide range of crafts, notably that of the armourer, but also to the fairly new trade of clockmaking, which was to take a great leap forward when the fusee was invented in Germany in the 1530s. This spindle mechanism enabled timepieces to be made quite small so that they could be carried, suspended about the person on a ribbon or attached to a girdle. Both armour (and arms) and timepieces (particularly small ones) offered scope for ornamentation, and much artistry was devoted to the embellishment of such goods, as it was also to be on a wide range of scientific instruments, many of them made of brass, which could be handsomely engraved. Elaborate clocks and ornamental scientific instruments were acquired by wealthy people as items to go in their 'cabinets of curiosities', where they kept their treasured possessions, rather than as objects of serious use.

The cities of Nürnberg and Augsburg became famed for armour, silverware, cabientmaking, clocks and printing – the last being a trade that also depends greatly on mechanical processes. The inter-relationship between

whole equal to those produced in Venice, Paris and Antwerp in the 16th century, or so it seems from the distance imposed by four centuries. Moreover, the copying and re-publishing of foreign patterns was a notable practice at Augsburg (less so at Nürnberg) from the 1520s until the 18th century. It must not be thought, however, that novelty was of no consequence to the printsellers, or indeed to the craftsmen of Nürnberg and Augsburg. Far from it. Many of the suites of designs published in the two cities – and in other German cities, be it noted – bore titles in which the *newness* of the compositions to be found within these usually slim volumes was stressed. The desire for new fashions and fresh patterns is not a modern one.

Nürnberg and Augsburg make to perfection the point that novel styles are mostly created within a community sharing approximately common aims. Engravers of silverware often worked for several master goldsmiths and thus might transmit new compositions to other workshops, almost inadvertently; masters in the same street could hardly avoid seeing each other's products, and every now and then one of them would buy a suite of engravings that had just come in from Antwerp or Venice, which would cause ripples of excitement in his circle. The work of important designers was also likely to be imitated, and suites of designs in much the same style would be brought out by lesser designers. They did not advance the history of design, but they speak for their times, and several patterns composed by these 'lesser men' are included here for that reason.

The styles of the Italian Renaissance reached Ger-

PI. 120 Model of cherrywood prepared by an Augsburg goldsmith about 1525–30 for casting a bracelet. In full Renaissance style, it embodies Classical profiles and vegetal scrollwork joined with semi-human figures. The central feature is missing.
Germanisches Nationalmuseum, Nürnberg

such trades is neatly demonstrated by the career of Daniel Hopfer, a particularly clever Augsburg artist (Pl. 117) whose chief occupation was etching ornament on armour (i.e. on steel). He used his experience in this medium to develop the technique of etching metal plates by means of which prints on paper could be produced. He had already become famous for his invention by 1493 and its potential was quickly recognised, to the extent that etchers soon joined the woodcutters and engravers of metal plates in producing printed images on paper for mass distribution. During the 16th century Nürnberg and Augsburg produced an enormous quantity of ornament prints and designs for decorative art objects, probably more even than Venice. It was this fact that led to their having such great influence, because the originality of their designs was probably not on the

many early. The style of Mantegna's followers (p. 15) inspired several designs for title-pages, notably the widely read works of Erasmus, the Dutch humanist, theologian and writer whose works in 1513 and 1518, for instance, were published (in Basle on the upper reaches of the Rhine, at the south-west corner of Germany), with title-pages in a style evidently based on engravings by Nicoletto da Modena. Of far greater competence, however, was the work of Daniel Hopfer, whose striking portrait of the young Emperor Charles V (Pl. 117) is a distinguished production and must have caused quite a stir when it first appeared. Hopfer's style was imitated by the brothers Beham at Nürnberg, from which city they were banished in the 1520s, Sebald settling eventually in Frankfurt and Barthel in Munich, where they continued to practise their trade. A score of lesser Nürnberg engravers, signing their work only with initials, later produced numerous engravings in the Beham style – with its small fleshy leaves. Sebald profoundly influenced two Nürnberg artists of some stature (Georg Pencz and Gilich Proger) as well as three

Pl. 121 Panelled room in Nürnberg, 1534; the first scheme of mural decoration that can be securely attributed to Peter Flötner. The scrolled frieze decoration with rinceaux and marine figures has features in common with the bracelet shown in Pl. 120 and with the woodcut friezes in Pl. 122. Traces of the original stencilled wall painting inspired the post-war restoration of this room. *Altstadtmuseum, Fembohaus, Nürnberg*

Pl. 122 Woodcuts printed in brown and beige with a frieze made to resemble wood and presumably intended to be pasted on to a wall as a decorative band. By Erasmus Loy of Regensburg (active *c.* 1520–70); probably about 1540. The text states that this sheet was produced under imperial licence, and warns 'Not to be re-printed' (i.e. do not copy). Sebald Beham of Nürnberg published a similar frieze about 1520–25 with a combat of tritons amid running scrolls. *The British Museum, London*

important engravers working in northern Germany, Jacob Binck and Johann Ladenspelder of Cologne, and Heinrich Aldegrever of Soest, which lies some 70 kilometres north-east of Cologne on the road to Hannover, Hamburg and the north. Aldegrever's reputation in Germany was very considerable during the second quarter of the century; he was principally an illustrator but also produced designs (with fleshy leaves in the Beham manner) for spoons, daggers and their sheaths, and panels in relief.

Albrecht Dürer, who lived in Nürnberg and had originally been trained as a goldsmith, was of course principally a painter and illustrator of books, but he designed some metalwork objects and his proposals for silver standing-cups set the pattern for such vessels in Germany for many decades. In 1521 he also designed an amazing throne for the Archbishop of Salzburg, which the eminent churchman must surely have rejected as unsuitable for the occupant of such a dignified post; its heavy shield-like arm-rests were to be supported with crouching lions while two long-necked birds with camels' heads supported an elaborate helmet-shaped canopy piled high with ornament including two dolphins and much foliage. It was not one of his happiest compositions. However, Dürer's influence on other artists was far-reaching. The Augsburg artist Hans Burgkmair, as well as illustrating books with many features in the new taste, designed sword pommels decorated with early Renaissance ornament in a Dürer-like manner, during the 1520s. More important was Albrecht Altdorfer of Regensburg, not far from Nürnberg, who etched some 20 plates for metalwork and ornament in the early 1520s which were reproduced again in the 1530s by Hieronymus Hopfer, Daniel's son, thereby making these elegant prints of standing-cups and jugs even more widely known. Unfortunately we could not illustrate an example here, but the forms Altdorfer espoused were in the Dürer style while the ornament on them was taken from Italian sources, chiefly of the Mantegna school (see Chapter 1).

Renaissance ornament may first have become familiar to many Germans from its use in religious works. We have noted that early manifestations of the style were to be seen on the title-pages of works by Erasmus, but the works of Martin Luther were of even greater importance in this respect because so many publications stemmed from his pen and numerous copies were printed. Luther was also a great believer in the power of music to inspire religious sentiments in churchgoers and insisted that this would popularize the church service. He therefore published a number of books of music including one for 'The German Mass', which came out in 1526 and has a charming title-page, said to have been designed by the elder Lucas Cranach (and certainly from his workshop), with some most curious versions of Renaissance grotesque ornament and a delightful depiction of red deer (Pl. 118).

One of the earliest German expressions of Renaissance ornament in furniture is the Emperor's Throne in the City Hall at Nürnberg, which dates from 1520–21 (Pl. 119). Its presence at the heart of the city's chief ceremonial building must have done much to encourage the citizens of Nürnberg to adopt this new manner of decoration for their own purposes. By the mid-1520s there was no longer any doubt that Renaissance motifs were being assimilated and used in the decorative arts in

Pl. 123 Bookbinding decorated with a moresque scrollwork pattern directly copied from an engraving published at Zurich in 1559, attributed to Peter Flötner who had, however, by this time long been established in Nürnberg. The binding covers a book printed at Augsburg in 1551. Printed from a single plate.
Österreichisches Nationalbibliothek, Vienna

Pl. 124 Detail of inlaid moresque and strapwork decoration in wood on a door from Schloss Neuberg on the upper reaches of the Danube, north-east of Augsburg. Executed in 1558 for a nobleman who presided over a small but cultivated court where exquisite work in an advanced taste was commissioned from highly competent master-craftsmen. The wrap-around scrolls of the central panel seem to betray a knowledge of contemporary French bookbinding patterns in the Grolier style (e.g. Pl. 86).
Schlossmuseum Berchtesgaden

but some artists/designers managed it very well. The Augsburg silversmith who cut the cherrywood model for a bracelet shown in Pl. 120 was one of them.

A leading figure in the development of the Renaissance style in Germany was Peter Flötner. He was trained as a sculptor in Augsburg and probably visited Italy about 1520. His reputation must already have been considerable by then because, in 1522, the Council of Nürnberg decided to grant him citizenship and he remained in that city until his death in 1546. His stature as an artist and his knowledge of the applied arts gave him the authority to act as a co-ordinator on large schemes, and he was responsible for interior architectural decoration in some of the most important houses in Nürnberg. One of the earliest schemes firmly attributable to him is that shown in Pl. 121 which was executed in 1534. Flötner was a prolific publisher of designs that included furniture and silverware, daggers, playing-cards and games-boards. It is very likely that he was in contact with Daniel Hopfer, who filled a somewhat similar position at Augsburg. Flötner also influenced the painter and sculptor Hans Brosamer, who worked at Nürnberg and Frankfurt, as the latter's *Neu Kunstbüchlein* of about 1545 makes evident; Brosamer's book enjoyed widespread success and was reprinted in 1570. Brosamer also influenced Aldegrever, who was working at Regensburg, as we noted. Flötner handled fluently a wide variety of ornament, including moresques, some fine engravings of which are often attributed to him (e.g. Pl. 123), including two for handsome games-boards. Superb moresque ornament is to be seen on much high-quality decorative art of the mid-16th century in Germany (Pls. 124, 127 and 130), a good deal of which probably derives from designs he published.

The presence in Nürnberg in the 1540s of Jacopo da Strada, who had probably worked under Giulio Romano at Mantua and who owned many of Giulio's designs on paper, must have given further impetus to the adoption of Mannerist forms in central and southern Germany, particularly among goldsmiths at Nürnberg and Augsburg. The taste for the bizarre, a common feature of many Giulio Romano designs, was taken up with especial gusto by Erasmus Hornick, a goldsmith who worked in both Nürnberg and Augsburg from the 1550s until 1582, and to a somewhat lesser extent by Matthias Zündt, who worked at Nürnberg until his death in 1572. Many of their designs embody the weird, often unpleasant-looking creatures so dear to the Mannerist heart, not to speak of fierce masks and contorted figures that rarely fail to give rise to a feeling of unease in the viewer. The Mannerist taste remained much in favour in goldsmiths' work in southern Germany and Austria until the end of the century, as Pl. 131 shows.

Many goldsmiths were of course jewellers. A popular form in the second half of the 16th century was the pendant. It was desirable that the pendant should

the major cities of Germany, even if the principles that governed their disposition were not always fully appreciated. There was a good deal of what, in another context, has been called 'Artisan Mannerism' about the German use of the Renaissance idiom until about 1540

Pl. 125 Engraved design for a pendant by Virgil Solis of Nürnberg, about 1550. This shows the pear-shaped form that was developed for pendants at about this time by Solis and Matthias Zündt, both of Nürnberg.

Pl. 126 Tankard of characteristic German form, with a body turned from a block of serpentine (a veined green stone). The silver-gilt mounts were probably made in London about 1575. Height 19.5 cm (7¹/₂in.)
By kind permission of the Master, Fellows and Scholars of Clare College, Cambridge

Pl. 129 The highly fashionable field-bed of the 16th century, which those who could afford such luxuries would take with them on their travels and have erected where they were to stay the night. German field-beds were in great demand among the princes of the Church in Rome, for instance, at this period. This superb example of about 1580, of ebony and ivory, must have been made at Augsburg; the form of its head- and foot-boards resembles that of other contemporary Augsburg work in inlaid ebony. It lacks its curtains and bedding.
Bayerisches Nationalmuseum, Munich

Pl. 127 Tazza, probably made at Augsburg in the 1560s, with moresques amid strapwork with 'breaks'; executed in the niello technique.
Musée du Louvre, Paris

Pl. 128 Design for a standing-cup dated 1543 by Augustin Hirschvogel, from a suite published at Nürnberg that includes several designs in the Mannerist style developed by Giulio Romano in the 1530s. Principally a painter of glass, Hirschvogel spent most of his life in Austria and was a learned and highly inventive man. Basket-work ornament was in favour with German goldsmiths at this period.
The British Museum, London

PI. 130 The Munich court portrait painter Hans Mielich compiled a colourfully illustrated inventory of the jewellery of the Duchess Anna of Bavaria. He set each item within a heavy framework and added dates in the early 1550s on several depictions. Here he shows the back of a pedant which has enamelled decoration in the most fashionable taste of the time, with moresques amid strapwork with 'breaks' (See PI. 84). The pear-shaped form favoured by Matthias Zündt and Virgil Solis at Nürnberg is well illustrated here.
Bayerische Staatsbibliothek, Munich Codex Monacencis (icon. 429)

PI. 131 Elaborate ewer in full Mannerist taste. Silver-gilt, set with mother-of-pearl ornament, made by Nikolaus Schmidt at Nürnberg around 1600.
Kunsthistorisches Museum, Vienna

always present its front face and should not swivel on its chain, although the backs were often beautifully worked as well (PI. 130). A cross prevented swivelling very well but not every woman wanted to wear such a symbol so prominently. It was in Matthias Zündt's time that the pear-shaped pendant was devised; some of his designs were on the ponderous side but nonetheless had much charm. The pear-shaped pendant retained its popularity beyond the end of the century.

A man whose enormous output of designs was of great influence during the middle decades of the century was Virgil Solis, a native of Nürnberg probably trained at Augsburg. He had a large workshop at Nürnberg, with a great number of assistants, and was closely linked with Flötner. He produced designs for objects of all kinds, from goldsmiths' work to playing-cards as well as illustrations for books. His oeuvre has been called 'the prime example of German decorative invention in the mid-sixteenth century', and his influence is to be seen throughout Europe.

Virgil Solis's production of engraved designs was of uneven quality, probably because so many assistants were involved, but his best work is delightful (PI. 125) and, as we see from this plate, he too favoured the pear-shaped form of pendant. He is also important for having republished Jacques Androuet Du Cerceau's evocation of the ruins of Rome, published at Orléans in 1550 and originally drawn by Léonard Thiry (see p. 34). In the foreword he explains that as 'this little book . . . is unavailable here [in Nürnberg] . . . it would be for the common good . . . if I were to publish it . . . so that our country should be as fortunate as the Italians and French have been. The designs are by Leonhart Theodorico [Léonard Thiry], an artful man. I mention this, so that he will have the honour and praise he deserves.' Virgil Solis evidently wished to behave in an honourable fashion; perhaps he had somehow met Du Cerceau. In general, however, Du Cerceau's designs were rarely copied directly in Germany, although the spirit of his compositions, and detail features, were undoubtedly a source of inspiration. By contrast, the work of Hans Vredeman de Vries (see p. 58) was rather more directly influential.

Augsburg had become famous throughout Europe for its joiners and inlayers, working in wood, and commissions for important features of interior architecture, panelling for grand rooms and pieces of furniture of especially high quality flowed to the city from far afield (Pls. 129 and 136).

From the middle of the 16th century until well into the next century there was a tendency in Germany to pile ornament on ornament that was especially prevalent in work produced in provincial areas (PI. 132). Towards the end of the century this trait was accentuated and this is also reflected in other media, for instance in jewellery, as PI. 133 shows. A book by an

Pl. 132 Massive two-tier oak and walnut cupboard made in Swabia, in south-west Germany, during the first quarter of the 17th century. The heavy ornamentation on the front of this expensive piece of display furniture epitomises German furniture at this period. We see here Northern Renaissance architectural elements at their wildest, handled by a skilled but untutored provincial craftsman.
Fürstl. Waldburg-Zeil'sche Sammlungen, Schloss Wangen im Allgau

Pl. 133 The heavy load of ornament common in German decorative arts at the turn of the century is exemplified here in small scale in a watercolour representation of an enamelled necklace with an emerald pendant. From an illustrated record of work done between about 1593 and 1608 by Jacob Mores, goldsmith in Hamburg, who had many clients at the courts of Sweden and Denmark.
Staatsbibliothek, Hamburg

Pl. 134 Title-page of a book of patterns for woodwork decoration which, although more Baroque in style, has much of the same overloaded character as the massive cupboard shown in Pl. 132. Dated 1602, the book is by Gabriel Krammer who was not only cabinetmaker to the court of Rudolph II at Prague but also apparently a piper in the Imperial Life Guard. Krammer was a joiner who came from Zurich, in Switzerland. His book was meant to accompany a volume on architecture and provided information for joiners fitting out rooms in a unified style. A second edition was published in 1611 in Cologne.
Victoria and Albert Museum, London (Mus. no. L.381–1860)

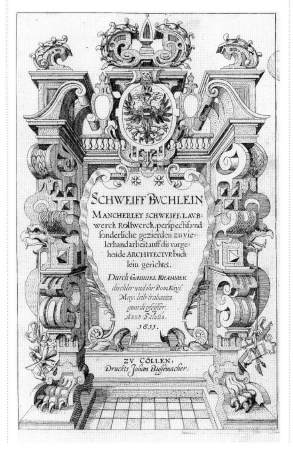

important joiner at the turn of the century provided designs for this kind of loaded ornament (Pl. 134). This particular style was given much impetus by the publications of Wendel Dietterlin in the 1590s. A mural painter by profession, living in Strassburg, the definitive edition of his work on architectural ornament was published at Nürnberg in 1598 with 94 plates of compositions of extreme complexity.

Alongside this tendency towards elaboration there existed an austere vein that came to the surface wherever taste was governed by a measure of Classical discipline. This is to be seen chiefly in high-quality

furniture, particularly that made at Nürnberg, Augsburg and Munich (Pl. 135). The widely admired ebony furniture of Augsburg, which included items of relatively small size, such as cabinets, writing-boxes and portable altars, also usually had rather severe lines, the decoration being provided by silver mounts, enamelled plaques or panels of semi-precious stones, which could sometimes be piled on thickly but were mostly disposed in a sober manner (Pl. 136).

When briefly discussing goldsmiths' designs (p. 66), we mentioned Jacopo da Strada and his large collection of designs by Giulio Romano. Jacopo joined the Nürnberg firm of Wenzel Jamnitzer, one of the most celebrated goldsmiths of all time, where he was probably employed for a decade or more from the mid-1540s.

Jacopo's main contribution was probably in the realm of design – Jamnitzer's business was receiving so many commissions for work at this period that fresh notions for their embellishment must have been extremely welcome. Jamnitzer himself was a fine designer (e.g. Pl. 138) so it was certainly not a case of his needing help except in order to produce greater variety in his firm's output.

Jamnitzer was in fact something of an intellectual and wrote a treatise on perspective which was published in 1568. The illustrations were engraved by Jost Amman, also of Nürnberg, a highly capable designer-illustrator who had, among many other things, provided numerous plates for a important edition of the Bible (a book that, of course, was to be seen in a huge number of households) published in 1564 at Frankfurt. The work on perspective contained illustrations of intricate geometric bodies that inspired inlayers of early marquetry work, who had recourse also to two other contemporary works containing illustrations of such forms – Hans Lencker's *Perspective Literaria*, published the year before Jamnitzer's treatise, which it in some ways excelled (its plates were engraved by Zündt), and the *Geometria et Perspectiva* published by Lorenz Stöer in 1567 at Augsburg (although he came from Nürnberg). These three works on perspective had a great influence on German furniture-makers in the second half of the century, Stöer's being the most influential, with its depiction of Classical ruins in the Léonard Thiry style (see pp. 42, 55 and 68 etc.) amid aggressive scrollwork.

A style that evolved more or less simultaneously at the end of the century at Antwerp, Stuttgart, Augsburg and Paris is well illustrated by Pl. 137. As explained on p. 58, it is known in Germany as *Schweifwerk*, and was a development of Northern Renaissance grotesque strap-work, with the junction points strengthened, often with blocks that have a halberd-like contour. One of the chief exponents of this style was Daniel Mignot, an immigrant French designer at Augsburg, whose enormous output of engravings for jewellery and other gold-smith's work dominated much South German production from the 1590s until about 1625 (Pls. 139 and 140).

Pl. 135 Not all German furniture of high quality was elaborate, as this elegant two-tiered cupboard made at Nürnberg in the mid-16th century shows. The basic form is of late Gothic origin, here given a Classical envelope of oak and ash veneers, which show off the shape handsomely.
Museum für Kunsthandwerk, Frankfurt am Main

Pl. 136 Ebony cabinet made for the Duke of Brunswick at Augsburg in 1631, almost certainly by the celebrated cabinet-maker Ulrich Baumgartner. Decorated with hardstones, paintings on marble and reliefs in silver, cabinets of this elaborate kind, made by a group of highly skilled craftsmen, were costly and much prized objects that would be prominently displayed by their owners.
Rijksmuseum, Amsterdam

Pl. 137 Exquisitely made silver-gilt casket, Augsburg, 1594, by Matthaus Walbaum. A splendid example of *Schweifwerk* ornament, with sweeping scrolls linked by an angular 'metal-like' framework with 'strengthened joints'.
Schatzkammer, Residenz, Munich (Mus. no. Mü.Sch.586–587)

Pl. 138 Silver frame for a dressing-mirror by the celebrated Nürnberg goldsmith Wenzel Jamnitzer; about 1568, the year in which he published his treatise on perspective, the title-page of which is of almost identical design.
The Metropolitan Museum, New York; gift of J. Pierpont Morgan, 1917 (17.190.620)

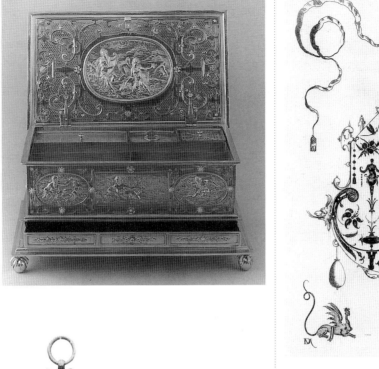

Pl. 139 Design for a pendant by Daniel Mignot of Augsburg, published in the mid-1590s. This composition carries on the tradition brought to Augsburg in the 1570s by the refugee Parisian designer Etienne Delaune.
Victoria and Albert Museum, London (Mus. no. E.2150–1911)

Pl. 140 Another design for a pendant by Daniel Mignot, this time displaying 'strengthened joints' with halberd-like details. One of a suite published in Augsburg in 1596 and again in 1616.
Victoria and Albert Museum, London (Mus. no. E.2150–1908)

Pl. 141 Title-page of a suite of patterns for goldsmith's work by Paul Flindt of Nürnberg; probably brought out in 1592 but published in reverse and with slight variations at Amsterdam in 1593 by Assuwerus van Londerseel (shown here) and in the same year by Andre Lüning at Vienna. This kind of overall strapwork became very popular around 1600 and patterns of this kind were still being reprinted in the early 18th century.
Rijksprentenkabinet, Rijksmuseum, Amsterdam

Pl. 142 Design of about 1600 by Hieronymus Bang, master goldsmith of Nürnberg, presumably for engraving on silver, but equally suitable for embroidery – indeed it resembles embroidery designs by Johann Sibmacher.
Victoria and Albert Museum, London (Mus. no. 21203.6)

His example was followed by Bernhard Zan, with two more pattern-books in 1580 and 1581, and by Jonas Silber who had been trained by Jamnitzer and who issued yet more patterns in this style between 1582 and 1590. The chief exponent of this fashion, however, was Paul Flindt who became a master goldsmith at Nürnberg in 1601 but had already brought out a large number of designs in this manner in the early 1590s (Pl. 141).

One of those who designed patterns for goldsmiths in the Flindt manner was Johann Sibmacher, also of Nürnberg. He is, however, more famous for the sets of patterns he produced for embroidery. His first work in this field came out in 1597 but an expanded version, which was often reprinted and copied, appeared in 1601; as late as 1736 a version appeared at Leipzig. Sibmacher's patterns range over a variety of embroidery techniques but quite a few have birds and flowers amidst wiry scrollwork. Much the same style is to be seen in designs of about 1600 by Hieronymus Bang, which are presumably for engraving on silver although might also serve very well for embroiderers (Pl. 142). Once again we see how closely the designing of patterns for use by craftsmen working in quite different trades could often co-incide in style. Theodor Bang, a goldsmith who was probably a son of Hieronymus, designed patterns in a similar style but more stiff in character, which were published in 1617 at Nürnberg. One of the designs included in this later work was copied from a pattern of 1601 by Sibmacher. Interwoven influences of this kind make the attribution of designs of this period extremely difficult, and often impossible.

A word must be said about engraving on glass, which became a speciality at Nürnberg in the early 17th century. Engraved ornament was cut with the aid of a spinning wheel, using fine sand lubricated with water as an abrasive – the lapidary's wheel. It was a technique adopted from the cutters of diamonds and other hardstones. The finest early practitioner of this art was Kaspar Lehmann, whose greatest achievements were executed while working for the Emperor Rudolph II at Prague from 1588 to 1622. At Prague he was succeeded by his pupil Georg Schwanhardt, who settled at Nürnberg in 1622 and continued to enjoy imperial privileges. The magnificent glass shown in Pl. 144 gives some idea of the stature of the latter's achievement. It will be seen that the form of this glass echoes that of contemporary silver.

One of the most important designers in Europe during the first third of the 17th century was Lucas Kilian, an engraver at Augsburg and, once again, the son of a goldsmith. He took the sweeping scrolls of *Schweifwerk* and the wiry scroll patterns of the Sibmacher style and added fleshy elements to produce a fresh form of ornament that looks forward to the Rococo of the mid-18th century. There is often a

His style somewhat echoes that of Etienne Delaune, who came to Augsburg from Paris in the 1570s (Pls. 79 and 81), but it seems that Mignot developed the halberd forms himself, and indeed they virtually take over the composition in his later work (Pl. 140). The dripping quality of Mignot's late style has an almost Gothic character and it is interesting to note that there was a curious revival of Gothic forms, and even to some extent of decoration, at the end of the 16th century in Germany. Quite a few heavy two-tier cupboards that are dated or datable testify to this phenomenon.

While Augsburg goldsmiths in the main adopted *Schweifwerk*, a new form of strapwork was developed at Nürnberg in the 1570s; this was essentially flat and was usually applied as overall decoration (Pl. 141). It can be monotonous but was popular at the time and widely imitated all over northern Europe. The goldsmith Georg Wechter has been credited with introducing this style, and published a book of 30 such patterns in 1579.

PI. 143 Title-page to a book of music for the lute published at Augsburg in 1617; an early composition by the talented Lucas Kilian. It betrays the influence of contemporary Italian cartouche designs with which he no doubt became familiar during his stay in Venice from 1601 to 1604. The heavy downward-sweeping scrolls at the sides show an awareness of the Auricular style that was at this time being developed in Holland (see Chapter 9).
Musikabteilung der Staatsbibliotek, Munich (Press mark 2 Mus.pr.110)

PI. 144 A particularly fine Nürnberg glass standing-cup with an enamelled finial, and with wheel-engraved and diamond-point decoration on the lid, by Georg Schwanhardt the Elder. This delicate object still has its original protective case of tooled leather. The glass was presented by the City of Nürnberg to the Swedish field-marshal, Count Carl Gustav Wrangel, in 1648.
Skokloster Castle, Sweden

strong downwards and inwards sweep to his compositions (Pls. 143 and 145).

In the early 16th century Augsburg products, and presumably also those of Nürnberg, were obtained from the city's goldsmiths and jewellers through the agents of large commercial organizations such as that of the Fuggers, the Imperial bankers; but gradually there sprang up a new class of middlemen who increasingly handled this part of the trade, commissioning work, giving credit to goldsmiths, providing the raw materials and generally supplying the trade with the capital it required.

Augsburg was badly hit by a plague in 1628 and the city's population was reduced by a third; it was then twice besieged in the 1630s, during the Thirty Years War, which cruelly affected the whole of Germany before it ended in 1648. After that dreadful upheaval, a new era began in which Augsburg continued to figure prominently while Nürnberg's fortunes declined.

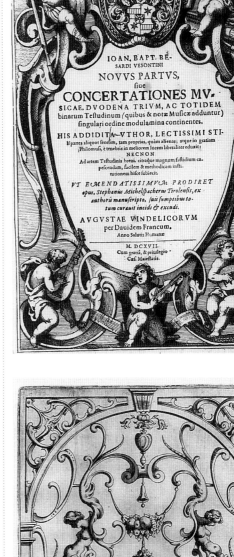

PI. 145 Another Lucas Kilian design, this time from a book of grotesques published in 1624.
Victoria and Albert Museum, London (Mus. no. E.3073–1938)

CHAPTER 7

ROME AND BOLOGNA

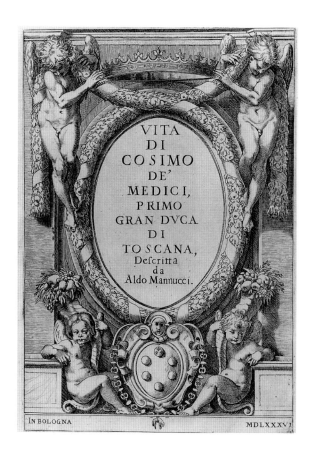

1580-1660

R ome was by far the most magnificent city in the whole of Europe by the end of the 16th century. Rocked at first by the intensity of the Protestant challenge, the Catholic Church was eventually strengthened by the need to mount an ideological counter-offensive while at the same time introducing far-reaching reforms within its own organization. Papal power was enhanced during the middle of the 16th century, as the Papacy exercised increasing control over Catholics throughout southern and western Europe, and soon even in many parts of the Americas (see Pl. 116). This control affected the spiritual life of the many millions of members of the Church and often also the social framework within which they lived because of the Church's involvement in politics. The revenues from this vast spiritual empire which, during the late 16th and early 17th centuries, flowed ever more strongly into the papal coffers and those of many cardinals and other members of the papal court (or Curia), ensured that the erecting of magnificent buildings in Rome – churches, palaces and villas – and their decoration and furnishing with ever greater splendour, continued uninterrupted during the period we shall now consider.

This period coincides roughly with the flowering of the Baroque style, which evolved in Rome early in the 17th century and was fully developed by about 1620.

Opulent forms, frequently grand in scale, richly tumbling in fluid contortions, characterize this style, which conjures up feelings very different from the nervous anxiety and discomfort evoked by Mannerism. Baroque was a style of confidence, not fearfulness, and its expressions can therefore sometimes seem overpowering; it was a style of propaganda designed to impress the viewer with the importance of a patron or the strength of the Catholic Church.

It is therefore no coincidence that the form most characteristic of Roman Baroque ornament is the shield-like cartouche that provided a central space on which a coat-of-arms could be proudly displayed, or a text recording an important event or benefaction could be inscribed. Large cartouches of this kind proliferate on buildings and monuments throughout the 17th century quarters of Rome (and of most other Italian cities, because the Roman example was widely imitated) and are also found on works of decorative art – on a smaller scale, to be sure – adopted for the same propagandist purpose (Pl. 147).

The Baroque cartouche, carved in stone or wood, has a heavy fleshiness that is different in character from early cartouches, which were made of cardboard, and also from the thick plates, seemingly of iron, as those designed at Fontainebleau and Antwerp in the mid-16th

Pl. 148 Painted pedestal for a portrait bust, bearing the arms of Pope Sixtus V, 1585–90. The criss-crossing straps, or bands, forming compartments within a border, produce a formula that was to become a European favourite with designers around 1680 (see Pl. 240), and continued well on into the 18th century. Moresques fill the intervals here.
Victoria and Albert Museum, London (Mus. no. A.40–1950)

Pl. 149 This highly grotesque and convoluted cartouche, designed by Daniel Rabel and published in Paris, probably in the 1620s, may have had an influence on such Italian designers as Agostino Mitelli (Pl. 150) and Stefano della Bella. *Rijksprentenkabinet, Rijksmuseum, Amsterdam*

century (see Chapters 4 and 5). The Baroque version has a zoomorphic character, parts of animals (eagles' wings, the masks of satyrs or marine beasts, the shells of molluscs, the beaks of birds and the pelts of dragons or lions) but human figures also often play a part in the composition – and here 'human' is stretched to include cherubs and merfolk. In fact a notable feature of Roman Baroque decoration is the way in which allegorical figures, usually represented with great naturalism, come to dominate schemes while the purely decorative ornament is increasingly relegated to the background (Pls. 147 and 151). Nevertheless, ornamental forms continue to provide the framework on which the figures rest.

The designers of Baroque ornament, particularly of cartouches, found it difficult to rid their compositions of all Mannerist traits. Fearsome or grimacing masks are often located at the top and bottom of shields. These are sometimes cleverly contrived by confronting two profile masks, that can also be read as a single mask facing the viewer (Pl. 150). Masks also wrap themselves pliantly around scrollwork (Pl. 153), while others are composed by the imaginative recasting of the folds of seashells.

Pl. 150 Agostino Mitelli published numerous designs for cartouches, in several suites, first in Bologna, then in Rome. This is apparently an example from the latter period, dating from 1640. Note the three concentric layers of framing and the confronted masks forming a single frontal mask.
Victoria and Albert Museum, London (Mus. no. E.3936–1907)

amidst voluptuous ornament; these were to inspire artists for a century or more. Annibale was often assisted in this and other schemes of painted decoration by his brother Agostino, who had been trained as a goldsmith and became famous as an engraver (Pl. 147); he may well have been responsible for much of the decorative structure of the two brothers' collaborative work. The celebrated artist Guido Reni, who was responsible for some of the most delightful painting in Baroque Rome, had also been trained in Bologna by Lodovico Carracci. A charming cartouche by Reni is to be seen in Pl. 151. Another of Lodovico's pupils, the sculptor Alessandro Algardi, moved to Rome after a period in Mantua and Venice, and enjoyed much success. He was also a distinguished designer of metalwork. Not associated in any significant way with the Carracci, on the other hand, but born near Bologna and active there for much of his life, was Agostino Mitelli, who was responsible for several popular and frequently reissued suites of cartouches (Pls. 150 and 152). Moreover, after his death in 1660, his son published many more of his father's designs.

The bold but disquietingly Mannerist designs for the façade of a palazzo in Rome by the 16th-century artist Polidoro da Caravaggio, who had worked with Raphael on the *Logge* at the Vatican and died in 1543 (see p. 26, Pls. 42 and 157), appealed also to people of the Baroque

Bolognese artists played an extremely important part in the development of the Baroque cartouche. Bologna, a major city within the extensive Papal State that was ruled from Rome, was the centre of the papal government in the rich northern province of Emilia. In consequence, while culturally more closely linked to Padua and Venice, it nevertheless had close political links with Rome and, while there were plenty of opportunities in Bologna for capable artists to exercise their skills locally, the possibilities in Rome were even more alluring.

The flowering of the Carracci family as the chief artists in Bologna at the end of the 16th century was significant for art history. Their main contribution lay in the creation of huge decorative schemes that depended largely on figure subjects within a complex decorative framework; as painters, they were no less masters of ornament than of human figures which loom large in the mainly allegorical narratives for which they became famous. Cartouches were a prominent element in these schemes, and because such flamboyant devices held enormous appeal for great people at that period, there was also a huge demand for cartouche designs in isolation. The Carracci satisfied this demand to perfection.

Ludovico Carracci was a painter who remained in Bologna, where he and his two cousins Agostino and Annibale founded an academy in 1582. Annibale, Lodovico's pupil, moved to Rome in 1594, where his outstanding achievement was the painting of two vast rooms in the Palazzo Farnese with mythological subjects

Pl. 151 A handsome cartouche with the coat-of-arms of a cardinal, designed in Rome by Guido Reni (d. 1642). The human figure now plays a major part in this composition. Note the mask at the base.
The British Museum, London

period, presumably on account of the seething energy possessed by these compositions which found an echo in Baroque sensibilities. For this reason Polidoro's designs were reprinted in 1582, 1658 and again in 1660. Polidoro's style became highly influential in the 17th century; the Genoese ewer shown in Pl. 158 is presumably evidence of this.

Pl. 152 A totally asymmetrical cartouche which looks forward to Rococo formulae of around 1740. From a suite by Agostino Mitelli published by Rossi in Rome in 1653. *Victoria and Albert Museum, London (Mus. no. E.151–1909)*

Pl. 153 Engraved design for a cartouche by Domenico Santi, in which the scrolls assume an almost fluid quality reflecting an awareness of the northern Auricular style (see Chapter 9). Probably about 1650. Santi was a painter and engraver active in Bologna; he was a pupil of Mitelli. *The Metropolitan Museum of Art, New York*

Pl. 154 Drawing by Agostino Carracci or Francesco Brizio of about 1600 for a title-page (subsequently engraved) where the human or near-human figure looms large. Note the flayed dragon's pelt at the base foreshadowing Auricular ornament (see Chapter 9) and the heavy garlands so characteristic of architectural designs in the first half of the 17th century. *The Royal Collection, Windsor Castle*

Pl. 148 shows a form of strapwork decoration that was to acquire great importance in the later decades of the 17th century. Such 'bandwork' may derive from the decoration of textiles with applied ribbon or galloon ornament. This would account for the way the straps cross each other to form circular, oval and fancily shaped compartments; the trimming of edges with an inset border was also a common form of embellishment for textiles from the late Renaissance onwards. Such bandwork ornament was later associated with engraved decoration on silver, or painted on faience and glassware, and became incorporated into late 17th-century grotesque patterns (Pl. 240). A variant of such ornament, without the 'crossings', is to be seen in Pl. 146.

A man who created ambitious and outstanding furnishings and decorative schemes in woodwork at this time was Giovanni Battista Montano. Born in Milan, he came to Rome in about 1572 and died in 1621. He was a skilled woodworker who was able to carve wood 'with the fluidity of wax'; he became a professor of carving and painting at the Academy in Rome, and practised as an architect – especially in commissions involving woodwork. Pl. 161 shows a page of sketches for bed-posts for the tall four-poster beds that had become an obligatory and extremely expensive feature of grand bedchambers by the end of the 16th century. Many very prominent people of the time gave Montano commissions; he worked for a least two popes, including Paul V, who ascended the Throne of St Peter in 1605. Although Montano was of course fully

Pl. 155 Title-page of a book of madrigals by the famous Ferrarese composer Luzzasco Luzzaschi, for 'two or three sopranos', members of the Duke Alfonzo d'Este's 'Music'. Published in Rome in 1601 by Simon Verovio, a Netherlander whose chief engraver was his compatriot Martin van Buyten.
Library of Congress, Washington

Pl. 156 Roman table of walnut made in the second quarter of the 17th century, with carved and gilded decoration in a Classical taste similar in general character to that of Pl. 159. Perhaps the work of Alessandro Nave, who worked for the Barberini family, whose arms are on the apron-piece.
Formerly in the Contini-Bonacossi Collection, Florence

conversant with the formal rules of Classical architecture, he was clearly sure enough of himself, as this illustration shows, to bend the rules and give his patrons designs that they could recognize as being in the forefront of fashion. Those artists who were able to help patrons achieve their ambitions in this way tended to find it a lucrative business.

Another preoccupation of the time (from about 1570 in Italy, and somewhat later elsewhere) was that of creating a unified effect in important rooms, following the precepts of Classical architectural theory. This could best be achieved by making the various components of decoration all the same colour. Thus a 'Red Bedchamber' would have a bed with red hangings at its focal point, and the wall hangings, the covering of seat furniture, a table-cover and (later on) window curtains all shades of the same colour. Any painted architectural elements of ceilings, walls, doorways, and so forth would then often also be of the same colour, but it was chiefly through the choice of textile furnishings made up in various forms that this now essential unity was achieved. Much responsibility for the appearance of rooms therefore came to be placed on the shoulders of an entrepreneur who could provide such decoration. He was at first known by various names but eventually came to be known as an upholsterer (*tapissier* in French), and filled the role today played, rather more grandly, by the interior decorator.

Mention should here be made of Giovanni Maggi, a painter and engraver who was born and practised in Rome. He published two series of views of the city

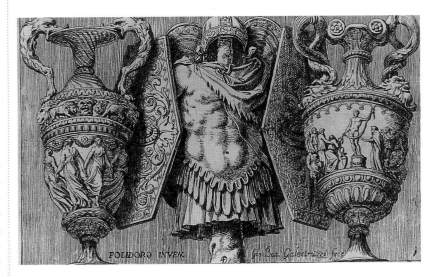

Pl. 157 Polidoro da Caravaggio (who died in 1543) decorated the façade of the Palazzo Milesi in Rome, a section of which is illustrated here. Probably originally published about 1540, these designs for fictive vases and trophies long continued to enjoy popularity with designers. One printing by Cherbino Alberti was published in 1582; the print shown here was brought out by Giovanni Battista Galestruzzi in Rome in 1658 and again in 1660.
Rijksprentenkabinet, Rijksmuseum, Amsterdam

and its embellishments, but he also worked in Florence for the Medici family, whose agent in Rome, Cardinal Francesco Del Monte, apparently commissioned from Maggi a large number of designs for glass vessels, some 2,000 of which, bound in four volumes, were presented to the Cardinal in 1604. The designs were probably intended for manufacture in Florence. Some are couched in a style similar to that of Buontalenti, distinguished designer to the Medici Court (see p. 27), but Maggi was evidently able to imitate a wide range of styles, and one has to remember that the possession of such a talent has been the good fortune of many

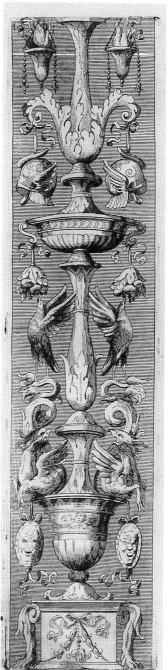

Pl. 158 Genoese silver ewer made in 1621–2, which is en suite with a large rosewater basin (not shown). It seems to owe much to the style advocated by Polidoro da Caravaggio (see Pl. 157). It was made for a member of the Lomellini family by Giovanni Aelbosca, who signed himself 'Belga', indicating his origins in the Southern Netherlands, presumably Antwerp.
Victoria and Albert Museum, London (Mus. no. M. 11–1974)

Pl. 159 Candelabra ornaments by Andrea Marchesi (d. 1559) in a church in Bologna begun in 1516, published in that city in 1645 by Agostino Mitelli. More fleshy than the early 16th-century compositions that inspired them, these representations are expressions of a renewed interest in Renaissance ornament that manifested itself during the second quarter of the 17th century.
Victoria and Albert Museum, London (Mus. no. E. 3349–1911)

Pl. 160 Title-page to a collection of keyboard music by Girolamo Frescobaldi, published in 1637 in Rome, where he was organist at St Peter's. Here again we see what appears to be revival of a Renaissance formula (the grotesque) in a fleshier form and with the addition of slender strapwork at top and bottom. Such compositions point the way to the work of French designers of the late decades of the century (see Pl. 240).
Library of Congress, Washington

designers through the ages, which makes the attribution of designs to a particular artist even more difficult than many people might suppose.

An important Venetian designer named Polifilo Giancarli composed two suites of scrolled acanthus friezes (one horizontal and the other vertical) of which the Venetian engraver Odoardo Fialetti produced prints in about 1628 (Pl. 162). These were forerunners of the ebullient acanthus scrolls characteristic of Roman late Baroque and were widely reprinted, first in Rome and then in Amsterdam, Paris and London, as we shall see in Chapter 10.

Pl. 161 Sketches of six columns for important beds by Giovanni Battista Montano; probably about 1600. The valances (pelmets) that hid the curtain-rods and rings are sketched in on the two left-hand proposals. The carved eagle forming the right-hand finial could be that of Camillo Borghese, who became Pope Paul V in 1605 and was a patron of Montano.
By courtesy of the Trustees of Sir John Soane's Museum, London

Pl. 162 The inclusion of human, or nearly human, figures amidst essentially ornamental forms is a notable characteristic of much Italian Baroque decoration. Sometimes the figures loom large, as here in the work of Polifilo Giancarli, a Venetian designer who died in 1650. Engraved by Odoardo Fialetti, also a Venetian, and first published in Venice about 1620, the suite of acanthus borders was later published in Rome, probably around 1628.
Metropolitan Museum of Art, New York; Harris Brisbane Dick Fund, 1946 (Mus. no. 49.149.4)

CHAPTER 8

PARIS

1610–1660

Pl. 163 Jewellery designs by Jacques Hurtu, known to have been active in Paris 1614–15 as a goldsmith and engraver. The 'strengthened joints' and halberd forms have been picked up from Augsburg designs, such as those of Mignot (Pls. 139 and 140). *Courtesy of C. G. Boerner GmGH, Düsseldorf*

Pl. 164 Enamelled leaf-shaped jewel design, probably for a lady's head-dress, decorated with forms like those favoured by Mignot and Hurtu, but here treated asymmetrically. By Jean Toutin who was working at Châteaudun when this was published in 1618–19; he later moved to Paris. *Museum für Kunsthandwerk, Frankfurt am Main (Mus. no. Loz 2836)*

Ever since the Middle Ages a lucrative branch of Parisian commerce has been directed at women and their needs, particularly their needs in the realm of luxury goods. Elite among those who supplied wares for this activity were the jewellers, and a great deal of attention was paid to the design of jewellery during the period which concerns us now.

Evidence of this manifests itself most obviously in the large number of printed designs published in Paris during this period (Pls. 163–4 and 166–9), but is also to be seen in the surviving jewellery itself, and in contemporary portraits. Some Parisian designs owed much to prints coming from Germany but, by about 1620, Paris was setting the fashion in this field. Parisian goldsmiths were adept at handling enamels and were becoming expert in the polishing of gemstones, notably diamonds, although this was a craft in which jewellers in Antwerp and, somewhat later, Amsterdam excelled (see Chapter 9).

For approximately the first third of the 17th century, jewellery designs printed in Paris concentrated chiefly on patterns for enamelled ornaments. Many of them feature the trumpet-volutes and C-scrolls that the Germans called '*Schweifwerk*', as noted earlier (p. 58). These sweeping motifs were to be seen in German designs at the very end of the 16th century, notably in the published work of Daniel Mignot of Augsburg. The

style is well exemplified by the gold cup inlaid with enamels to be seen in Pl. 165, which was made by an Augsburg goldsmith working in Salzburg around 1600. A Parisian design in a similar style is shown in Pl. 163; it is by Jacques Hurtu and dates from 1614. A characteristic of many French patterns of this general class is that they often have small independent figures at the bottom; in this case there are insects, while those in Pls. 164 and 168-9 are of human beings. A notable feature of Hurtu's delightful patterns are the strings of pearls that decrease in size sequentially and describe scrolls amid the halberd-forms and 'metalwork scrolls' of his grotesque ornament. The French today refer to the pearl patterns as *cosse-de-pois* [i.e. pea-pod patterns]. Jean Toutin published some suites of jewellery designs incorporating *cosse-de-pois* and halberd forms used asymmetrically (Pl. 164) in a very lively manner.

Towards the middle of the century, a greater degree of naturalism pervaded French jewellery design – and much other design, as we shall see. The charming patterns of François Lefebure (Pl. 168-9), demonstrate this assertion well, as do some designs by Gédéon L'Egaré, also of Paris, which probably date from the 1630s. L'Egaré's style was copied by Peter Aubry of Strassburg and published by him around 1640. The Toutin style was still popular in the 1630s, as Pl. 167 shows.

Pl. 165 Gold bowl with inlaid enamel decoration about 1600. Attributed to Hans Karl, who worked for a while for the archbishop of Salzburg. The ornament is in the style of Daniel Mignot of Augsburg (see Pl. 139), a designer probably of French descent, whose patterns were imitated in Paris. Height 12 cm (4¾ in.) *Schatzkammer, Residenz, Munich (Mus. no. 502)*

Pl. 167 Toutin's style (Pl. 164) is here seen taken up by a Leiden goldsmith, Guillaume de la Quewellerie, adopting a symmetrical structure. Published in 1635.

Pl. 166 Parisian design for a cap ornament, or aigrette, of the early 17th century, engraved by Pierre Firens (who also published Hurtu's designs). The colourful enamelled flowers and leaves must have shimmered on their wiry stems in an exciting manner. *Victoria and Albert Museum, London (Mus. no. E. 1216–1923)*

The tapestry illustrated in Pl. 178 was woven in Paris in 1625–6 and presented by Louis XIII to a papal legate to France. Its borders are remarkable for the Italianate cartouches in a style that would have seemed familiar to the recipient of this splendid diplomatic gift.

The presence of Stefano della Bella (Pl. 171) in Paris between 1639 and 1649 forged another strong link between Italy and France. He was the son and nephew of sculptors who had worked in the widely celebrated studio of Giovanni Bologna in Florence. He himself was trained as a goldsmith and became an outstanding engraver, producing a very large number of charming etchings, most of his later work being published in Paris. He first worked for the Medici family, then went to Rome where he spent six years, before going to Paris in the train of the Florentine Ambassador Extraordinary to France in 1639. Ten years later he was forced to leave France, which was by then suffering from the disturbances of the Fronde, an often violent civil war that from time to time seriously upset life in the French capital. Della Bella's style derives to a large extent from Florentine Mannerism, and seems also to have been

Pls. 168 and 169 Plates from two small books published by Balthazar Moncornet in Paris in 1665 of 'new goldsmiths' work by the best masters of the day', although both designs are believed to be by François Lefebure, who was indeed a celebrated master. The pendant was probably to be executed in colours on a white ground; the diamonds shown on the second plate would have been polished in the 'rose cut' technique, in which Parisian jewellers were leading the world. That Moncornet expected an international circulation is indicated by the fact that the text is in both French and German. Note the view of the formal gardens at Ruel, a small palace on the edge of Paris.
Victoria and Albert Museum, London (Mus. no. E. 2330–1912 and 1974–1914)

Pl. 170 Tapestry woven at Paris in the workshop of Marc de Comans and François de la Planche, presented by Louis XIII to Cardinal Francesco Barberini who was sent as Papal Legate to France in 1625–6. A year later the Cardinal set up a tapestry works in Rome.
By kind permission of Rainer Zietz, London

influenced by Mitelli (see p. 77). His etchings have a sculptural quality, which, however, is rendered with great delicacy of line producing an almost smoky effect. His style also carries echoes of the contemporary Dutch Auricular taste (see Chapter 9), and looks forward to late Baroque and Rococo forms of the early 18th century, and was immensely influential in his lifetime and later.

A great deal of rebuilding took place in Paris from the 1620s onwards in spite of the disruption caused by the Fronde in the late 1640s and early 1650s. Whole new quarters sprang up and many fine new buildings, all richly furnished, were erected at this time. This of course greatly stimulated the luxury house-furnishing and decorating trades. We must therefore take a look at Parisian residential architecture of the grander kind in the time of Cardinal Richelieu, who was Chief Minister from 1629 until his death in 1642, and of his successor, Cardinal Mazarin.

It is in chimneypieces and ceilings that we find the clearest expressions of contemporary fashion at this time. Several suites of engravings showing designs for chimneypieces were published in the 1630s and 1640s, including those in Jean Barbet's *Livre d'Architecture* of 1633, which was dedicated to Cardinal Richelieu and purported to show 'that which is beautiful in Paris today', with the implication that the features illustrated had actually been constructed and were new. A *Livre des divers ornemens pour Plafonds…* [book of various ornaments for ceilings] was published in about 1640 by Jean Cotelle, a painter-decorator (Pl. 175). This was dedicated to Anne de Rohan, Princess of Guémené, in whose town residence he had executed much painted decoration. He was later to work for the Crown at the Louvre, Tuileries and Fontainebleau. Barbet's designs for chimneypieces were republished in Paris in 1641 and, in a simplified form, also in Amsterdam during the same year by Cornelis Danckerts. At least one design for a chimneypiece very similar in style to that of Barbet (Pl. 173) was sent from Paris to London in 1637 where it was imitated by Inigo Jones, the Court Architect, who was at that time decorating the celebrated villa at Greenwich for the French-born Queen Henrietta Maria. The office of the Court Architect, either in the time of Inigo Jones (died 1652) or of his successor John Webb, had on its shelves a group of colourful Parisian drawings of this period for chimneypieces, ceilings and mural decoration (many of them by Cotelle), which had presumably been acquired as a source of inspiration for the English draughtsmen working in the office (Pl. 175). Henrietta Maria was the daughter of Marie de' Medici, for whom the Luxembourg Palace in Paris was built (from 1615 until well into the 1620s), a building that embodied many extremely advanced features in its ground-plan and decoration and became a model for splendid building elsewhere in Europe for much of the 17th century. Henrietta Maria paid great attention to the embellish-

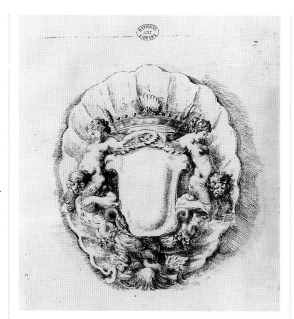

Pl. 171 Cartouche designed by the Florentine artist Stefano della Bella, who spent much time in Paris and whose work was mostly published there, as was this delightful composition – in 1644.
Victoria and Albert Museum, London (Mus. no. E. 1304–1897)

Pl. 172 Title-page of 1627 to a work on carpentry for buildings, by Mathurin Jousse, displaying current motifs of French architectural ornament of a somewhat provincial character; the plinth bears decoration based on Italian early 16th-century prints, such as those of Marco Dente.
Courtesy of Marlborough Rare Books Ltd, London

ment of her surroundings and in many cases paid the bills from her own private account.

Pl. 172 shows the title-page of a book of 1627 on structural carpentry, which characterises the Classical style in French architectural ornament at this stage in a rather provincial version; the author worked in the small town of La Flèche which lies about 250 kilometres (150 miles) south-west of Paris. The doorway shown in Pl. 174 is more sophisticated; it appears in a treatise on architecture published in Paris in 1645 by the important

the 16th century, with fewer elements and greater plasticity. An early suite of engravings showing this new formula illustrates painted mural decoration in the glamorous bathing apartment of the Queen Regent (Anne d'Autriche) at the Palais Royal in Paris, carried out in 1644 by the celebrated painter Simon Vouet. He had spent the period 1612 to 1627 in Rome (with a pension from the French Crown), where he had been in close contact with intellectuals possessed of strong antiquarian interests. He was thus familiar with grotesque ornament in each of its many manifestations, from the

architect Pierre Le Muet. By this stage a sober form of Classicism with bold ornament handled rather severely permeated fine building in and around the French capital. It was onto formal framework of this nature that lively, robust ornament, derived from the Roman Baroque style of the second quarter of the 17th century, was liberally heaped to produce a new court style of decoration that began to make its appearance at Paris in the middle of the century (Pl. 176).

Decoration of this new kind to a large extent follows the principles of grotesque ornament, although its general character is much more monumental than that of

S.Vouet In.   10   M.Dorigny Jc.

of his pupils, Charles Le Brun, to become the tri-umphant court style of Louis XIV in the 1660s.

In some of its versions the Vouet style may owe some-thing also to that of the Fontainebleau School, notably where strapwork cartouches frame central scenes. Plenty of engravings existed to show what the Fontainebleau style looked like but this line of influence could also have reached Vouet in prints.

The engravings in Le Muet's book of 1645 were exe-cuted by Jean Marot, at that time about 25 years old. His output of engravings was enormous and ranged from illustrations of entire buildings to architectural ornament of many kinds, including vases, chimneypieces, locks for doors, and ceilings; Pl. 177 shows a doorway. He was also an architect and can be said to represent the standard French mid-century upper-class taste. His style is not as luscious as that of Vouet; indeed, Marot's dry delineation speaks for French Classicism while Vouet's more volup-tuous forms reflect his extensive personal knowledge of Roman Baroque. Marot's almost exact contemporary, Jean Le Pautre, who was equally prolific, seems to have felt the pulse of fashionable taste in the 1650s and into the 1670s more sensitively (Pl. 178).

Further impetus to the spread of Italian influence at the French court was provided by two Italian artists who

Antique versions down through those of Pinturicchio, the Raphael School and Pirro Ligorio, to patterns like that of 1637 shown in Pl. 160. He must also have studied the most recent work in Rome of the great painter-decorators such as the Carracci and Pietro da Cortona.

On his return to Paris in 1627, to become the King's principal painter, Vouet was soon engaged on impor-tant assignments at the royal palaces. The painted dec-orations he executed at the Palais Royal in 1644–5 were extremely influential, not least because they were the subject of the suite of prints that first came out in 1647 but which was later copied and published at Antwerp and, in 1691, at Augsburg. Vouet's elegant Italianate style was to be developed at the hands of one

Pl. 176 Published illustration of mural decoration in Anne d'Autriche's *appartement des bains* at the Palais Royal, Paris, executed in the mid-1640s by Simon Vouet, then principal painter to the French court. Engraved by Michel Dorigny, 1647.
Metropolitan Museum of Art, New York; Harris Brisbane Dick Fund, 1934 (34.70.3 [11])

T 122 J. Marot: Portal, aus *Ornemens ov placarts*, M. 17. Jh.

Pl. 177 Design for a doorway, published in the mid 17th century, by Jean Marot (see also Pl. 174) – the son of a joiner.
From Ornemens ou placarts

apartments at the Louvre for Anne d'Autriche, which he completed in 1657. Between them, Romanelli and Grimaldi did much to transmit the ebullient spirit and rolling forms of Roman Baroque to mid-century Paris. The example they provided was keenly noted by a number of ambitious French artists and designers who were to become important in the 1660s.

Let us for a moment turn to ornament on a smaller scale, like that shown in Pl. 180, which is an engraving of 1660 showing the chased ornaments on pistols made by Thuraine and Le Hollandois (note the Netherlandish connection; the family name was apparently Reynier), gunsmiths to the King, by that time Louis XIV. The lively, luscious style of Vouet is here seen executed in the somewhat intractable medium of chiselled steel.

A much lighter form of decoration than that introduced by Vouet, with its Roman Baroque overtones, was that of which Charles Errard seems to have been the

Pl. 178 Title-page of a book of designs for mural decoration by Jean Le Pautre, probably published in the 1660s and claimed as his own invention. Whether true or not, the style depicted is that developed in the middle of the century from that introduced by Vouet in the late 1640s (see Pl. 176).
From Lambris à la Françoise Nouvellement Inventée et Gravée par Iean le Potre

Pl. 179 Bookbinding of crimson morocco leather with gold tooling producing a so-called 'fanfare pattern' consisting of interlaced strapwork. The ground is filled with delicate and sparkling *pointillé* punched work composed of small dots. On an edition of Tasso's *Gerusalemme Liberata* published in Paris in 1644.
Reproduced by permission of the Provost and Fellows of Eton College, Windsor

worked for Cardinal Mazarin, the Italian who ruled France as Chief Minister from 1642 until 1661. Mazarin built his own palace close to the Palais Royal (Anne d'Autriche's residence), and it became celebrated for the magnificence of its decoration and furnishing in a predominantly Italian taste. The principal Italian artist working for Mazarin was Giovanni Francesco Romanelli, who had studied painting in Rome under both Domenichino and Pietro da Cortona. Romanelli's powerful patron in Rome, Cardinal Francesco Barberini, appointed him chief designer of a new tapestry workshop that he founded in 1627. A decade later Barberini arranged his appointment as director of the painters' academy in Rome, the Accademia di San Luca, a post that undoubtedly acknowledged his high standing in his profession, despite the means by which it was secured. In 1647 Romanelli followed Barberini into exile in Paris where he was soon engaged on the decoration of the gallery in Mazarin's new palace. He had executed a substantial part of the decor before he returned to Rome in 1648; the work was completed by Giovanni Francesco Grimaldi, another painter trained in Rome, who also designed important ornamental features, such as cabinets, mirrors and buffets for the palace. Romanelli returned to Paris in 1655 in order to decorate two new

chief exponent. He was engaged on decorating the apartment of Anne d'Autriche at the Louvre palace in the 1650s and a suite of engravings based on his work was published about 1660 (Pl. 181). Errard, a painter of a scholarly cast of mind who had spent much time in Rome, was a founder member of the French Royal Academy and carried out a great deal of work at the French royal palaces although he was gradually eclipsed by Charles Le Brun in the early 1660s, after which he returned to Rome to take up the post of Director of the French Academy there. The light style he used at the Louvre follows the candelabrum formula with symmetrical scrollwork, now furnished with fairly naturalistic flowers and foliage. Yet, for all its naturalistic detail, Errard's decoration adheres more closely to the severe French version of the Classical tradition than to the Baroque richness of Vouet (Pl. 176). Its wiry scrollwork is tightly controlled and lacks the generosity that Vouet's, and later Le Brun's, work so gloriously possess. However, Errard's designs prefigured the wiry grotesques to be seen in some of Berain's engravings of the 1690s (Pl. 241), and a step on the way to this development is represented by the design shown in Pl. 182, which is the work of Georges Charmeton. Charmeton not only executed painted decoration in various important Parisian buildings but also designed embroidery patterns that may perhaps owe something to the wiry embroidery patterns of Johann Sibmacher, which were published in Nürnberg around 1600 (Pl. 142). Patterns of this kind derive ultimately from moresque designs (Pls. 55 and 123).

Overall decoration of a rather different kind is to be seen on fine Parisian bookbindings of the second quarter of the 17th century (Pl. 179). Of great delicacy and amazing precision, this so-called 'fanfare pattern' does not possess the bravura of fine French binding of a century earlier when this art-form was in the forefront of design (Pls. 84, 86 and 90). The niggling fanfare patterns have their charm but are the output of skilled tradesmen rather than artists of talent, or, rather, highly competent craftsmen working to the designs of brilliant designers. They are interesting, however, because they echo on a small scale those used in contemporary garden-design and for parquetry floors and large areas of painted wall-tiles. A variant of such bookbinding patterns is one with motifs resembling a fan; a splendid Roman binding of this type is to be seen in Pl. 183.

Pl. 182 Panel of ornament, essentially grotesque in style, with wiry scrolls set in a framework of metal-like strapwork; designed by Georges Charmeton, who died in 1674. Published shortly after his death; engraved by Nicolas Robert.

Pl. 183 Contemporary Roman binding on a book published in 1658; red morocco with gilt tooling including fan-tool corner decoration and a *rinceaux* pattern in the border. Binding made by the Andreoli brothers, who both in turn became binders to the Vatican. Bound for the discriminating Queen Christina, who had abdicated the Swedish throne and was by this time living in intellectual circles in Rome.
Courtesy of Sotheby's, London

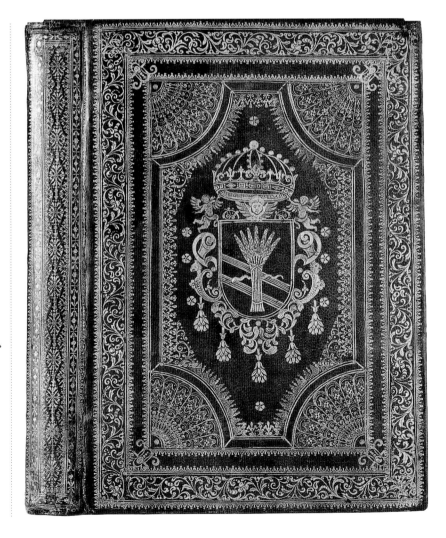

CHAPTER 9

AMSTERDAM

1610-1670

Pl. 184 Portrait of a botanist of Leiden University, executed as a print in 1601 by Jacques de Gheyn when he was established in that city, although it was published at Antwerp. The exotic plants and gourds forming the head-dresses of the mermaids are a reminder of how fascinated Netherlanders were by distant parts of the world across the seas, and their elongated tails are early examples of the curvaceous marine forms characteristic of a new style – the Auricular – that appeared in its fully fledged form in Holland around 1610–15. De Gheyn had previously worked under Hendrick Goltzius at Haarlem (see Pl. 187). *The Bodleian Library, University of Oxford (RSL.RR.x.307)*

Pl. 185 The underside of the bowl of a tazza made in Prague in 1607 by the Utrecht silversmith Paul van Vianen. The three naturalistic scenes in shallow relief are surrounded by novel forms – early expressions of the so-called Auricular style. Similar framing ornament is to be seen on the tazza's foot and stem. *Rijksmuseum, Amsterdam*

We have seen how the great city of Antwerp, focal point of trade routes and with its ample deep-water harbourage on the estuary of the River Scheldt, held the dominant commercial position in the Netherlands in the 16th century (Chapter 6).

The revolt of the Netherlands against Spain ruined Antwerp, and the centre of international trade and finance shifted gradually to Amsterdam, which became the principal city of those northern provinces that finally succeeded in winning their independence from Spain in 1609. The strength of the new republic (then known as the United Provinces but commonly called Holland) rested chiefly on its command of the sea, one result of which was to enable the northerners to exert a stranglehold on the shipping-route that connected Antwerp to the sea. The northerners had speedily developed this power not only in order to defend their coasts and control their sea entries, but also to exploit their increasingly extensive sea-borne trade, which was to make Holland the greatest maritime state of Europe in the 17th century. They came to command the sea-borne carrying trade; freight was their chief business. This was backed by a lively and lucrative entrepôt trade, as goods were trans-shipped at Dutch ports to other parts of Europe. All this required financing, often in

daring and imaginative ways, and this in turn made the Dutch the most enterprising bankers of the time in Europe.

The northern provinces became increasingly and emphatically Protestant while the southern remained largely Catholic, and many southerners moved north to avoid religious persecution, but the fact that the northern provinces now seemed to offer far more favourable conditions for commercial enterprise must also have proved an equally powerful magnet that attracted bold and energetic people northwards. Among the immigrants were many skilled craftsmen and not a few artists. It needs to be said, however, that despite this shift to the north, the city of Antwerp remained a great artistic centre throughout the 17th century (think of Rubens, a son of that city, to name only the foremost).

On the direct route northwards from Antwerp lie the important cities of Breda and Utrecht, with Tilburg and Hertogenbosch to the east, and Dordrecht, Rotterdam, Delft and Leiden on the westerly route. West of Amsterdam itself lies Haarlem. Immigrants from the south took up residence in all these cities, many of them later moving on in the pursuit of their calling; indeed, the continual movement of immigrants from one city to another in the northern provinces is a feature of the time, not least among artists.

Pl. 186 A formal portrait of 1610 framed with Auricular forms, showing that these were deemed entirely appropriate for the purpose. The sitter was a counsellor to the Emperor Rudolph II at Prague, and the artist, Aegidius Sadeler, describes himself as engraver to the Emperor. Sadeler was in close contact with prominent artists in the Netherlands, notably Hendrick Goltzius. The heavy festoons and swags of fruit become characteristic features of early Baroque ornament around 1620.
Rijksprentenkabinet, Rijksmuseum, Amsterdam

Pl. 187 Engraving by Hendrick Goltzius, famed artist of Haarlem, of about 1595, showing a bowl in an early form of the Auricular idiom, which in turn derives from certain Italian Mannerist designs of the mid-16th century. Note the drinking-glasses depicted in the lower corners.
Rijksprentenkabinet, Rijksmuseum, Amsterdam

Pl. 188 Drawing of Auricular ornament for a basin to be executed in silver, designed by Adam van Vianen or his son Christiaen; c.1627–1630. The Auricular ornament frames panels that were presumably to be decorated with small scenes. The cartilaginous character of such ornament is well exemplified by this design, as are the marine motifs that frequently appear in such decoration.
Nationalmuseum, Stockholm

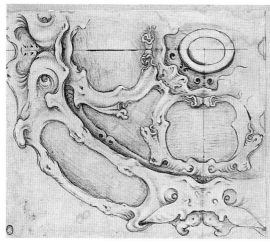

ear, with its soft and rounded folds and fleshy parts, all built upon a cartilage-like understructure, with no angles or sharp edges. Sometimes marine animals have been the source of inspiration, sometimes the designers' fantasies were evidently prompted by anatomy, with visceral or skeletal elements much to the fore. It is difficult to describe the style; its strange and almost disquieting character is best conveyed by studying the objects themselves, or illustrations of them (Pls. 185, 189 and 191) although the contorted three-dimensional forms are not all that easy to capture in a photograph.

The Auricular style seems to have been developed chiefly by members of the van Vianen family, goldsmiths at Utrecht. Adam van Vianen remained at Utrecht, having become a master goldsmith there in 1593, following in the steps of his father. His younger brother Paul, who may have been the actual pioneer of the style, went to work abroad, first at the Bavarian court at Munich from 1596, then moving on to Salzburg, and ending up in Prague in the service of that great patron of the arts, the Emperor Rudolph II (see p. 72). Paul died at Prague in 1613 but he had by then created works in silver that are superb early expressions of the new style (Pl. 185). Adam himself died in 1627,

but his son Christiaen collected some of his father's designs and published them at Amsterdam in about 1652, adding a few compositions of his own, it is now thought. By this time the style was widely familiar in Holland and in many European cities, but Christiaen's publication (with a text in Dutch, French and German) gave further impetus to the spread of the style. It was to a large extent a goldsmith's art-form, but in the middle of the century could also be found in carved woodwork (table-stands, cupboard-fronts, balustrades, picture-frames; Pls. 192 and 193), in stuccowork and in engravings of ornaments, which led to its application as two-dimensional decoration on flat surfaces such as stained glass.

Auricular decoration on Paul van Vianen's work at

In Utrecht, at the beginning of the 17th century, the goldsmiths evolved a style that was highly remarkable and seemingly unlike anything that had ever been seen before, although of course it had its roots in earlier styles, as we shall see. Today, the style is known as the Auricular because its forms often resemble the human

PI. 189 A delightful shell-like cup in the Auricular style by Adam van Vianen; Utrecht, 1625. The fluid decoration, brilliantly worked in silver, shows to advantage in this small object, only 16.5 cm (6 ½ in.) high. *Rijksmuseum, Amsterdam*

PI. 190 One of a suite of Auricular designs by Gerbrand van den Eeckhout, the son of an Amsterdam silversmith, published in about 1650. The forms at the bottom may well be ear-like, but they may also seem to be made of dough. The figures flanking the central 'mask' give an impression of animal carcasses. From a 'new' suite of cartouches (*Veelderhande Nieuwe Compartiment*) which was followed in 1655 by a further suite. *Rijksprentenkabinet, Rijksmuseum, Amsterdam*

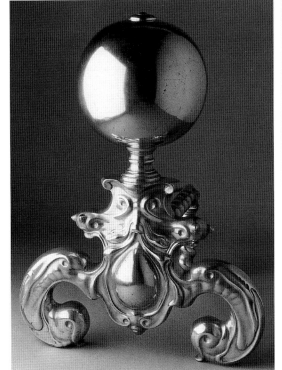

PI. 191 Silver fire-dog with legs of Auricular form; probably Dutch, 1640s. The ornament is very much in the style that Jan Lutma made famous at this time and this object (one of a pair) was probably made in Amsterdam. *The Danish Royal Collection, Rosenborg Castle, Copenhagen.*

Prague in the decade before his death in 1613 mostly took the form of surface ornament in shallow relief (PI. 185) but occasionally spread into truly three-dimensional form on the stems of cups and the like. It was Adam van Vianen in Utrecht who seems to have been the first to develop a style that affected the shape of entire vessels of goldsmith's work (PI. 189). There are indications that he was already experimenting with such forms in 1610, and it may be no coincidence that it was in the same year that Paul van Vianen returned to Utrecht from Prague on a short visit. Did Paul introduce Adam to new forms during his visit?

Adam's *tour de force* in this vein was executed in 1614, when the Amsterdam goldsmiths' guild invited him to produce a cup for guild use, and what is remarkable about this exercise is that the cup he created was a fully evolved Auricular object, in the same taste as a cup of his shown here in PI. 189 of about a decade later. The fact that the Amsterdam guild invited a master from another city to make this cup shows how greatly van Vianen was respected at the time (the sheer technical achievement of creating such a vessel out of a single ingot of metal was in itself astonishing) but that they were prepared to accept a vessel in this still novel style also suggests that other prominent members of the profession were not totally ignorant of the Auricular idiom by 1614. Guilds were normally very conservative institutions, but those of Amsterdam at this period were perhaps rather less so, as they cannot have been unaffected by the excitement of living in that city, in a country essentially free from oppression and where almost anything seemed possible to men of courage, whether it be in business ventures or sailing the high seas – or experimenting in the various realms of art.

If members of the Amsterdam guild were aware of the existence of this new style by 1610–14, when fully-fledged examples could presumably be seen in their city, precursors must have appeared somewhat earlier and here we switch our attention to the city of Haarlem, not far from Amsterdam, where a group of artists had been interested in simpler versions of such forms in the 1590s (PI. 187). The two most prominent Haarlem artists at the time were Hendrick Goltzius and Karel van Mander, both of whom were in close contact with Netherlandish artists working for Rudolph II in Prague, notable among whom were the Antwerp artist Bartholmäus Spranger and the Netherlandish engraver Aegidius Sadeler (PI. 186), both of whom were playing leading roles in artistic creativity in Prague. Many of the artists working in Prague were Italian or were strongly influenced by Italian art, especially that in the Mannerist taste embodying strange and frequently grotesque beasts, contorted stems and handles, and an apparent disdain for stability and practical purpose. The influence of earlier Italian Mannerism was also exerted by the presence in Prague of a vast collection of designs by Giulio Romano dating mostly from the 1530s (Pls. 35 and 36), which were in the hands of the antiquary Jacopo Strada and to which the court artists must presumably have had access. Strada's son Ottavio published 82 of Giulio's designs in 1587, thus making a selection of them widely available. It may be that such a

Pl. 192 Portrait of John Maitland, future Duke of Lauderdale, painted by Cornelis Janssen (Cornelius Johnson), about 1640, with a contemporary frame in the Auricular style. Janssen, the son of émigré parents, was born in London and was at this time still living in England (he later moved to Middleburg in Holland to escape the English Civil War), so the frame is presumably English. It is possible that someone in the circle of Christiaen van Vianen was responsible for its design. *Victoria and Albert Museum, London, on loan to the National Trust, Ham House, Richmond*

Pl. 193 A characteristically Dutch form of side-table with an elaborately carved wooden frame supporting a marble top; about 1660. The carved ornament appears to owe much to Gerbrand van den Eeckhout's engravings. Later examples acquire an overlay of naturalistic decoration. The carving of such stands was carried out in sculptors' workshops rather than those of furniture-makers. *Centraal Museum, Utrecht (Mus. no. 4501)*

source of inspiration, added to their own fertile inventiveness, induced such Haarlem artists as Goltzius and van Mander to devise forms that seem to be new and to introduce them at first as subsidiary motifs in their own work (Pl. 187).

The Auricular style of the van Vianens was further developed in Amsterdam by the equally skilled goldsmith Jan Lutma, who had established himself there in 1620, after five years working in Paris. He died in 1669, by which date a suite of engravings after his designs had been published (1653); a further series was brought out in 1684, suggesting that designers were still interested in these forms. With both Lutma and Adam van Vianen's designs being published in the 1650s, a second wave of inspiration fed the imaginations of designers and not only in the Netherlands. The wave was made bigger by the publication in the same decade of two

suites of Auricular compositions by Gerbrand van den Eeckhout, the son of an Amsterdam goldsmith, who must certainly have known Lutma; the second suite appeared in 1655 (Pl. 190). Gerbrand's designs included several for carved table-stands (Pl. 193), and his style was applicable to works in a wide range of materials. So, while the fresh and exciting first fruits of fully developed Auricularism were to be seen in metalwork during the second and third decade of the century, other manifestations of the style were mostly produced in the third quarter of the century. It was, moreover, a style that was popular chiefly in northern Europe and in Protestant areas, rather than in the Catholic lands of southern Europe – although traces of Auricularism may be found in works produced all over Europe.

Refugees from the Spanish-dominated Southern Netherlands fled not only northwards to Holland, but in other directions as well, and there can have been no major Protestant city in Europe where they were not to be found by the early 17th century. They chiefly went eastward and the large cities of western Germany became home to many important Netherlandish enterprises, as we shall see. With regard to the spread of the Auricular style, the city of Hamburg was notable for goldsmiths' work in this style and, indeed, one of the earliest pattern-books containing designs with Auricular elements was published in that city in 1621 by Gotfried Müller, who had come to Hamburg the year before from Brunswick. It is not at present clear where he found his sources of inspiration, but they are likely to have come from Amsterdam or Haarlem. Augsburg was also early to show a keen interest in the Auricular style but it was a German, Lucas Kilian, rather than a Netherlander who played the most important role there (Pl. 143). Kilian published several suites of engravings in the Auricular taste at Augsburg in the 1620s. Indeed, he was an important pioneer of the style in Germany, where some especially wild confections in this taste were later produced, for example those of Donath Horn and of Friedrich Unteutsch, both of Frankfurt am Main, a city where many Netherlanders were established (Pl. 196). Unteutsch's work was published in about 1645; Horn's work was issued in Nürnberg before he moved to Frankfurt in 1673.

French goldsmiths seem not to have adopted the Auricular style to any great extent but the Parisian goldsmith Daniel Boutemie published a pattern-book in 1636 that he called an '*Ouvrage Rare et Nouveau*' [A rare and novel work] in which he included Auricular cartouches of an unpleasantly spiky character, explaining that his 'capricious' designs would be of interest to goldsmiths, engravers, chasers of metalwork, sculptors and makers of furniture. At about that time another Parisian designer, Daniel Rabel, a celebrated engraver in the 1620s and early 1630s, produced a book of cartouches with Auricular features that are rather less wild than Boutemie's (Pl. 149). He also executed illustrations for Honoré d'Urfé's pastoral romance about the shepherdess Astrée (1633). The fame of d'Urfé's book may have made printsellers receptive to Rabel's suites of ornament, which were certainly in themselves influential both in Germany and the Netherlands; Mitelli, in Italy, may also have derived inspiration from them.

A third Frenchman who flirted with the Auricular style was Jacques Callot, who was born at Nancy, which lies much closer to the German frontier at Strassburg than to Paris. He settled in Florence in 1612, and much of his production was executed there. Although Callot's designs are more akin to the work of Italians (e.g. Mitelli), an Auricular character may be recognized in some of his published work (Pl. 195).

It is probable that English designers who followed developments on the Continent will have seen examples of Auricular forms before 1630, but in that year a highly skilled goldsmith who was a master of the style was invited to London by Charles I. He was Christiaen, a son of Adam van Vianen of Utrecht. Christiaen stayed in London until 1641, and returned in 1665 to work briefly for Charles II after the monarchy had been restored. In the 1630s Christiaen was employing at least 11 people, one of whom (John Bodendick) remained in England when his master returned to Holland. On his second visit, Christiaen left behind his son-in-law, Jean-Gérard Coques (or Cooqus) who was extremely competent, as a wine-jug made by him in about 1670 clearly shows (Pl. 194). The picture-frame shown in Pl. 192, which displays unmistakable Auricular features, surrounds a portrait that may have been painted around 1640 in London; if so, this suggests that van Vianen, or someone working close to him, was willing to provide designs for objects in materials other than silver. Christiaen van Vianen was sometimes listed as a 'Norimberger' in the goldsmiths' records because Nürnberg silver enjoyed such a high reputation in England and the city's name became a generic term for all Germanic silver of fine quality, including that of a great Dutch master such as van Vianen. The English, incidentally, often did not distinguish Dutchmen from Germans (their languages sounded very similar to English ears, no doubt, and many Dutchmen worked in Germany, as we have seen), which accounts for the people of Holland being called 'Dutch' in England – a corruption of *deutsch*, which means German.

The Auricular style did not develop and had no derivative of any sort. It was an unruly style which had its roots at the bottom of the sea among strange monsters, crabs and conger eels, or in dripping caves, in the slime of estuaries, in crypts, butchers' shops, anatomy theatres and other eerie and discomforting places. It was anti-conventional and appealed particularly to the essentially middle-class people of Holland, who had triumphed against heavy odds at sea, and in the banking-

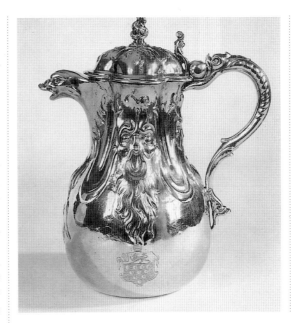

Pl. 194 Wine-jug of silver made in the workshop of Jean-Gérard Cooqus in London, about 1670. Cooqus's mastery of the Auricular style, rendered in repoussé-work, was scarcely less spectacular than that of his father-in-law, Christiaen van Vianen.
Rijksmuseum, Amsterdam

Pl. 195 Scene by Jacques Callot framed with gristly Auricular ornament, published in 1629. Although he settled in Florence in 1612, his influence was powerful – not least on Parisian *ornemanistes* like Rabel and Boutemie (see Pl. 149). This cartouche combines a Netherlandish form with a spooky character often found in Italian Mannerist ornament.

Pl. 196 Designs for brackets in the Auricular style by Donath Horn, a cabinetmaker who worked at Nürnberg before moving to Frankfurt in 1673. During his Nürnberg period he published a pattern-book with 39 plates of such ornament, which exemplifies the German form of the Auricular idiom; it tends to be more vigorous than the Netherlandish version. Probably executed in about 1660.

houses where they so adroitly handled the finances of much of Europe. By the second half of the 17th century, when Europe sought stability after the turmoil of the wars of religion and civil commotions of the previous 100 years or so, unconventionality was, however, no longer desirable. Now the tough, centralized command of courts, hedged in with formality and ceremonial, became the pattern required for centralized control of a nation, and Louis XIV's splendid example at Versailles was the epitome of that way of ordering matters (see Chapter 11). In order to achieve stability, moreover, courts invoked the benefits of tradition, order and discipline in their support, and in the arts Classicism (which was a style based on rules) served their purpose best, as we shall see.

Of course, the Classical style had not completely disappeared after the 16th century, even in Holland; while the Auricular style evolved, flourished and died away, the Classical tradition remained dominant in many

places, ready to be further developed in a manner suited to the new needs of an aristocratic and courtly culture. The Auricular idiom, along with the sentiments that lay behind it, retreated to the grottoes and other hidden places whence it had come, and remained there as a subculture, awaiting the time, almost a century hence, when it would inspire artists who were working in what was to become the Rococo style (see Chapter 13).

Classical forms are to be seen in many Northern Netherlandish designs and artefacts from the period under discussion (Pl. 200). The Dutch took a particularly strong interest in Italian illustrated treatises on architecture such as those of Serlio, Palladio and

Scamozzi; and it will be remembered that in both Holland and England there were many great admirers of Palladio during the second quarter of the 17th century, including the Englishman, Inigo Jones.

Dutch translations of the chief works on architecture in Italian, French and German appeared from the late 16th century onwards in Amsterdam. These were augmented by the publication of copies of suites of engraved ornament from abroad, including much architectural decoration (suites of chimneypieces, for instance, rendered either precisely or more often in slightly simplified form more suitable for a middle-class clientele). The name of Cornelius Danckerts appeared on many such suites in the second quarter of the century. This famous Amsterdam publisher and printseller not only produced copies of foreign work but also commissioned new work from contemporary Dutch designers. His customers could be found all over Europe, one of them being Robert Pricke, a leading publisher in London between 1646 and 1700. Pricke in turn copied Danckerts's prints, which always bear the marks of Dutch taste even where Danckerts had copied the subject from a French or German original. This flourishing print trade in Amsterdam, which disseminated information about various forms of ornament, soon overshadowed all other centres of such trade except Paris.

A particularly good designer of ornament active in Amsterdam from about 1630 was Hans Janssen (b. 1605), who became a prominent publisher in Amsterdam, as well as a designer. The design for a dish shown in Pl. 203 is excellent and is also a reminder that grotesque ornament continued to evolve after the end of the 16th century.

The northwards shift of Netherlandish stylistic creativity at this period is exemplified in the history of

Pl. 197 One of three dishes attached to a silver table-fountain to catch drips from the taps. Made by the celebrated goldsmith Hans Peters III of Augsburg. Acquired by the Danish Crown in 1649. The influence of the Dutch Auricular manner is here very marked. Indeed, this is one of the finest examples of silver in this taste. *The Danish Royal Collection, Rosenborg Castle, Copenhagen*

Pl. 198 Portrait by Crispijn de Passe the Elder, executed in 1598 at Cologne about three years after his move from Antwerp. The enframing cartouche has all the hallmarks of the late Antwerp version of Northern Mannerism. The Count Schwarzenberg, here portrayed, was a successful leader of the Imperial forces combating the Turks in Hungary.

Pl. 199 'Summer', from a suite of the Seasons by Crispijn de Passe the Elder, executed either at Antwerp or Cologne late in the 16th century. The frame surrounding this emblematic subject is in the manner of contemporary northern Mannerist grotesque designs.
Victoria and Albert Museum, London (Mus. no. E. O. 100)

the de Passe family. The elder Crispijn de Passe was born in about 1570 in the Amsterdam region but moved to Antwerp where he became a member of the painters' guild in 1585. He learned much during his Antwerp years, at that time still the chief creative centre of the region, before setting up as a book-illustrator and engraver in Cologne, where he flourished until about 1612. He then moved to Utrecht at the time when Adam van Vianen was creating exciting forms in goldsmiths' work (see p. 94). De Passe handled the Mannerist cartouche with brilliance, sometimes investing it with grotesque features (Pls. 198 and 199). He had a large trade with France and had contacts with England where two of his sons, Willem and Simon, later worked as engravers (Simon also worked in Denmark for a while). Crispijn's eldest son, Crispijn II, was born at Cologne and later collaborated with his father (d. 1637) at Utrecht, though the younger man's compositions incline more towards Classicism (Pls. 200 and 201) than his father's. After moving to Rotterdam for a while, he settled in Amsterdam around 1640. Between about 1617 and 1630 he had taught drawing in Paris, and a third edition of his influential furniture pattern book, *Oficina Arcularia* … (first published at Utrecht in 1621, then at Amsterdam in 1642), appeared at Paris in 1651. Clearly the family's influence was enormous and it emanated largely from the northern Netherlands.

In the field of jewel-making, the great technical advances in the 16th century had been in the realm of enamelling (see p. 59). The 17th century saw the art of diamond-cutting and polishing reach new heights and this affected the forms adopted by jewellers in order to take advantage of the enhanced light-reflecting brilliance of the now more subtly shaped stone. Great attention was paid to the polishing of the underside of diamonds which, it was realised, made them shine more brightly; it therefore also helped if light could reach the stone from behind as well as in front, and this

Pl. 200 Design for a hanging cupboard or a wall tabernacle from the influential pattern-book *Oficina Arcularia…*, issued at Utrecht in 1621 by the publishing house of Crispijn de Passe the Elder but compiled by his son, Crispijn the Younger, who adhered to the Classical tradition, as we see here. Note the broken pediments, and the caryatid of his left-hand version. The gadrooning of the supporting console on the left is inspired by silversmiths' work, for which the motif was in great favour.
Victoria and Albert Museum, London (Mus. no. E. 2175–1929)

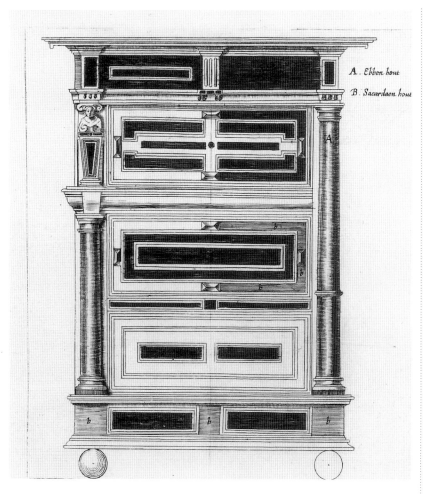

A. Ebben hout

B. Sacardaen hout

Pl. 201 Design for a cabinet or writing-desk (with alternative treatments) from the same source as Pl. 200. This, with its columns and carefully planned panels, adheres even more strictly to the Classical architectural idiom. Intended to be executed in ebony and rosewood, as the key to A and B tells us, furniture built on these general principles is relatively common.
Victoria and Albert Museum, London (Mus. no. E. 2175–1929)

encouraged the development of yet more ingenious settings. In so far as the shaping of the stones is concerned, the 'rose cut' had certainly evolved by the 1620s and the 'brilliant' had been devised by the 1680s. The chief centre of diamond-cutting and polishing in the 16th century had been Antwerp, but it seems that by about 1600 the centre where the most important innovations were made was Paris. Even as late as 1660 a young Antwerp diamond-polisher is known to have become apprenticed in Paris in order to perfect his art. He would not have taken this step had he not expected to learn something important from the Parisian jewellers. However, the principal centre of diamond-working was now Amsterdam, which had overtaken Antwerp in this activity, as in so many others, early in the 17th century. The Dutch imported the diamonds and exported what they did not need; obviously they kept the best stones for themselves.

Diamonds and other hardstones were often engraved, and here also techniques improved dramatically in the first half of the 17th century, and were eventually applied to the engraving of glass, at which the Dutch excelled in the second half of the century, although the best German and Bohemian glass-engravers of the time were in no way inferior.

While it is tempting to ascribe all anonymous 17th-century works decorated with naturalist flowers to the flower-loving Dutch, such decoration was, of course, popular in many other nations. Naturalistic flowers became increasingly common on decorative art objects from the 1640s onwards. The beautifully engraved jug shown in Pl. 202 displays a superb example of such ornament; it is dated 1650 and was probably made in northern Germany.

During the middle years of the 17th century the city of Delft became the principal centre of production for high-class pottery in northern Europe. Once again we see a northward emigration of talent as potters from Antwerp, making tin-glazed earthenware in the Italian *maiolica* tradition, moved first to Middleburg at the mouth of the Scheldt (1564), then to Dordrecht and Haarlem. Haarlem potters in turn colonized Delft (1584) and Rotterdam (1612). So famous did the Delft factories become, and so productive were its many factories, that the term 'delftware' has been applied to these products, which are technically akin to *maiolica* and faience (see p. 131).

The golden age of Delft pottery fell largely after 1670 so is here dealt with later (Chapter 12), but the technical achievements leading to greater refinement in the Delft products took place during the first two-thirds of the century. The chief source of inspiration came in the form of Chinese porcelain, large quantities of which were reaching Amsterdam by sea from the early 17th century onwards. The Delft potters learned to make their wares thinner, more like the porcelain importations; and they learned to copy Chinese decoration, sometimes with astonishing precision. This purely imitative phase lasted until mid-century, and the wares were chiefly blue and white, but it was not until well into the second half of the century that forms and decoration springing from the European tradition come to the fore in the Delft products.

The persecutions of the late 16th century had also encouraged the emigration of skilful linen-damask weavers from Courtrai, in the south, to Haarlem. The number of weavers who moved was quite small, but included several of the most talented masters, including Passchier Lammertin, who made napkins and table-cloths and numbered many princely clients among his customers. Linen-damask is notoriously difficult to photograph, so no illustration is included here.

The Dutch contribution to European culture during the first three-quarters of the 17th century lay primarily in having set an admirable pattern for middle-class life. In its most exalted manifestations it can be called patrician but it was never aristocratic. The culture that the Dutch established and which found favour with the middle classes all over Europe, from Lisbon to Moscow and beyond, and from Trondheim to Bayonne and Bergamo, was, in effect the antithesis of the French,

PI. 203 Design for a dish with alternative circular and octagonal borders, by Hans Hendrick Janssen of Amsterdam; about 1630. A particularly pleasing composition, with its centre based on the grotesque formula, it is evidently intended to be displayed upright. *From Jessen,* Meister des Ornamentstichs, *Vol. I, pl. 200*

PI. 204 A Dutch breast-ornament; about 1630. Gold, decorated with black and white enamel, set with diamonds. Height 13 cm (5½ in.). By this stage, the Dutch had become pre-eminent at polishing diamonds. *Victoria and Albert Museum, London (Mus. no. M. 143–1975)*

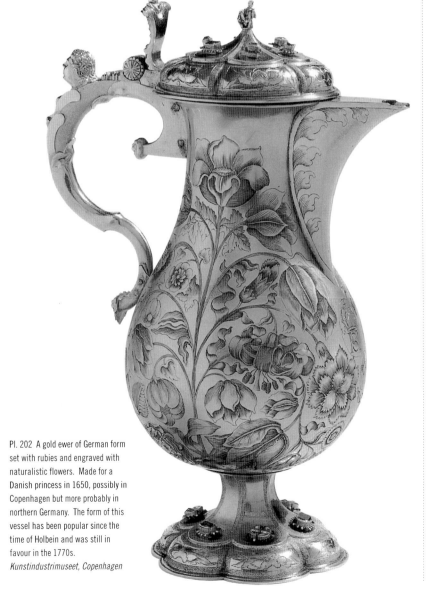

PI. 202 A gold ewer of German form set with rubies and engraved with naturalistic flowers. Made for a Danish princess in 1650, possibly in Copenhagen but more probably in northern Germany. The form of this vessel has been popular since the time of Holbein and was still in favour in the 1770s. *Kunstindustrimuseet, Copenhagen*

essentially aristocratic, culture. It was a sober, even a calculating pattern; it was sound, unfussy and spoke of solid values. It was also colourful, clean, yet it could encompass opulence. It had much to recommend it. And the country where the Dutch example in many fields was to have the most far-reaching effect was England and, by colonial extension, North America.

CHAPTER 10

ROME

PI. 205 One of the most celebrated Renaissance monuments in Florence, the tomb of Piero and Giovanni de' Medici in the family chapel, executed in bronze by Andrea del Verrocchio in 1471–2 and here shown in an engraving produced a century later by Cornelis Cort, a Flemish artist working in Rome. Based on an antique Roman sarcophagus, the robust acanthus-plant decoration of this tomb-chest has inspired designers ever since it was new, but this was particularly the case in the 17th century.
The British Museum, London

PI. 206 Engraving of acanthus decoration by Pietro Antonio Prisco, who worked in Naples; published in 1624. The stalks are becoming less evident and the leaves scroll over three-dimensionally. See also PI. 162.

There was nothing fundamentally different about circumstances in Rome during the 50 years before 1660 and the 50 that followed, with regard to the history of design. One might say that things remained much the same only more so. The Catholic Church's victories over reforming Protestantism had come to be taken for granted; the status quo now had to be preserved at all costs. A deeply conservative society that was to become all but moribund in the 19th century accepted change with increasing circumspection. Artistic patronage remained chiefly in the hands of princes of the Church and the only noteworthy change during the second half of the century was that the great patrician families now joined the ranks of the popes and cardinals in the matter of building themselves magnificent residences and furnishing them with the utmost splendour. In earlier centuries the patrician families of Rome, whose roots in many cases went back to Classical times, greatly resented the growing temporal power of the Church in what they regarded as their city. By the middle of the 17th century this antagonism had largely died away; it was no longer in anyone's interest. Secular and ecclesiastical princes mixed freely, members of their families intermarried, and together they made Rome an even more splendid city than it had been in the 16th century. The sumptuous furnishing of the gallery

in the Palazzo Colonna still provides a spectacular example of a secular prince imitating the princes of the Church in creating magnificent surroundings for himself (PI. 211). The gallery was completed shortly before the end of the 17th century.

The stream of pilgrims to the Holy City that we mentioned before grew even larger during the 17th century. While Rome had no industries to speak of that could boost its economy, the pilgrims brought substantial 'invisible earnings' to the city, just as tourists do today – they required lodging and food, guides, porters, shops of all kinds, and, in many cases, works of art, books, prints and antiquities that could be carried home. Moreover, when they got back, all would speak of the splendours of Rome, thus encouraging others to visit the city. This last factor must have played an important part in making Roman design more widely known. So, while no great historical break affected Rome around 1660, the dominance of the ornamental cartouche discussed in Chapter 7 waned, and emphasis now switched to a vegetal form, the acanthus leaf, which assumed a Baroque character and turned from being the comparatively tightly controlled, two-dimensional motif it had been since Classical times into one that was vigorously convoluted, sometimes even wayward, and very apparently three-dimensional. This rejuvenated form of acanthus reached the extreme of its development in Rome about 1680, but earlier forms were enjoying great favour by the 1660s and this lively motif had rapidly become a principal ornamental motif in the decorative arts in many parts of Europe by the 1670s.

Acanthus ornament was much used in Classical times and is an essential element of the so-called Corinthian order in Classical architecture. It was never entirely absent from the designer's repertoire. Scrolling vegetation was a common motif in Gothic art and sometimes took on an acanthus form. In heraldic ornament the mantling (originally a free-hanging textile component attached to the back of a rider's helmet) was usually represented as billowing around the helm and coat-of-arms, and was sometimes transformed into a representation of heavily scrolling acanthus (Pl. 220). The acanthus motif based on direct observation of Classical examples became common in Italy during the early Renaissance (Chapters 1 and 2). The supreme example of this must be Verrocchio's bronze tomb of 1472 that is based on a Classical formula for sarcophagi (Pl. 205). An important Classical monument from the time of the Emperor Augustus was the Ara Pacis, an altar inaugurated in the year 9 BC, fragments of which came to light during the Renaissance and then entered important collections of antiquities; part of its spiralling acanthus ornament was closely followed in an engraving by Agostino Veneziano in the 1530s (see p. 22). But acanthus leaves figure prominently in a great number of early ornament prints, from those produced by followers of Mantegna, through the prolific output of the Raphael School (of which Agostino was a member) and on to mid-century publications such as those of Giovanni Battista Pittoni. Designers in Germany, sensitive to Italian influence, were quick to adopt the motif; Aldegrever was among the first, in the late 1520s, and he had developed the concept brilliantly by the 1540s. In France acanthus was not commonly used before the 1550s, it seems, but then it is found used as ornament in such advanced architecture as the Italianate château at Ecouen, and was subsequently published by Jean Bullant in his book on the rules of architecture of 1564. Du Cerceau also relied greatly on acanthus decoration in his furniture designs of the 1560s.

However, those configurations are for the most part lean, tight ornaments springing from wiry, scrolling stems; the opulence of the Baroque form with which we are dealing is quite different in character. Early heralds of this change were Pietro Antonio Prisco, whose acanthus ornament in a suite of prints published in 1624 is richer and more three-dimensional than hitherto seen (Pl. 206), and also Polifilo Giancarli, whose engravings were published during the same decade (Pl. 162), while the astonishing work of a calligrapher named Vincenzo Morandi takes this opulence a step further (Pl. 213). The motif at this stage in its development was carried

Pl. 207 Drawing of a tripod-stand or table carved with a naturalistic tree trunk and oak leaves (possibly a reference to the Chigi family). Bernini, or his assistant Schor, designed a stand for a statue similar to this. Roman work of the second quarter of the 17th century. *Nationalmuseum, Stockholm (Tessin No. 1086)*

Pl. 208 Sketches for a ceremonial cradle by a Roman designer in the Bernini/Schor circle, active during the third quarter of the 17th century – perhaps by Giovanni Paolo Schor himself. It has been suggested that the design is for a salt cellar, but this seems unlikely. *The Royal Collection, Windsor Castle*

to France by Stefano della Bella, an Italian who was in Paris in the 1640s but continued to have his prints of ornament published there after he had returned home, which of course meant that the French were the first to see his new etchings (see Pl. 171). Della Bella's work certainly influenced that of Jean Le Pautre, who will figure largely in the next chapter, which is about France (see Pls. 178 and 231).

Painters who executed large schemes of interior embellishment at this period tended to be especially

Pl. 209 German versions of Roman acanthus ornament published at Augsburg in 1678; designed and engraved by Johann Conrad Reuttimann, who was probably a silversmith. *Victoria and Albert Museum, London*

Pl. 210 Design of part of a state coach decorated with acanthus leaves carved in the Roman manner. From a suite of designs by Mathias Echter of Graz dated 1677.

Pl. 211 Interior of a room of state in a Roman palazzo in the full-blown Baroque manner of about 1670. Possibly a theatre design, this undoubtedly reflects contemporary fashion in the furnishing of splendid rooms.
Victoria and Albert Museum, London (Mus. no. D316–1887)

Pl. 212 Design of a state coach (with alternative treatments for the corner-finials) by Filippo Passarini, Rome, 1698. State coaches in this style were in fashion in Rome already in the 1670s.
Victoria and Albert Museum, London (Mus. no. E. 1529–1923)

good at inventing designs for purely decorative features. Even if the paintings for a ceiling or wall, for example, were entirely pictorial, they needed framing in some way and it was in the borders, frames and in-fillings between the fictive scenes that imaginative and often highly innovative forms of ornament were introduced. It was when working on these border-areas that many young artists assisting a celebrated master like Pietro da Cortona learned their trade and, in the case of Cortona's pupils especially, often came to be inventive designers of ornament themselves. Cortona, indeed, trained some of the leading designers of ornament in Rome who were to become active during the period that now interests us. Pietro da Cortona worked mainly in Rome but spent much of the 1640s and some of the 1660s working on the decoration of the Pitti Palace in Florence. He was engaged on most of the great decorative enterprises of the day. His chief patron was Cardinal Francesco Barberini, who became Pope Urban VIII (1623–44).

Pl. 215 Carved-frame design by a Nürnberg cabinetmaker Georg Caspar Erasmus; published in 1695. *Victoria and Albert Museum, London* (Mus. no. E. 3315–1913)

Pl. 213 Pen and ink drawing by a master calligrapher named Vincente Morandi, about whom nothing is known except that he worked in the second quarter of the century. Probably Florentine. *Private collection*

Pl. 214 Superbly carved frame with sinuous stretched acanthus decoration, not quite like the tumbling motifs of the Schor, Ferri and Cerini school. Note the mask framed by this ornament at the top. Probably made in Florence, possibly in the 1650s and almost certainly not later than the mid-1660s. It betrays a knowledge of the Auricular style, which had reached the height of its popularity in Holland and northern Germany at this time. *Uffizi Gallery, Florence*

Cortona's painted ceiling in the Saloon at the Palazzo Barberini (completed in 1639) made him famous throughout Europe, and his decoration of the Quirinale Gallery in the 1650s was scarcely less celebrated.

The other artistic giant in Rome in the second quarter of the century was Gian Lorenzo Bernini, Cortona's contemporary and likewise a man who profoundly influenced design in the decorative arts. Primarily a sculptor but also an architect, his most influential work was undoubtedly the huge tabernacle [*baldacchino*] over the centralized high altar in St Peter's, a *tour de force* of bronze-casting and of a form and with detailing that was to be widely imitated. A pupil of both Pietro da Cortona and Bernini was Carlo Fontana, who became

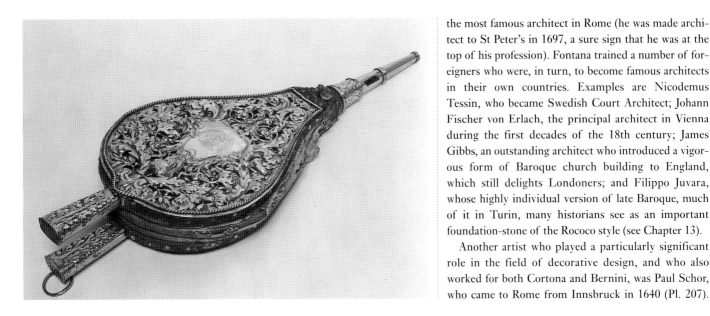

the most famous architect in Rome (he was made architect to St Peter's in 1697, a sure sign that he was at the top of his profession). Fontana trained a number of foreigners who were, in turn, to become famous architects in their own countries. Examples are Nicodemus Tessin, who became Swedish Court Architect; Johann Fischer von Erlach, the principal architect in Vienna during the first decades of the 18th century; James Gibbs, an outstanding architect who introduced a vigorous form of Baroque church building to England, which still delights Londoners; and Filippo Juvara, whose highly individual version of late Baroque, much of it in Turin, many historians see as an important foundation-stone of the Rococo style (see Chapter 13).

Another artist who played a particularly significant role in the field of decorative design, and who also worked for both Cortona and Bernini, was Paul Schor, who came to Rome from Innsbruck in 1640 (Pl. 207).

PL. 216 Bellows with chased silver mounts with openwork acanthus foliage. Made in London between 1672 and 1677 (or 1679) for Elizabeth, Duchess of Lauderdale. Among the original furnishings of Ham House.
Victoria and Albert Museum, London, on loan to The National Trust, Ham House, Richmond

Pl. 217 Engraved design by Pietro Cerini, published in Rome in the 1680s or 1690s, in a lighter style than that previously used in Italy for acanthus decoration. Perhaps influenced by French patterns such as that illustrated in Pl. 248.
Victoria and Albert Museum, London, (Mus. no. E. 2741–1908)

PL. 218 Title-page for a suite of designs of 'new ornaments… invented… by Johannes Unselt, sculptor; published and obtainable from Johann Ulrich Strapff, engraver and art-dealer in Augsburg, 1696'. In the light style favoured by Cerini (see Pl. 218).

He was a painter with a strong sculptural sense who came to enjoy a high reputation as a designer of decorative art ranging from amazing beds to ephemeral table-decoration of sugar-paste. Schor was responsible for imparting to acanthus ornament the full power of the Baroque manner. Pl. 208 shows this manner well although acanthus happens not to be very evident in these particular compositions. Another clever designer in much the same powerful vein was Ciro Ferri, a Roman artist who worked under Cortona at the Pitti Palace in Florence in the 1660s. Ferri was responsible for introducing the florid style of late Roman Baroque to that city, a notable expression being a bronze altar-frontal made in Rome in 1683 for the chapel in Santa Maria Maddalena de' Pazzi in Florence; it is decorated with rich acanthus ornament that yields nothing in exuberance to similar work by Schor. Ferri designed a number of state coaches in this ebullient taste, one for an English ambassador's procession to the Vatican in 1687, the designs for which were engraved and published in Rome in that year and in London a year later (and at Augsburg in 1700), while another suite of coach designs by Ferri was published in 1691.

Ferri's formula for state coaches was closely followed by another Roman designer, Filippo Passarini, who

Pl. 219 Frame carved with especially complex acanthus foliage in a light and open style, forming part of the furnishings of the Gesu Church at Mirandola, near Modena, made about 1696. Attributed to Giovan Battista Salani and Felice Francolini.
Il Gesu, Mirandola

Pl. 220 Funeral escutcheon carved in 1703 at the Stockholm workshop of Burchardt Precht, the most capable carver in Sweden at the time. Based on a well-established German formula, the mantling of the helms and blasons takes the form of richly tumbling acanthus leaves.
Turinge Church, Södermanland, Sweden

published 'new designs' (including that for a coach in Ferri's style shown in Pl. 212) in 1698 that were intended to help 'goldsmiths, carvers and embroiderers'. However, that this style was by no means novel in the 1690s, in spite of Passarini's claim on his title-page, is proved by the detail of a coach design using flamboyant acanthus which was published at Graz (in southern Austria) in 1679 by Mathias Echter (Pl. 210), who had probably been to Rome and may have met Schor (d. 1674) and perhaps also Ferri. The parallels between the work of these three designers seems too close for coincidence, and the title of Echter's suite of engravings does in fact make reference to '*fogliami Romane*' [Roman foliage] that is 'of new invention', showing that he was well aware of the origin of this kind of ornament. The style, moreover, is reflected in an Augsburg publication of 1678 by Johann Konrad Reutimann (Pl. 209), which reproduced bold floral designs for silversmiths' work.

A less heavy variant of the Schor and Ferri style evolved towards the very end of the century and co-existed with the heavier version still championed by men such as Passarini; this new variant is well exemplified in designs by Pietro Cerini, published in Rome in the 1680s or 1690s (Pl. 217). Cerini may have known Parisian designs such as that shown in Pl. 248, which may be of a decade or so earlier. Cerini's style seems to have influenced Johann Unselt, a cabinetmaker working in Augsburg, who produced several books of designs decorated with vigorous but now rather lighter acanthus foliage (Pl. 218). Another cabinetmaker who used this acanthus formula was Johann Indau in Vienna. He actually entitled his own publication of designs 'New

Roman Ornaments' [*Neue Romanische Zierraten*]. This was published before 1685, while a fresh suite of 'New designs for... Roman foliage' (note the parallel with Echter's title) came out in 1686 and was subsequently reissued at Augsburg. Indau must surely have visited Rome and may well have met Cerini while he was there.

While novel styles could be, and often were, transmitted by printed patterns, in order to understand the nature of a new form of ornament and thus be able to reproduce it as intended, it helps to see executed work in the round. This applies especially to ornament of the

Pl. 221 Design for an octagonal silver dish with a richly chased border in the Baroque taste, executed in Rome about 1690. The double-headed eagles are the blason of the Ottoboni family; the presence of the papal tiara indicates that Alexander VIII, Pope from 1689 to 1691, commissioned this design.
Courtesy of the Lodewijk Houthakker Collection, Amsterdam

Pl. 222 Carved and gilded frame attributed to Lorenzo Aili, which surrounds a painting at the castle of Soragna, not far from Parma, where Aili was working in 1701. The separate stalks of acanthus (now freely interpreted) running outside the main frame give a foretaste of frame design in the Rococo style. *Meli Lupi Collection, Rocca, Soragna, Parma*

Pl. 223 and 224 Two plates from Giovanni Giardini's *Disegni Diversi*, a collection of 100 of his designs, published in Rome in 1714. Some of the designs will, of course, be of an earlier date. The collection was re-published in 1750; both editions were very influential. William Kent was in Rome when the work was first published and was clearly inspired by Giardini's designs for console-tables which he imitated on his return to London. The chocolate-pot on the stand of the 'cabaret' is of French form. *Victoria and Albert Museum, London (Mus. no. E. 5549–1908 and E.5524–1908)*

Pl. 225 Neck of a baryton (a large cello-like fiddle with sympathetic strings) made in Berlin in 1720 by Jacques Sainprae. There are now breaks in the acanthus scrollwork. *Victoria and Albert Museum, London (Mus. no. 1444–1870)*

Pl. 226 Woven silk damask bearing a pattern that was to enjoy enormous favour all over Europe for decorating rooms of the finest sort from the 1720s until at least the 1770s; indeed, it must be regarded as the most popular pattern of all time for a woven textile of any complexity. Probably woven in Genoa, although the pattern was imitated at other centres of silk weaving.
Victoria and Albert Museum, London; Department of Textiles' archives

kind we are considering here. Even if Echter and Indau saw Roman acanthus decoration on its native soil, many of their compatriot fellow-artists did not; they had to rely on printed patterns. For those working in Augsburg, Graz and Vienna, for example, prints of ornament reached them via the well-established trade-routes and printsellers' network. Prints published in Rome reached Venice very early and could then have been acquired in that city by visiting foreigners from the north, and we know that many northern artists made that journey even if they went no further south. Moreover, prints being taken directly to cities in the north might sometimes have been shown to people in cities en route.

On the route north through the Veneto lies the small city of Belluno, where a woodcarver's son was born in 1662; he was to become famous in Venice, where he arrived in 1677 aged about 15. Andrea Brustolon may possibly have seen prints of 'Roman foliage' before his departure and will certainly have seen them in Venice. He visited Rome in 1679–80 and will have seen

examples of the real thing at every hand. He was to become the chief practitioner in this style in Venice and later in his native Belluno where he set up practice in 1695. He trained a whole school of carvers in the management of this powerful style, which spread to places such as Parma and Bologna (Pl. 219).

That knowledge of 'Roman foliage' patterns had reached England by 1679 is demonstrated by a pair of silver-mounted bellows at Ham House, near London, which are mentioned in inventories of 1677 and 1679, and which cannot be earlier than 1672 (Pl. 216).

Heavy Baroque forms did not die out after 1700 in Rome even though a lighter variant of acanthus scrolls and related patterns had made its appearance in the last decades of the 17th century. The design for a silver dish shown in Pl. 221 must date from about 1690, as the double-headed eagles probably refer to Alexander VIII, who was Pope from 1689 to 1691. Although not composed with acanthus, the design of this dish has a similar density to other Roman late Baroque patterns, as do the two designs illustrated in Pls. 223 and 224, which are by Giovanni Giardini, a leading Roman goldsmith, metalworker (he became bronze-founder to the papal court in 1698) and designer, active from the 1660s until the second decade of the 18th century.

Readers may have noticed that 'Roman acanthus' ornament appears so natural that no 'breaks' are present in the scrolls. It was apparently only in the 1720s and 1730s that breaks were introduced, as the elaborately carved peg-box of a baryton made in Berlin in about 1720 shows (Pl. 225); here breaks, or abrupt changes in direction in the scrollwork, are clearly visible. This must have been designed under the additional influence of northern late Baroque designs, such as those of Berain and his imitators, both in France and Germany (see Chapter 11).

Textile patterns, especially those woven on a loom, for the most part followed fashionable design only in a most general way. Woven patterns tended to have much the same density of design as contemporary patterns in other media, but the motifs used were stylised and remained so until a satisfactory method of rendering shading made it possible to impart a degree of naturalism to vegetal and other figurative patterns (see Chapter 13). In the 17th century patterns on woven textiles appeared entirely two-dimensional; this was especially the case with patterns designed for furnishing purposes, notably hangings for walls and round beds (Pl. 226). At Genoa a speciality was made of furnishing materials of silk, principally of velvet or executed with the damask weave. Damask has a ground for which a satin weave is used while the reverse of satin weave (which is dull rather than shiny) produces the pattern. This arrangement can be reversed so that the satin weave forms the pattern.

A Roman speciality in the middle and late decades of the 17th century was the production of richly decorated cabinets which wealthy people would place at strategic points in their apartments. They were often the subject of magnificent gifts which spread the Roman Baroque taste most effectively. The Roman model was imitated

in Florence, as Pl. 227 shows, and cabinets of the same opulent kind were made for the French king at the Gobelins in Paris, and elsewhere. Such furniture was extremely expensive, so a range of less costly, but nonetheless showy, cabinets was produced, notably at Antwerp (Pl. 228).

Pl. 227 Richly decorated cabinet veneered with ebony, rosewood and *pietre-dure* ornament, made in the grand-ducal workshops in Florence between 1642 and 1646 to the designs of the architect Matteo Nigetti. Such splendid confections set a pattern for large ornamental cabinets that was widely imitated. *Galleria degli Uffizi, Florence*

Pl. 228 Cabinet of about 1680 made at Antwerp in general imitation of superb cabinets like that shown in Pl. 227 but with the use of less expensive materials – tortoiseshell instead of marble, for instance, and stamped and gilded sheet-metal ornaments made to resemble gilt-bronze mounts. The finials standing on the bottom shelf do not belong to this piece. *The Swedish Royal Collections, Gripsholm Castle, Sweden*

CHAPTER 11

PARIS AND VERSAILLES

1660–1720

L ouis XIV became King of France as a small boy so his highly capable mother, Anne d'Autriche, was made Regent with Cardinal Mazarin acting as her chief minister. She was Austrian, he was Italian, and having two foreigners in charge was an affront to the pride of many Frenchmen, although the state's affairs were well run, and certain nobles, aggrieved by their exclusion from high office, rebelled. The civil wars of the so-called Fronde were intermittent but often vicious and when Louis took up the reins of government after Mazarin's death in 1661, he was determined to check the power of the nobility so as to ensure that never again would threats to the royal power arise from that quarter. One way of accomplishing this was to keep the chief noblemen close to his royal person and occupied with the many rituals that he imposed on the court. This to some extent prevented them scheming against him although they often became involved in jockeying for position among themselves. The King viewed with extreme disfavour absence from the court without good reason, and those, moreover, who wanted to speak to him found that the best passport to an audience was to have spent lavishly on clothes, entertainments, gambling and any other activity that could be expected to dissipate the petitioner's personal fortune and thus weaken any inclination he might have to plot against the monarch.

An important element of this framework was the King's provision of magnificent surroundings for himself and his court. This he set about doing in 1661, with improvements first to the Louvre Palace and, soon after, on a more modest scale, to the adjacent Tuileries. But the chief focus of Louis's attention was the palace at Versailles, some 15 miles (20 kilometres) from the centre of Paris. In successive waves of building, a fairly small hunting lodge on the edge of an extensive forest was turned into a vast palace, a veritable city which could house the King and his family (many of them with their own apartments, some of which were scarcely less splendid than those of the monarch), a court with numerous extensive rooms of parade in which complicated ceremonial could be performed, the offices of a government that had been moved down from Paris to be close to King and court, and a huge supporting cast that serviced the whole of this great complex. Building activity never ceased until the very end of Louis's reign in 1715, but the main work of building an entirely new palace, which first enveloped and then extended vastly out from the small hunting lodge, began in 1678. Prodigious sums of money were spent and the greatest artistic talents of France were thrown into achieving the spectacular edifice that dazzled all who saw it, even Italians who were used to palatial magnificence. And it

Pl. 231 From a suite of designs of keyhole escutcheons designed and engraved by Jean Le Pautre, closely following the style of Charles Le Brun. Aimed at a much wider range of skilled craftsmen than locksmiths, this is one of numerous suites of designs for the decoration of a variety of classes of objects produced by Le Pautre, mainly in the 1660s.
Private collection

Pl. 232 Decorative panel in the Salle des Buffets at Vaux-le-Vicomte designed by Charles Le Brun; painted in about 1660. Note the bandwork elements resembling ironwork.
Vaux-le-Vicomte, Maincy

Pl. 233 Four proposals for console-tables to be made of silver for the state rooms at Versailles, at least one version of which was made and placed in the Galerie des Glaces between 1678 and 1684. Although based on a sketch by Le Brun, these finished drawings are by one of the top goldsmiths of the time, either Claude Ballin or his successor, Nicolas De Launay.
Nationalmuseum, Stockholm
(CC 2389)

create furnishing of equal excellence, which they achieved with no mean success. The result was that the decorative arts in France at this time came to be regarded as on a par with the fine arts, and Versailles became a superb showcase for French luxury goods of every kind. Frenchmen swelled with pride at their countrymen's achievements; foreigners tended to return home and do what they could to emulate the brilliant French example. As we shall see in the next chapter, even rulers of nations opposed to French territorial and political ambitions – the Dutch, the English and sundry German principalities – were very ready to try and reproduce, as best they could, imitations of the Château de Versailles and its magnificent contents, and this amazing exemplar remained an ideal of princely building through the whole of the next century.

Louis XIV took a close personal interest in all this activity. Designs were usually submitted to him for approval and his assent is often noted in writing on the

drawing concerned. Sometimes he made comments, often astute. On ornament for a room at the small house at the zoo in the park at Versailles, he suggested that it ought perhaps to be more light-hearted (that it should smack more of youthfulness). This observation, made in 1699, is often cited as an early expression of the spirit that was to lead French designers into creating the Rococo style early in the 18th century. But it could, of course, also be seen as a perfectly sensible comment to make; in those day a zoo was rather like a fun-fair, not a place where one was expected to be serious, especially as this particular building was being turned into a play-

was not just the building itself that dazzled; because it now became the fashion to hang pictures by the great masters of the past – Italian, Flemish and French – on the walls of the principal rooms rather than in specially designed galleries, French designers now strove to

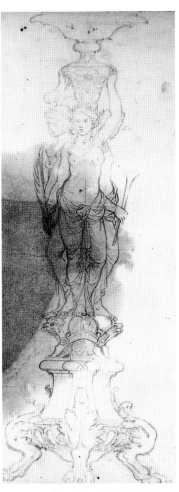

Pl. 234 Drawing by Charles Le Brun, or a close assistant, of a silver candle-stand that stood in the King's audience chamber at Versailles in the 1680s. This and other stands were made by the leading goldsmiths working for the Crown, including Ballin and De Launay. They were of man's height.
Nationalmuseum, Stockholm (CC 502)

palace for a little girl, the Duchess de Bourgogne, who had captivated the whole court, including Louis, and on whom much attention was being bestowed at that time. Another instance of his attention to detail in matters of decoration concerns some pull-up curtains in one of his own suites of rooms; he insisted that the upholsterer be given precise instructions as to where in the pelmet-board holes for the cord should be drilled. The King was, however, in no sense a designer; he was the initiator whose strong will forced through the numerous schemes of building and renewal, several of them vast in scale and of enormous complexity.

Assisting most ably in all this was his chief minister, Jean-Baptiste Colbert, who had served under Mazarin. Colbert soon assumed the superintendency of the Royal Building Works in which role he could control, stimulate and initiate work in the Royal Buildings Office, an organization that was normally directed by an Architect-in-Chief. That post was held by Louis Le Vau until his death in 1670, but it was not filled again until Jules-Hardouin Mansart was appointed in 1683. During that interval the office was, in effect, run by a small committee under Colbert, and by the various officers of the organization, who found it advantageous to collaborate with each other for the common good. However, an 'outsider' in the form of the chief royal painter, Charles Le Brun, had begun to gain enormous influence within the Royal Buildings Office during the 1660s. By 1661 he had been entrusted with the decoration of a central space at the Louvre, the Galerie d'Apollon, which still survives: in 1664 he was made Painter-in-Chief and he had already, during the previous year, been appointed Director of the royal workshops at the Gobelins, which not only made tapestries but now also furnishings of all kinds, from silverware to marble-topped tables, magnificent cabinets, lacquerwork and much else. Once he was able to influence what was being done at the Buildings Office, and working as he was with the approval of the King and Colbert, it could truly be said of Le Brun (as it was in a newspaper at the time) that 'all the Arts are carried on under him . . . there is no aspect with which he is not concerned'.

When Jules-Hardouin Mansart was appointed Architect-in-Chief just before Colbert's death in 1683, Le Brun's influence on the building works was already on the wane although he retained the King's favour and remained in charge of the Gobelins until his death in 1690.

Mansart had the approval of Colbert's successor as chief minister, Louvois, an administrator with no experience in the realm of the Arts but who managed to increase the staff of the Royal Buildings Office and to re-organise it to good effect. Mansart and the other principal architects had now perforce to delegate much work, so large were the tasks being entrusted to the office staff. Mansart, and no doubt the other senior offi-

cers, had to have assistant draughtsmen who tidied up and re-drew designs produced by their masters. After the restructuring Mansart was established as director of an efficient centralized organization that produced many stupendous buildings during the last 30 years of Louis XIV's long reign.

Robert de Cotte, Mansart's brother-in-law and himself a brilliant young architect, rose to become Mansart's collaborator and ultimately his successor in 1708. He must have the credit for some of the major architectural conceptions of the 1690s and early 1700s and certainly presided over the transition from the heavy academic style of the central years of Louis's reign to the much lighter manner of the early 18th century.

Besides the Royal Buildings Office and the Gobelins, another royal organization was that which looked after court entertainments and similar, for the most part, ephemeral commissions; it had the title of Menus-Plaisirs. Here Jean Berain was the leading creative force; he was to carry forward one branch of French design in a striking form, as we shall see.

We noted in Chapter 8 that Le Brun had worked under Vouet. Both were strongly influenced by the Italian Baroque manner of painting, particularly by the work of Pietro da Cortona, and notably that in the great hall of the palazzo Barberini in Rome of 1633–9. Cortona's decoration of some of the principal rooms at the Pitti Palace in Florence, executed chiefly in the 1640s, also made a powerful impression on French artists. It was the manner in which the normally hard lines of framing were disguised, so that the composition of the decor as a whole assumed a fluid and un-architectural character, that seemed so noteworthy to visitors from abroad. Both Vouet and Le Brun's styles reflected a knowledge of this Italian idiom and Le Brun was a brilliant exponent of a French version of it during the 1660s and 1670s (compare Pls. 229 and 230).

Le Brun was responsible for virtually everything that was carried out at Versailles until well into the 1680s, even if the finished design for an object might be by a different hand. Good examples of this are the drawing of a console table to be executed in massive silver for the Versailles Gallery (Pl. 233) and the sketch of a candle-stand for the King's Audience Chamber (Pl. 234). The door of a fine marquetry cabinet illustrated in Pl. 235 shows the same taste in a different medium. Le Brun's genius lay behind the whole conception of how the rooms at Versailles should look, and he controlled the output of the workshops serving the Crown so that a unified look – the 'Le Brun Look' – was achieved when all was assembled.

Le Brun's decorative style was disseminated across the western world by the highly competent engravings of Jean Le Pautre, whose output was enormous. Although his first dated engraving is from 1643, and his many suites of engravings are rarely dated, most of

royal interiors from 1684 to 1699, and whose style is shown in a suite of engravings of 1684, of 'Doors and Chimney-pieces designed by Mr. Mansard newly executed in certain royal buildings' (Pl. 236). The walls and doors are decorated with a multiplicity of rectangular panels arranged in tiers, each with bold mouldings, the only carving being in the overdoors, the frames of inset pictures and around the inset mirror over the fireplace, which was a new feature – one that was to be taken up enthusiastically within a few months of its first appearance at Versailles in the King's new bedchamber and his billiard room. The Mansart-Lassurance form of chimney-breast no longer projected forward into the room. A further development of the chimneypiece, which was to have a profound effect on the appearance of rooms all over Europe shortly after its introduction, was achieved by lowering the fireplace opening in proportion to the height of the room (Pls. 237 and 239). Credit for this invention should almost certainly be given to Pierre Le Pautre, son of Jean Le Pautre, who had given his son an excellent grounding in the principles of design and a sound knowledge of the repertoire of ornament. When

Pl. 235 The central panel of a marquetry and ebony cabinet made by Pierre Gole, the principal cabinetmaker to the French Crown in the 1670s and early 1680s. Like most other furnishings of a sumptuous nature produced for the Crown at this time, the decoration of this piece betrays the influence of Le Brun, even though he may not have had a direct hand in its design. Gole was a Dutchman who had moved to Paris about 1640.
Rijksmuseum, Amsterdam

Pl. 236 Design by Lassurance for mural decoration in a room at Versailles executed in the early 1680s under the direction of the Royal architect-in-Chief, Jules-Hardouin Mansart. Engraved by Pierre Le Pautre in 1684. Note the mirror over the fireplace.
Victoria and Albert Museum, London (Mus. no. E.5814–1908)

them were probably executed before 1670. His style rests on that of Le Brun; within an academic framework is a rich assemblage of High-Baroque ornament usually incorporating pairs of human figures. What Le Pautre published was taken up less as a series of models than as 'ideas that are intended to fire the imagination'. His work was often copied abroad. The original versions could of course be obtained in Paris; Christopher Wren did just this sort of thing on a visit in 1665.

Mansart's first major work was his extension in 1675 of the château at Clagny, just outside the park at Versailles. This important small château had been built to the designs of Antoine Le Pautre in 1674, for Louis XIV's mistress Madame de Montespan. It was in an advanced taste and was truly a 'house of delight' as someone put it at the time. Thereafter Mansart's star rose fast; he represented the academic tendency, favouring elegant compositions with bold and simple lines. His chief assistant was a man named Lassurance who was apparently responsible for the design of all the

Mansart was made Superintendent of the Royal Buildings Office in 1699, Pierre Le Pautre was employed as a designer and engraver and remained a star figure in the Office until he died in 1716. Both Mansart and his assistant Robert de Cotte called on him personally to

PI. 237 Design by Pierre Le Pautre, working under the direction of J.-H. Mansart, for two chimneypieces in French royal palaces. Note the low proportions of the fireplace opening and the tall glass fixed to the wall above; also the quite deep mantel-shelf that can accommodate a garniture of ornamental vessels. The mirror is framed with carved mouldings and a cresting which owe much to the decorative style of Jean Berain (see PI. 242). About 1698. *Victoria and Albert Museum, London (Mus. no. E.5796–1908)*

PI. 238 Top of a folding writing-table made for Louis XIV's private study at Versailles c.1685 by the exceptionally skilled cabinet-maker Alexandre-Jean Oppenord[t], who had come to Paris from Flanders. It is quite probable that the design for this brass and red marquetry work was provided by Jean Berain, who had been designer 'for the King's Bedchamber and Study' (i.e. for his private rooms) since 1674. Note the bandwork structure from which the foliage springs (compare with PI. 242). *The Metropolitan Museum, New York; Gift of Mrs Charles Wrightsman, 1986 (1986.365.3)*

Vouet and assistant of Errard, had been commissioned to design a suite of tapestries for weaving at the Gobelins with 'arabesques in the style of Raphael', and, possibly inspired by these, Berain began developing a new form of grotesque pattern that became a central class of ornament in French decorative creativity and was soon widely imitated.

In taking up and developing the grotesque formula, Berain looked back to grotesque ornament as used by Le Brun. Berain had engraved representations of Le Brun's decorations of the 1660s and early 1670s in the Galerie d'Apollon at the Louvre and at the Tuileries (see p. 50). An element in this formula that had been novel was the inclusion in the composition of strapwork, or bandwork, used as a subsidiary pattern to that of the main grotesque conformation (see PI. 232).

It has been said that Berain did not at first adopt grotesque patterns for his work at the royal palaces. PI. 238 shows the top of a table made for Louis XIV's private study in about 1685, which has paired bandwork with the intersections and breaks that were to

PI. 239 Design of 1699 for a chimneypiece by Pierre Le Pautre, working to Mansart's instructions, for the small pleasure palace at Marly. The mirror is now enormously tall, and has had to be made of three large plates, but each is far bigger than anything that was available 20 years earlier – a measure of French technological achievement as much as the brilliance of the designer. The elaborate panel with carved ornament above incorporates an outline once again inspired by Berain, as is the form of the mask and the characteristic diapered background.

make drawings for all the most important interior work undertaken during these years when such great changes were taking place, mainly as a result of Le Pautre's inventiveness (PI. 239).

Pierre Le Pautre knew Jean Berain, who was chief designer at the Menus-Plaisirs. From his appointment in 1674 until the early 1680s, Berain was chiefly concerned with designs for royal pageantry in connection with the numerous ceremonies and entertainments with which Louis XIV impressed visitors to his palaces and kept his own entourage busy. Berain's great contribution to the history of design lies in his development of the grotesque, which the French, confusingly, at this time began to call 'arabesques'. In 1684, Noel Coypel, a pupil of

become so characteristic of Berain's style – indeed it seems very likely that he was responsible for this design. However, Berain tried out his own variant of the grotesque formula mainly in private commissions, and the first important manifestation of this was at the Hôtel de Mailly in Paris, in 1687–8, where one ceiling thus decorated survives. His work there has all the hallmarks of the style for which he became famous. PI. 240 shows the style fully developed; the paired bandwork is evident, and one sees how it often breaks and abruptly changes course, and sometimes interlaces. Some of the bandwork has assumed a girder-like character, and scrolls often end in a billhook, which is sometimes even developed into a bird's head with a hooked beak.

ing framework – what remained of bandwork – was flimsy in the extreme. An informed commentator, writing in 1713, said of Audran that he was one of the principal designers of the time, especially in the realm of grotesques in the style of Raphael, and praised particularly his work at the small château of the Menagerie – the zoo in the park at Versailles – which was executed in 1699 (Pl. 245). Berain's style remained hugely popular in France and elsewhere (see Chapter 12), not least because it was spread through the medium of numerous printed designs published by Berain himself, or copied from such prints in Germany. Many exercises in this vein only owe a small debt to Berain directly but can all be called Berainesque.

An aspect of the building of the great palace at Versailles that has not been sufficiently stressed is that the irksome nature of pomp and ceremony breeds a corresponding need for relaxation, informality and comfort. Innovatory design often first appeared in buildings where an informal way of life tended to be the norm – notably at the château at the Menagerie (the Zoo) which was done up for a little girl; the château at Marly

Pl. 241 Berain engraving, probably of the 1690s, in a far lighter and more open style than that of his earlier work (e.g. Pl. 240).

The subsequent development of his style is indicated in Pl. 242; the pattern is lighter and more airy, the bandwork eventually gains the upper hand and provides a framework around which floral motifs play and light-hearted figures cavort; herms support substantial ironwork structures implausibly on their heads.

Berain was eventually eclipsed by a younger and equally brilliant designer, Claude Audran, at the very end of the century. Audran had worked under Le Brun at Versailles and had been engaged on many projects at the royal palaces before it became brutally clear, in 1699, that Louis XIV's favour had now been transferred from Berain to the younger man. The latter's style was truly light, his figures were attenuated, and his connect-

which was a place where great informality reigned; and that at Clagny which was built for the liveliest of the King's mistresses. Innovation has always tended to blossom in informal settings rather than in grand buildings where conservative notions usually delay change. Fresh ideas were also often first tried out in closets and other rooms of an intimate nature; this was very much the case at Versailles (Pls. 244 and 246), but it is a phenomenon that can be traced back to Renaissance times.

We have noted how the use of naturalist flowers for the decoration of works of applied art spread across Europe in the middle decades of the 17th century (p. 100). An interesting manifestation of this is some sheets of designs

Pl. 243 This imposing title-page in a book of motets published in 1710 may seem a little old-fashioned, but was dedicated to Michel-Richard de La Lande, the chief musical figure at the French court, a factor that may have weighed with the designers – either the Jean Berain we have been discussing, or his son, of the same name. Bandwork, enclosing a diaper pattern, has here taken over the borders.
Bibliothèque Nationale, Paris

Pl. 245 Design by Claude Audran for a ceiling composed of ultra-light bandwork with small figures, a style that gained him great favour in French court circles around 1700. The design may possibly have been produced in connection with the redecoration in 1699 of the small château at the zoo in the park at Versailles.
Nationalmuseum, Stockholm (CC II 34)

Pl. 247 Back of a dressing-mirror, probably made by the cabinetmaker André-Charles Boulle and delivered in 1713 to the Duchesse de Berry. Decorated in a lightweight Berainesque manner developed at the turn of the century, the marquetry is of tortoiseshell and gilt copper; the mounts are of gilt bronze. Probably commissioned by the *marchand mercier* La Roüe and sold to the duchess.
Reproduced by permission of the Trustees of the Wallace Collection, London

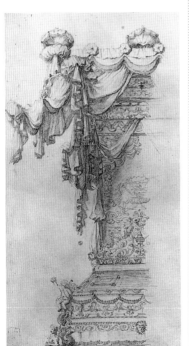

Pl. 244 This bed, with its fantastic and highly un-serious bed-hangings (totally unsuitable for a normal bedchamber), stood in Louis XIV's love-nest, the Trianon de Porcelaine, in the grounds of Versailles, built by Le Vau for Louis's mistress Madame de Montespan, and furnished in 1672. It is likely to have been more of a day-bed than a bed in which to sleep and it was certainly very different from the box-like beds to be found in formal rooms of state in French royal buildings.
Nationalmuseum, Stockholm (THC 1070)

Pl. 246 Mirror of silver filigree (wire formed into patterns) laid onto a lacquered surface, originally black (but painted blue in 1839); made in Paris in 1669. Decoration of this kind was to be seen in a small room at Versailles carried out in the 1660s during Louis XIV's first wave of refurbishing. The room caught the fancy of many who saw it, and the King of Denmark was no doubt aware of its fame. He apparently commissioned this mirror in Paris in 1669; it is a rare survivor of a technique that was admired at the French court in the mid-17th century.
The Danish Royal Collection, Rosenborg Castle, Copenhagen

by Paul Androuet Du Cerceau, a late member of the distinguished designer-family, probably of the 1660s (Pl. 248). These were intended chiefly to inspire embroiderers but one is stated to be suitable for weaving in silk at the then famous silk-weaving establishments at Tours. The silk-weavers were not yet technically able to render the flowers decorating their materials with such a high degree of naturalism (the embroiderers could do so because the techniques they employed allowed greater freedom of execution) and it was not until the 1730s that this could be achieved (see p. 146). Naturalistic flowers could also be rendered in the knotted-pile technique of carpet-weaving. The fine and enormous carpet shown in Pl. 251 demonstrates this. A series of such carpets, all woven at the Savonnerie workshops (so-called because they were established in an old soap factory), were laid on the floor of the Galerie d'Apollon at the Louvre at this time (the 1660s), and were certainly conceived as furnishings to play counterpoint to Le Brun's splendid ceilings and mural decorations for that celebrated room, which still survives. However, it has to be said that, in textiles, naturalism in the rendering of flowers, although more prevalent in the mid-17th century, was not a dominant taste; stylized flowers remained pre-eminent until the 1730s.

Turning to furniture for a moment, one finds examples of top-quality French pieces of this period outside

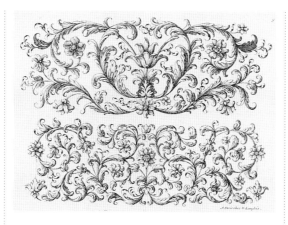

France more readily than in their country of origin. Diplomatic gifts from Louis XIV provide further examples of the excellence of the work being produced in the chief furniture workshops in Paris at this time. Pl. 249 is a specimen of the new form of seat-furniture by that time coming into being in Paris, setting a new standard for comfort that was to be developed with great success by Parisian chairmakers during the next seventy years so that the French *fauteuil* of the 1740s and 1750s became the most comfortable as well as elegant form of seating ever devised.

In the realm of silverware much has been written about the massive pieces of silver furniture that were made for the principal rooms at Versailles in the 1670s and 1680s (Pl. 233). These were all melted down in 1690 when Louis's fortunes declined after several expensive and largely unsuccessful military campaigns. Only one such piece of French silver furniture survives from that period and that is a baptismal font in the Royal Chapel in Stockholm, made by a French goldsmith temporarily resident there; but the character of such furniture is conveyed in small by a delightful frame of solid silver (Pl. 250). The silver furniture at Versailles had no great influence on design and was replaced by pieces carved in wood and gilded, a newer taste. It was, rather, in smaller items that French goldsmiths' work set an example that was to inspire later generations, both in France and abroad (see Chapter 12). Particularly inventive seem to have been Parisian goldsmiths active in the 1670s. For example, it was at this period that the shapes of most classes of table silver acquired their definitive form, and are still being produced in these forms today in France and elsewhere. A good example of this is the *ecuelle*, a vessel that can serve many purposes from eating soup to serving small portions of vegetables. In its characteristic form it has two handles and a domed lid (Pl. 255).

The handsome sconce of about 1710 (Pl. 255) is a reminder that French bronze-casters were inferior to none at this period, notably in making or embellishing items for the furnishing of rooms. This mirror-backed light-fitting is a work of distinction in an advanced taste but its maker is unknown. The use of mirror-glass as a backplate to reflect light from the candle inserted in the projecting arm at the bottom was new in the 1670s (hitherto the backplates had been of polished brass or silver). This was one of the ways in which mirror-glass came to be used to such astonishing effect in France, where the making of mirror-glass overtook the Italian production of this material (hitherto an Italian monopoly) due to fresh technological accomplishments late in the century. The principal advance lay in the development of techniques for making plate-glass by casting it

Pl. 251 Savonnerie carpet sent in 1669 by Louis XIV to Cosimo III, Grand Duke of Tuscany. The scrollwork has a similar weight to that shown in Pl. 248. The overall design could very well have been executed as a ceiling. Indeed, correspondence between a ceiling and the carpet on the floor below was often the way of achieving greater unity in grand rooms at this period.
Palazzo Pitti, Florence

on a flat metal surface. This made it possible to produce sheets of far larger dimensions, and although the cost of making glass in this new way was at first extremely high (the breakage of such large sheets, especially during the silvering and polishing processes, was heavy at first), the availability of large plates opened up new opportunities for the interior architect, and we see how skilfully its potential was exploited in rooms from the late 17th century into the second quarter of the next century (see Pls. 236, 237, 239, 259 and 260). The framing of mirror-plates to form free-hanging items of furniture (as opposed to their being inset) also developed in handsome ways, as indeed did the making of frames for pictures. The glass-backed sconce, incidentally, became a highly fashionable item in the middle decades of the 18th century; three early proposals put forward in about

Pl. 252 Table and pair of candlestands of carved wood, partly gilded on a blue ground. This splendid group was apparently ordered in Paris for the Danish Queen Sofie Amalie in about 1670. The scagliola (imitation marble) table-top is dated 1672. The lion's paw feet of the table are of a form characteristic of Parisian furniture of the time (e.g. Pl. 249).
The Danish Royal Collection, Rosenborg Castle, Copenhagen

Pl. 253 Table of the 1680s entirely faced with superb marquetry in tortoiseshell, brass, silver and various woods, some of them stained. Ascribed to the workshop of André-Charles Boulle, the most celebrated cabinetmaker of all time, who produced the finest furniture for the French Crown after the death of Pierre Gole (see Pl. 235). Height 72 cm (28³/₈ in.) Width 110.5 cm (43¹/₂ in.) Depth 73.6 cm (29in.)
Collection of the J. Paul Getty Museum, Malibu, California

121

Pl. 254 Small silver flasks (about 14 cm [5½ in.] high) forming part of a made-up dressing-service owned by the Duchess Hedvig Sofia of Holstein-Gottorp, born a Swedish princess. Made by the Parisian goldsmith Vincent Fortier in 1675–6. The decoration in bold relief is a delightful expression of fashionable taste in Paris during the 1670s, and the spiralling gadrooned ornament on the neck points the way for later use of this formula in many parts of Europe.
The Danish Royal Collection, Rosenborg Castle, Copenhagen

Pl. 255 Wall-light of silvered bronze with a glass mirror-plate supported on oak. Paris, about 1710. A handsome example of the taste at this late stage in the reign of Louis XIV. Height 50 cm (19½ in.) Width 29.5 cm (22½ in.) Depth 17.2cm (6¾ in.)
Collection of the J. Paul Getty Museum, Malibu, California

Pl. 256 Two-handed covered bowl (*ecuelle*) from the same service as the flasks shown in Pl. 254; Parisian, 1672–7, also by Fortier. Note the 'cut-card' decoration, applied so as to produce shallow relief decoration; this type of embellishment was to be greatly in demand far into the 18th century.
The Danish Royal Collection, Rosenborg Castle, Copenhagen

Pl. 257 Medal-cabinet in the form of a commode with drawers behind a pair of doors, attributed to A. C. Boulle; of about 1710–15. The two gilt bronze mounts on the doors are replacements. Belonged to Robert de Cotte's son, who held an important post in the Royal Buildings Office from 1718.
J. Paul Getty Museum, Malibu, California

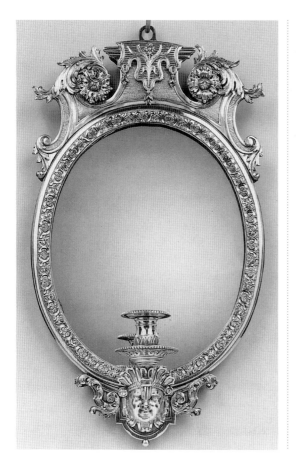

1730 are to be seen in Pl. 258. They are by Nicolas Pineau, one of the most brilliant Parisian designers of the early Rococo period, whose work we shall study in Chapter 13.

A new class of furniture was invented in France early in the 18th century. It was heavy and, in its definitive form, rested on short legs so that it looked like an old-fashioned chest, yet it was a 'chest-of-drawers', a far more convenient piece of furniture to use than the chest had been. The fact that it was '*plus commode*' [more convenient] than a chest gave it its French name but in fact commodes were to a large extent ornamental features of rooms taking the place of pier-tables, which usually stood beneath the tall mirrors (pier-glasses) fitted between the windows of grand rooms. The large front face of commodes offered a splendid expanse for decoration, and the opportunity was soon seized upon, to great effect (Pl. 257).

After the death of Louis XIV in 1715, his nephew the Duc d'Orléans was appointed Regent and he soon set about redecorating his residence at the Palais-Royal which, once again, became the site of important innovations in the field of interior decoration. His architect Gilles–Marie Oppenord was responsible for the changes made from 1717 to the early 1720s. As the son of a leading cabinetmaker under Louis XIV, Oppenord was familiar with all the artistic innovations at the court. He had been a pupil of Mansart, and he spent much of the 1690s in Rome. Oppenord was well qualified to produce exciting new schemes for the Regent, who wanted to dazzle his countrymen and to seem in no way inferior, in terms of magnificent surroundings, to his defunct uncle. Bringing to the task a deep knowledge of the work of Pierre Le Pautre (Pls. 237 and 239), as well as that of Bernini and Borromini in Rome, Oppenord produced a richer, more sculptural form of decoration,

Pl. 258 Engraved designs for wall-lights by Nicolas Pineau, showing his light rendering of Berainesque ornament to which he added a more graceful character. Note the use of shell-like ornament as a border. Probably from the late 1720s. *Victoria and Albert Museum, London (Mus. no. E.5936–1908)*

Pl. 259 Design by the architect Gilles-Marie Oppenord for the Salon à l'Italienne at the Palais Royal, Paris. The building was refurbished in 1717 for the Regent, the Duc d'Orléans. Note the strongly sculptural element, the lively contours and the bold ornament on the panels. *Victoria and Albert Museum, London (Mus. no. E.5936–1908)*

with altogether livelier contours (Pl. 259). After the death of Le Pautre in 1716, Robert de Cotte, by then Architect–in–Chief to the Crown, came to rely greatly on Oppenord.

The loosening of contours continued in the work of Antoine Vassé, who was a sculptor. He also worked under de Cotte and in 1718–19 designed and executed the panelling for the residence of a son of Louis XIV – the Comte de Toulouse (Pl. 260). Indeed, the whole feeling of Vassé's work is towards a greater plasticity of form. A new feature often seen in his designs is the rim of shell which enlivens borders and became a notable feature of decoration in the 1720s and 1730s. The innovative work of Oppenord and Vassé helped lay the foundations for the advent of the Rococo style.

Pl. 260 The magnificent Gallery at the Hôtel de Toulouse, Paris, designed by Antoine Vassé in 1718–19. The intricate contours of Vassé's panels and the full-blooded nature of his figure-subjects reveal his training as a sculptor.

CHAPTER 12

THE HAGUE, LONDON AND THE CHIEF CITIES OF GERMANY

1670-1730

France had become a superpower under Louis XIV, and was the chief power to be reckoned with from the 1670s onwards. She also became the primary source of new fashions in the whole wide realm of the Arts – from architecture to silk-weaving, music to cooking, from literature to the making of faience. We shall now see how the French court style, a Parisian creation with the Château de Versailles as its main showcase, spread to a handful of bustling, energetic and enterprising communities in the Northern Netherlands, in England and in Germany.

The dominance of France was greatly feared by the other European nations, especially as Louis XIV's armies pushed their way into neighbouring lands with a success that hugely gratified Frenchmen but appalled almost everyone else. The country most affected by these incursions was the Dutch republic.

However, the Dutch, led by William of Orange, eventually checked Louis's expansionism. In 1678 the Peace of Nijmegen was signed and Louis, exhausted, and with his exchequer almost empty after having waged war on three fronts (in the Netherlands, in northern Italy, and in Spain), was only too pleased to conclude peace – for a while.

William's court was at the Hague which lies some 35 miles (50 kilometres) south-west of Amsterdam and became an important centre while William was, in effect, the principal officer in the land. In 1677, he had married Princess Mary, a daughter of James II, of England, and the Dutch court took on at this period a strong measure of princely grandeur, even though it in no way matched the splendour of Versailles. So notable were William's achievements as leader of the Dutch struggle against France that he was therefore an obvious candidate to replace James, whose pro-Catholic actions, including marriage to Mary of Modena and the promotion of Catholics to government, had alienated most of England. James fled the country and went to live at the French Court with his Queen where they were welcomed, well housed and given a handsome pension. Matters were so arranged that William assumed the Crown of England without much resistance and became King William III. The 'bloodless revolution' of 1688 left William (now crowned jointly with his wife) with increased standing, both in rank and reputation; and he was gradually to turn England from a minor, rather pro-French state into a great power that came to dominate the anti-French coalition of states. Thus it was an English general, the Duke of Marlborough, appointed by William to lead the allied forces shortly before his own death, who finally defeated Louis XIV, a fact that was reinforced by the Treaty of Utrecht in 1713.

Thus, the Dutch Republic, which had been the most

powerful Protestant nation in Europe and dominated the North Sea during the first two thirds of the 17th century, yielded its position to Britain without a fight and introduced to the city of London modern finance, thereby enabling the British economy to expand enormously. By 1700, Britain was poised for the world-wide colonial expansion that changed her from a largely agrarian economy to one based on industries, many of which were new or greatly extended. With Dutch know-how and financial backing, Britain's new financial institutions enabled her to raise capital far beyond what was possible from taxation and domestic loans. It was the lack of a strong credit structure and consequent financial exhaustion that ultimately led to the defeat of Louis XIV; it was not through any failure on the battlefield or at sea.

Once King of England, William of Orange set about improving the palaces, both in Holland and in England, in order to reflect the new dignity of himself and his Queen and to encompass the heightened court ceremonial that this entailed. Although the Dutch and the English were engaged in a bitter war with the French, it was paradoxically the French court style that they sought to introduce into their stately residences. This style was naturally enough also adopted by the principal members of William's court, who in several cases had residences of their own both in Holland and in England. Indeed, it is the interlocking relationship between the two countries in the realm of the Arts, particularly those to do with the interior of houses, that is so striking a feature of this period – the years from approximately 1685 to 1715.

Greatly assisting in the process of introducing French court taste to Holland was the arrival of a man who must have worked for Berain as an engraver and later probably as a designer in the Menus-Plaisirs (see Chapter 11). Daniel Marot came to Holland in 1686 as a refugee from the French persecution of Protestants at that time. His father had been an important architect in Paris (see Pl. 177), and he himself will have known a great deal about the architecture and decoration of Versailles and the other French royal palaces. Soon after his arrival in Holland Marot was employed by William. Marot evidently visited England several times and therefore there is really very little that distinguishes the court style in Holland from that of England during this phase (which came to an end when William died in 1702), but it has to be remembered that, at first, this style was confined to court circles. It took a little longer for it to spread to the more conservative merchant classes, even the wealthiest of them, in Amsterdam and the other principal Dutch cities, and likewise to their opposite numbers in England.

Many fine buildings, with contents to match, were erected and furnished in this period; and the style which pervades all this new work is extraordinarily homogeneous, presumably because of Marot's all-per-

Pl. 263 Design for a wrought-iron gate by Jean Tijou, published in London in 1693.
Victoria and Albert Museum, London (Mus. no. 25082–11)

Pl. 264 The ceiling of the White Closet at Ham House, Richmond, by Antonio Verrio, painted in the mid-1670s. Note the formal elements of the surround, reminiscent of Le Brun's style and that of Jean Le Pautre.
The National Trust, Ham House, Richmond

vasive influence. In buildings where he had a measure of control he normally co-ordinated the work of the artists and craftsmen and so produced rooms of unified appearance and of great distinction (Pl. 261). Indeed, Marot was the first architect to produce engravings for

Pl. 265 Two-handled cup, its lid with *repoussé* decoration and a cast finial of formalized acanthus leaves; London, 1683–4. A characteristic English type, bowls of almost square silhouette being popular for English silver vessels of several kinds at this period.
Victoria and Albert Museum, London
(Mus. no. M.129–1922)

Pl. 266 Tea-caddy of silver with both *repoussé* and 'cut-card' ornament, made at The Hague in 1695. Although the form derives from that of Chinese stoneware tea-caddies, the ornament is typically French in style. Height 90 cm (3¹/₂ in.)
Rijksmuseum, Amsterdam

Pl. 267 Silver-gilt jug made by Lorenz Biller, the second goldsmith of that name working at Augsburg who, together with his brothers Ludwig and Albrecht, amongst other things supplied several courts (including that at Dresden) with silver furnishings. This handsome vessel, with bold acanthus decoration, dates from about 1685–1700.
*The Hermitage Museum,
St Petersburg (Mus. no. E.7951)*

lent architect Jacob Roman and, of course, had a team of assistants and trusted sub-contractors who could faithfully execute his designs. The chief upholsterer working for the court at The Hague at this time was a Frenchman named Pierre Courtonne. His counterparts in London were also French – John Poitevin who succeeded Jean Casbert as Chief Upholsterer to the Royal Household in 1670s, Francis Lapierre, and Philip Guibert who filled a similar role in the 1690s (Pl. 262). Marot seems to have been associated with Lapierre on at least one occasion – to do with designing a state bed in 1706.

Marot was connected by marriage to the celebrated Parisian cabinetmaker Pierre Gole (see Pl. 235), who was a Dutchman, and Gole's son Cornelis was established in London as a leading cabinetmaker at the end of the century. In 1712 Cornelis Gole published some designs with a French title 'for the use of artisans of several kinds' which he dedicated to the Duke of Devonshire (Pl. 277). This was one of several links between Paris and London, with a Dutch connection; furthermore Pierre Gole and Gerreit Jensen, an important Dutch cabinetmaker established in London, apparently had some sort of business relationship. Perhaps Gole provided the elaborate marquetry panels incorporating veneers of engraved metal and wood for Gerreit Jensen's fine furniture that he was making at this time. The painter Pierre Berchet, who had worked for the French Crown in the 1670s, came to England in 1682 or 1683, returned to France in order to execute decorative painting at Marly (see p. 118) and then came back to England after 1685. He then went to work at Het Loo, William of Orange's country residence in Holland where the interiors were largely designed by Marot, and was subsequently one of the competitors for the decoration of St Paul's Cathedral in London.

Many other cases of French artists and artisans coming to work in England at this period can be cited. Some, like Simon Delobel, who had made Louis XIV's state bed and came over with several beds for James II in 1685, only paid a quick visit; others, like the Pelletier brothers, executed large quantities of superbly carved and gilded furniture for the English royal palaces and various 'courtier houses' in England over many years. The brilliant French smith Jean Tijou, whose wrought iron gates grace Hampton Court, Chatsworth and St Paul's Cathedral, seems to have returned to France in 1712, by which time he had published a suite of engravings of his own work (see Pl. 263) that was brought out again in Paris in 1723 when the designs were described as being 'English compositions', although Tijou's work in fact drew heavily on earlier French pattern-books and has many references to the designs of Berain.

The greatest influx of French citizens into Protestant countries, which included many North German states and both Denmark and Sweden as well as Holland and England, took place in the 1680s when French

every conceivable class of decoration so that there was no excuse for sub-contractors to get it wrong when asked to contribute to an integrated Marotesque ensemble. Many of Marot's engraved suites of the 1690s were assembled and published in 1703 (Pl. 273), shortly after William's death, when he no doubt saw a need to promote himself more widely in order to reach a broader clientele. The same designs, supplemented by many fresh ones, were brought out again in 1712 (Pl. 270). Thereafter, Marot's inventiveness started to wane although he lived on until 1752. But many houses in Amsterdam of the 1720s and 1730s have Marotesque decoration and his style spread across the borders of Holland into Germany and Scandinavia (largely through his engravings), where it continued to be popular deep into the middle of the century (Pl. 275).

In Holland Marot often worked alongside the excel-

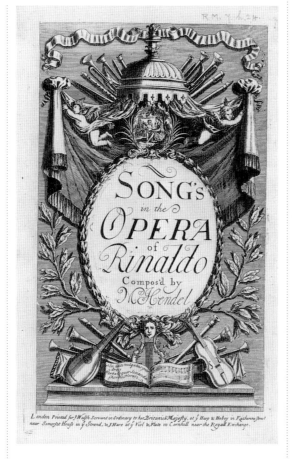

dominated by Protestants who could rarely find any other way to make use of their talents. When even just a handful of such key people departed as refugees, the effect of their loss could be devastating. The silkweaving industry at Tours, for example, never recovered from the loss of its chief personnel. The damage done to Paris-based industry seems to have been smaller and, in this connection, it is noteworthy that some of the most celebrated Huguenot silversmiths who came to settle and work in England at this period came, not from Paris, but

persecution of Huguenots came to a head. This persecution, which started in the 1660s, must surely have been one of the most ill-advised acts of government perpetrated under Louis XIV, because France lost many exceptionally able citizens as a result. Forbidden to join the professions, the higher positions in industries were

from such places as Rouen, Metz and the Poitiers area. Being skilled at their trade, these clever men had little difficulty in mastering the new Parisian styles as they became known to them, whether they were living in the French provinces or in London. It has to be added that by no means all the French artists working in London at this time were Protestants; quite a few Catholics were among them. Some were invited to execute special commissions; others came simply because they perceived that working conditions in England – and in Holland – were likely to be better for an ambitious and skilled person than was the case in France.

The switching of the dominant position in the decorative arts from Holland to England, as far as innovation is concerned, is demonstrated by the cabinetmakers' guild at The Hague which, in 1711, stipulated that those seeking to become masters should build, as evidence of their competence, 'an English cabinet six feet high . . . with drawers below . . . veneered with walnut'.

Pl. 271 Painting of the overmantel of a chimneypiece in the Marot style with delftware vessels arranged in close array. The small figures (presumably of Chinese porcelain) on the miniature brackets produce an effect like carved ornament. By a Dutch artist; dated 1719.
Amsterdams Historisch Museum

This is quite clearly what is today called a bureau-bookcase, a tall piece of furniture with doors fronting the top section, a fall-front for writing upon, and 'drawers below', as the regulations put it. But the form was one that the English had adopted from Holland! The form, incidentally, was imitated by cabinetmakers in many German and Scandinavian centres, where its origin was perceived as being English so that it was generally called 'an English writing desk'.

At this point we must just look back to the 1660s and 1670s, the years before England began to adopt more directly the French court style, in the 1680s. Of course there had been borrowings from France before but not on the same scale. Influence on England at this earlier period came largely from Holland. The reason for this, apart from Holland's geographical proximity and the generally similar national characteristics of the two peoples, lay in the fact that many Englishmen of the kind who would normally be patrons of the arts spent the years of the Civil War and the subsequent Commonwealth period (i.e. the late 1640s and 1650s) in Holland. There they saw and evidently approved of the current style in Dutch architecture, and an Anglicized version of this later spread to England as the refugees returned home and started to rebuild their country under a restored monarchy. The Dutch buildings were of red brick with stone dressings; they tended to be plain and owed much to a Classical tradition that was established in Holland in the 1620s and 1630s, as a reaction to the spiky exuberances of the Northern Netherlandish Renaissance taste (see Chapter 5). An important contribution to the formation of this style, as we have already noted (p. 61), was that made by Rubens in publishing a two-volume book in 1622 and 1626 with engraved elevations of fine houses in Genoa which, although embodying many flamboyant features, possessed proportions and silhouettes similar to those of typical later Dutch buildings. Rubens intended that the plates in his book

Pl. 272 Water-cistern for rinsing glasses, and a basin or wine-cooler for cooling bottles of wine, made in London in the years 1701–3 by the Huguenot goldsmith Pierre Harache. The massive shape of wine-coolers at this period, particularly in England, is noteworthy; Marot shows this characteristic clearly in his engraved plate of about 1685(?), which is reproduced in Pl. 270.
By kind permission of the Earl Spencer

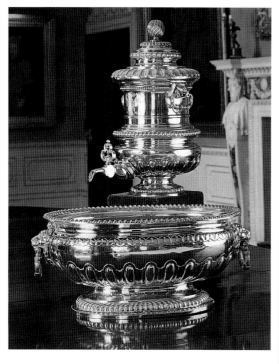

Pl. 273 A plate of designs for a counterpane and a bed-tester with bandwork decoration by Daniel Marot, from his *Nouveaux Livre de Licts de Differentes Pensseez* published in 1703, although the designs could well be earlier by a decade or more.

Pl. 275 Teapot made by Andreas Wall, a Stockholm goldsmith, in 1720. It was his 'masterpiece' (i.e. the object he had to make to prove his competence to become a master in the Stockholm guild). He couched it in a German form with which he could well have become familiar while working in Germany, as he will almost certainly have done when he was a journeyman. Note the Berainesque or Marotesque interlaced bandwork ornament. Height 23 cm (9 in.)
Hallwyl Museum, Stockholm

Pl. 274 Neck of a theorbo (a form of lute) made in Hamburg in 1734, which has a finger-board decorated with marquetry of ivory and tortoiseshell still using a Berainesque formula. The instrument-maker was Jacob Heinrich Goldt.
Victoria and Albert Museum, London (Mus. no. 4274–1856)

should be taken as guidance also by those building much smaller edifices. The English architect Hugh May was the principal exponent of the Dutch red-brick style and was responsible for building King Charles II a palatial block in this taste at Windsor Castle, incorporating apartments for the King and his Queen. These were laid out on the very latest principles governing room-distribution and guaranteed great comfort for the monarchs while at the same time providing a satisfactory setting for court ceremonial. The interior decoration was of considerable splendour, much of the carved ornament on the oak panelling being carried out by the Dutch-trained Grinling Gibbons. The gilding was done by a Frenchman (René Cousin), however, and the

extensive areas of fictive painting by Antonio Verrio who was Italian but had worked for a while under Le Brun at Versailles (Pl. 264). Hugh May has been somewhat overshadowed by Christopher Wren but the apartments he and his collaborators created in the late 1670s must have been the most impressive and glamorous ever produced in England. Unfortunately, what they created has largely been destroyed or overlaid by later work.

It was of course not only in architecture that Dutch influence was seen in England during this period. It affected the shape and decoration of silverware, furniture, faience and ornament generally. One characteristically Dutch form of decoration was that carried out with Chinese and Japanese porcelain or with lacquerwork. The importation of these wares from the Far East to Amsterdam was largely in the hands of the Dutch East India Company, whose warehouses were stacked with these exotic artefacts whence quite a lot were trans-shipped to other parts of Europe. The shapes and decoration of Far Eastern porcelain were closely imitated on a large scale at Delft in tin-glazed earthenware (faience, or delftware), which in turn was copied in a smaller way in other parts of Europe. Lacquerwork was similarly imitated (but in a technically different technique called japanning) both in Holland and several other countries, notably in Germany (see Pl. 281). But

more remarkable was the way that, in Holland, whole rooms were decorated with porcelain vessels and figures deployed up the wall or around chimneypieces as architectural ornament, like carving. Panels of Oriental lacquer were likewise set into the panelling of a room, not infrequently cut up and reassembled in an incongruous manner, no regard being paid to the direction in which scenes were originally intended to be seen so that sometimes they were on their sides and even occasionally upside down. Many a fine Japanese screen was sacrificed to such exercises. It is curious to note that the fashion for dressing rooms in this way was espoused particularly by the women of the House of Orange, so that the wife of Prince Frederik Hendrik, Prince of Orange, already had a room decorated with Japanese lacquer in her palace at The Hague before 1660, and Princesses of Orange of the next generation had closets and chimneypieces decorated with formally arranged masses of porcelain wherever they resided, be it at The Hague or in London, at Lieeuwarden, Berlin or Koblenz. Of course this Chinamania caught on among people of fashion and, by the early 18th century, 'everyone' had to have a 'China closet'; a fairly modest essay in this manner is to be seen in Pl. 271. That this form of decoration was characteristically Dutch in the eyes of other Europeans at an early date seems to be confirmed by the existence of a 'Dutch Banqueting Room' at the Earl of Arundel's town-house, Tart Hall, in 1641, where an inventory reveals that glassware, brassware, basketwork and porcelain were displayed in groups up the walls and on shelves, in one place 'in the manner of a column'. Such formally organized art-treasures – for porcelain and lacquerwork were expensive and highly prized – followed those of Renaissance princes and their successors but the emphasis now was on playfulness and light-hearted make-believe (Let's go to my China Closet and drink tea and pretend we are Chinamen!) rather than on serious collecting.

We saw that Delft was the chief centre of pottery making in Northern Europe by the third quarter of the 17th century and that its products were mostly made to resemble real Chinese porcelain (p. 100). From about 1670 or so, some Delft potters adopted European forms and sometimes also European types of decoration. Delftware is delightful and decorative and was much imitated by other potteries throughout Europe, but it also chips easily, leaving the granular ware beneath the white tin-glaze exposed and vulnerable to unsightly staining. An altogether more robust material was needed and early steps towards developing this were taken in the late 17th century by a potter named Arij de Milde. He managed to produce a robust red-coloured stoneware (a dense, strong material) in imitation of Chinese stoneware from Yi-hsing in the Kiangsu province, which had become extremely popular with those Europeans who could afford the luxury of drink-

Pl. 278 The amazing inlaid floor of different coloured woods laid between 1714 and 1719 at Schloss Weissenstein, Pommersfelden, near Bamberg in Franconia. The work was carried out by Ferdinand Plitzner and his assistants. It will be seen that motifs favoured by Marot, notably the bandwork, have been a potent source of inspiration to this exceptionally skilful German master woodworker.
Schloss Weissenstein, Pommersfelden

ing tea. It took a much harder blow to chip stoneware and it was from this refined ware, with its essentially simple forms, that the great strides towards producing practical industrial pottery were taken in England in the 18th century (see Chapter 15). Arij de Milde's technical breakthrough seems to have been brought to England by two Dutchmen, John and David Elers, in about 1686.

In the 1690s they moved to Staffordshire and there produced red stoneware in the Dutch/Chinese manner, but their workshop closed in 1698. Their example was, however, not lost on certain enterprising and astute Staffordshire potters, as we shall see.

Another innovation that took place in England at this period, also the result of a technological development,

Pl. 279 Music title-page; Nürnberg, 1725. Piano and organ pieces by Wilhelm Pachelbel, organist at St Sebald's Church in Nürnberg. The cartouche form has now acquired Berainesque detailing (the diapered ground and the broken bandwork borders).
Civico Museo Bibliografico Musicale, Bologna

A few imitations of Chinese porcelain were produced in Florence in the late 16th century (see p. 27) but it was not technically a porcelain at all and nothing came of the enterprise after its very brief flowering. Further attempts were made to produce true 'hard paste' porcelain during the 17th century but all to no avail, although some very pleasing 'soft paste' wares (based on crushed glass) were produced in France. Discovering how to make porcelain was at that time seen as being a miracle akin to discovering how to make gold from lead and mercury, and those who guided such experiments were called 'arcanists' because of the arcane nature of their studies. In the end, of course, one arcanist managed to do it; his name was Johann Friedrich Böttger and he had, in fact, been engaged earlier in trying to transmute lead into gold. He was not alone in making this scarcely less valuable discovery of how to produce porcelain, as he was directed by a celebrated physicist, and their years of experimenting were carried out in Saxony, where a glassmaking industry could supply the facilities they required. Böttger's discovery of 1710 changed the history of European ceramics dramatically. In that year his princely master, the Elector of Saxony, set up a manufactory for the production of porcelain at Meissen, a small town close to the Saxon capital of Dresden, and soon fashionable attention all over Europe was trained on the curious and delightful wares emanating from that city. The goldsmiths of Augsburg were, as usual, quick off the mark for, by 1711, a crate of undecorated porcelain had already been sent to an Augsburg goldsmith for decorating and selling on to his own customers. Much Meissen porcelain was decorated at Augsburg in the early years; later, Augsburg was viewed as a damaging competitor, but she continued to buy up finished Meissen porcelain and fit it into travelling-cases and cabinets as complete sets, offering them for sale as Augsburg confections, which in a sense they were.

It is astonishing that the Meissen factory was able to successfully transport its wares across Europe in great quantity, especially within Germany where there were so many territorial hindrances, in the form of frontiers charging duties, that freight-wagons and barges had to cross. It must have been the enormous success of the Meissen enterprise that made it possible to absorb these tolls in the high retail price. Other less fortunate industries had difficulty in bearing this substantial burden, and German trades in the decorative arts suffered badly throughout the 18th century as a result.

Pl. 280 Title-page to a book of 'entirely new' designs for '*Laub und Bandlwerck*' [Foliage and Bandwork] published in Augsburg in 1727. By Johann Jacob Baumgartner, who has here paid rather more attention to contemporary Italian three-dimensional cartouche forms than to those of France, but the proposals for plate-rims (in the four corners) betray Berainesque influence. Baumgartner's numerous engravings had a wide circulation (see also Pl. 282).
Victoria and Albert Museum, London, (Mus. no. E.677–1916)

was the making of glassware incorporating a high level of lead. It thus became less malleable than soda-glass, and this dictated the forms that glassware of this new type could take; the forms had to be simpler while the walls and stems of vessels had to be thicker. English drinking glasses now assumed a characteristically plain form, often elegant and always a great deal more robust than the more delicate and often fussy Continental forms although, once the English type became familiar abroad (and English glasses were exported in great quantity during the 18th century), it was imitated elsewhere, notably in Holland, Germany and Scandinavia. This was probably the first important example of the English manufacturing a product that was plain and sturdy and exporting it to Europe and the American colonies where these properties were admired in what were for the most part middle-class circles.

The international character of ornament throughout Northern Europe at this period is here illustrated in the plates. We see the baldachin-formula favoured by Berain (see p. 117 and Pls. 240 and 242) quickly picked up in Augsburg around 1700, used by a leading cabinet-maker at Würzburg in 1716, displayed on a London title-page for a Handel opera in 1711 and employed (numerous times) in the designs of Daniel Marot (Pls. 268–70). The general indebtedness to Berain and his school is everywhere evident but, by 1703 at any rate, Marot's engravings were doing much to spread knowledge of this style which he himself had helped to develop further (Pl. 273); a superb marquetry floor in the Schloss at Pommersfelden, executed between 1714 and 1719 shows how the Berain-Marot formula could be adapted in the hands of a skilled artisan (Pl. 278).

Interlaced bandwork is characteristic of this type of ornament and is to be seen in Pls. 274–6, which show objects produced in Stockholm, Hamburg and London – in two cases, as late as 1734.

A rather different type of ornament, based on the cartouche, was given fresh life by a number of designers; again, they worked in widely separate regions yet were all clearly aware of recent developments of the formula. Here we see designs by a Dutchman working in London who was the son of a celebrated Parisian cabinetmaker, and engravers working in Nürnberg and Augsburg (Pls. 277, 279 and 280).

Furniture began to take on less cumbersome and

Pl. 281 Japanned cabinet from the Elector of Saxony's 'Dutch Porcelain Closet' at Dresden, painted by Martin Schnell, one of the most accomplished japanners imitating Oriental lacquerwork; about 1715. Schnell had worked for a while at Berlin under Georg Dagly, the most celebrated japanner on the Continent at the beginning of the century, before settling in Dresden in 1710 and working both on furniture and Meissen porcelain. The Chinese scenes are painted on a white ground.
Kunstgewerbemuseum, Berlin

Pl. 282 Another pattern by the Augsburg designer J. J. Baumgartner (see Pl. 280), this time with chinoiserie subjects set amid the entwined scrolls of a late Baroque cartouche. Published in 1727. This is for the back-plate of a wall-sconce.
Victoria and Albert Museum, London (Mus. no. E.677–1916)

Meissen, being first in the field, set the pattern for other porcelain manufacturers to follow all over Europe. It is not possible here to discuss the many forms or patterns Meissen favoured but the figures made of porcelain deserve to be mentioned, as they were an almost totally new departure. They were the descendants of those sugarpaste figures (*trionfi*, in Italian) that sculptors produced to decorate the tables at grand dinners in the 17th century. Now they were produced in porcelain, prettily painted and less easily broken so that they could be used over and over again. The chief new class of vessels that the Meissen potters developed in so many varieties were those used in the taking of tea and coffee, a class for which exotic decoration with chinoiseries was a frequently adopted obvious choice. These beverages taste better when drunk from porcelain and the white ware shows up the coloured liquid to advantage. Pl. 282 shows the kind of pattern that inspired the decorators of German porcelain and faience at this time.

Pl. 283 Plate from a German book about ornament for joiners and cabinetmakers, published at Nürnberg in 1695 with designs by Georg Caspar Erasmus (see Pl. 215). He was interested in architecture and published a book for craftsmen on the Classical Orders. Here he shows doorways and cupboard fronts.

more elegant forms in the late 17th century, as we saw from the illustrations to the previous chapter dealing with French products. An English version of a French ensemble, made specially to occupy a dominant position in a fine room, is shown in Pl. 284 (cf. Pl. 253). The four designs for massive cupboards (Pl. 283), a Germanic form favoured from Holland to Lithuania and from Norway to Northern Italy, illustrate a tradition hardly affected by French taste at all, on the other hand; a degree of Classicism is to be seen in the examples shown here although that is more likely to be present through Netherlandish influence (cf. Pls. 200 and 201). What is curious about these patterns is that the top right-hand example seems likely to have influenced some English cabinetmakers in the second quarter of the 18th century (see Pl. 369).

England and Holland must probably continue to vie for the position of 'inventor of the cane-seated chair' which evolved into its definitive form around 1680 (Pl. 285). My impression is that the earliest European chairs with cane seats date from the 1660s and are to be seen in several English houses. They may have been made in Holland before that but I have not seen any specimens in Dutch collections. The point is of no great consequence; what matters is that both countries were making very similar cane-seated (and backed) walnut chairs by the 1680s and England certainly exported large quantities of them to Northern Germany, Scandinavia and the colonies on the East Coast of North America. In all these countries imitations were eventually being produced and chairmakers in many places on the Continent began to call themselves 'English chairmakers', even though they had never visited England. A Dutch variant of slightly later date, with an upholstered seat but a caned back, is to be seen in Pl. 286 and it will be noticed that, by this time (the 1690s), the Anglo-Dutch walnut chair had become more elegant. The elegance increased in the early 1700s, as the fine armchair shown in Pl. 287 demonstrates. One can appreciate more readily why chairmakers in Bremen and Copenhagen were proud to call themselves 'English chairmakers' when one sees this fine piece of seat-furniture. It is less easy to appreciate that the chair shown in Pl. 288 could have been regarded as elegant but it certainly was when it was new, in 1737. This rather poor drawing comes from the records of the guild of chairmakers at Leiden, in Holland; it was for record purposes within the guild only.

The Dutch excelled at marquetry decoration with veneers of wood. The technique probably first evolved at Antwerp, and Parisian cabinetmakers may have been early practitioners of this art form. But the Dutch made it very much their own and their most skilled craftsmen achieved pictorial miracles with this technique, as Pl. 290 shows. The form of this large cabinet is somewhat ungainly because it is derived from the heavy cup-

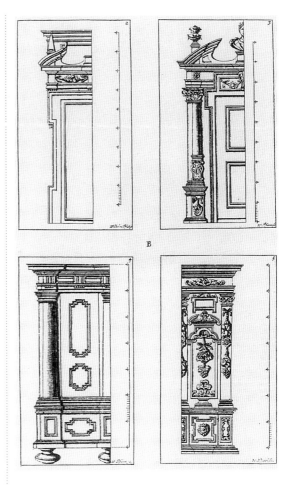

B

boards we discussed above in connection with Pl. 283 but such broad cabinets offered an extensive 'canvas' on which the marqueteurs could execute their art. This cabinet dates from about 1700. A cabinet made in Copenhagen in 1679, presumably by a Dutchman or a skilled craftsman familiar with the best Dutch practices, shows the less naturalist style used earlier, although the birds and moths are pretty naturalistically treated (Pl. 289), and the foliage on the drawers inside is exquisite in its 'formalized naturalism'.

However, Dutch and more especially British furniture of the period relied largely on the patterns found in wood veneers to provide the decorative element on their furniture. The handsome walnut cabinet of about 1700 shown in Pl. 291 shows this admirably. It does not appear to be English; it may well be Dublin work.

As for Germany, Dresden had become 'world-famous' for its porcelain. Berlin was still not a city that had much to offer Europe but it was warming up. Munich was fairly dormant although the works of the architect Joseph Effner were often delightful. Many other cities maintained their production of high-quality luxury goods with distinction, notably Hamburg. However, the outstanding success story at this period was once again the city of Augsburg. Centre of one of the world's foremost goldsmiths' industries, serving important patrons all over the civilized world, it was also a powerhouse of publishing in the field of design. Not only were copies of prints that had been produced originally in Paris and The Hague republished there; Augsburg designers such as Decker took French patterns and developed them, and others like Johann Schübler borrowed schemes put forward by Marot and evolved designs (for beds, for example) that would serve a Germanic clientele well past the middle of the century. It was amazing what Germany could achieve in spite of being politically fragmented, and having suffered so grievously from warfare, from sporadic famine and much destitution, and from the fearsome presence of large Turkish armies not far from her eastern borders.

Pl. 284 Pier-table, mirror and pair of candle-stands, carved and with japanned panels and detailing amidst the gilt scrollwork, probably made about 1703 by John Guilbaud, a Huguenot working in London. This set formed one of the principal decorative features of the earliest rooms at Hopetoun House, outside Edinburgh.
The Hopetoun House Preservation Trust

Pl. 285 English walnut armchair of characteristic form with caned seat and back; about 1675. Intended for use with a cushion. The carving is of above average quality and this chair has arms, but chairs of this type, varying only in the details of their carving, were made in enormous quantities; many were exported to Europe and the American colonies.
Courtesy of William H. Stokes, Cirencester

Pl. 286 Dutch, or possibly English, walnut chair with caned back and upholstered seat; about 1690. This chair was intended for rooms of higher standing than the chair shown in Pl. 285 but it belongs to the same tradition.
Cooper-Hewitt, National Design Museum, Smithsonian Institution, New York; gift of Irwin Untermeyer (Mus. no. 1950–4–1)

Pl 287 English walnut chair with caned seat and back of about 1700, exported to Hartford, Connecticut, where it remained in the Wyllys family's possession until acquired by the Boston Museum. Intended for use with a cushion or squab.
Museum of Fine Arts, Boston, Massachusetts

PI. 290 Cabinet of specifically Dutch form (broad, with no central legs) favoured around 1700, decorated with exceptionally fine marquetry firmly attributed to the cabinetmaker Jan van Mekeren, whose speciality was the extremely naturalistic depiction of flowers in wood. No one else ever quite matched his skill in this direction.
Rijksmuseum, Amsterdam

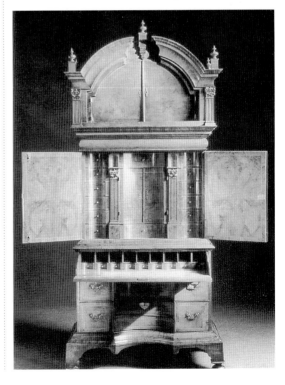

PI. 289 Cabinet-on-stand of a form adopted all over Europe, decorated with very fine marquetry in the Dutch taste; dated 1679. Probably made in Copenhagen by a Dutch or North German cabinetmaker. The name of Lorenz Corbianus has been proposed; from Altona (now part of Hamburg), he worked for the Danish Crown between 1673 and 1693; he was paid impressive sums for cabinets.
The Danish Royal Collection, Rosenborg Castle, Copenhagen

PI. 288 Drawing of a Dutch walnut chair with upholstered seat. This was the form of masterpiece being set by the chairmakers' guild at Leiden, Holland, in the second quarter of the century. It is of the form that had been fashionable in England for about a decade. Dated 1737.
Gemeentearchief, Leiden

PI. 291 Walnut writing-cabinet, of unusual form that is, however, in its plainness characteristic of the Anglo-Dutch taste in carcass furniture in general. With virtually unadorned veneers of fancily veined wood, the panels being merely framed with cross-banding edged with feather-banding. Probably made in Dublin, about 1700.
Courtesy of Messrs Arthur Brett and Sons Ltd, Norwich

CHAPTER 13

PARIS AND THE GERMAN COURTS

Pl. 292 Sketch by Antoine Watteau for a 'grotesque' composition; 1715–20. In spite of the marvellous freedom with which the artist has drawn this composition, it is essentially akin to Berain's patterns for grotesques centring on a pavilion (see Pl. 240) and, indeed, in its engraved form, this design became relatively stolid.
National Gallery of Art, Washington, Ailsa Mellon Bruce Fund, 1982

1720-1760

This chapter is about the Rococo style, its genesis in France and its spread across Europe. What we have to say here could perfectly well have been added on to the end of Chapter 11 but it seemed necessary to pause and say something about what was going on in Holland and England around 1700 before taking up the French story again. So there is no discernible break in our tale, but what can certainly be called a new style evolved in Paris in the 1720s and numerous expressions of it were to be seen there by the mid-1730s.

The new style grew out of that which was fashionable in Paris during the first quarter of the century, and we noted how ornaments became more lively and on the whole lighter during that time. The Berainesque formula for grotesques (see p. 117), grew more delicate in the hands of Claude Audran and Claude Gillot, and already possessed much of the Rococo spirit before 1720 (Pl. 293). Comparison between Pl. 240 and Pl. 292, the latter showing an ethereal drawing of a similar subject by Antoine Watteau from the late 'teens of the century, make the development plain. How this kind of grotesque decoration developed in the second quarter of the century is indicated by the panel of about 1730 painted by Audran who was then about 60 (Pl. 294).

We noted how seashells of various kinds were often present in carved mural decoration executed by François-Antoine Vassé (see p. 123) around 1720. Shells and other marine motifs come greatly to the fore from that time until well past the middle of the century. Pl. 295 shows that even a Parisian bookbinder, admittedly a brilliant one, has taken up a scallop-shell motif, treating it formally in a repetitive arrangement separated by bandwork with 'breaks' in the Berain–Marot tradition; he did this on the binding of a book from the year 1728. A chocolate-pot with its warmer (Pl. 297), produced by a leading Parisian goldsmith in 1729, is decorated with marine subjects that include shell ornaments treated asymmetrically. The plastic ornament is largely confined to the stand and spout, and dolphins play an important role because this fine piece of work was made as a present when the Queen of France (Marie Leszcynska, wife of Louis XV) gave birth to an heir to the throne, in France called a Dauphin – hence the dolphins. The engraved framing on the body of the vessel resembles that on contemporary panelling in the new taste.

It was in fact in goldsmiths' work that the most startling stylistic advances were made in the French capital during the decade from 1725 or so. This was first and foremost due to the presence there of a young goldsmith who had been brought up in Turin and was thus very familiar with Baroque ornament in its Italian

Pl. 295 Tooled leather bookbinding on a book published in Paris in 1718, with an addition made in 1728. This very attractive binding with an orange ground, the pattern executed in black and gold with red dots, is probably the work of Antoine-Michel Padeloup, a famous binder of the time; about 1730.
Bibliothèque Nationale, Paris

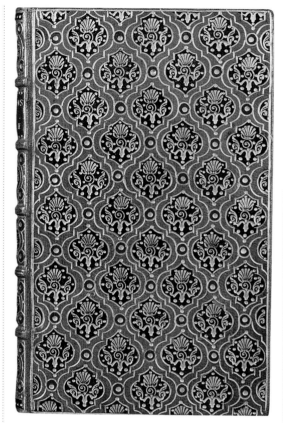

Pl. 296 Sketch by Juste-Aurèle Meissonnier for a small flask or casting bottle, or just possibly a finial for a fire-dog or roof of a Sedan chair. About 1730?
The Metropolitan Museum of Art, New York; Rogers Fund, 1986 (Mus. no. 1986 1032.1)

Pl. 297 Chocolate-pot made for the birth of the Dauphin in 1729; note the dolphin-feet and spout, and other marine subjects. Produced in Paris by the celebrated goldsmith Henri-Nicolas Cousinet, and given to Queen Marie Leszcynska. The engraved royal arms on the body were removed during the French Revolution.
Musée du Louvre, Paris

the King (Louis XV), in 1724, and then in 1726 became personal designer to the King, succeeding in this post the two Jean Berains, father and then son. Although he had ambitions to be an architect, it was as a designer of silver and gold items that Meissonier exerted the most powerful influence, with energetic designs of amazing plasticity and vigorous spiralling movement (Pls. 296 and 303). In the 1750s, when this new manner had largely run its course in Paris, an astute observer could still recall that it was Meissonier who had been 'the first to banish symmetry' in contemporary design.

Very little of his silverwork has survived (and none of that made for the Crown as far as is known), so we rely for the most part for our assessment of his style on the many engravings of his work published from the mid-1720s until 1735. His *oeuvre* was first published as a body in 1734 and was republished in about 1750. When they were novel, his designs attracted much attention, even excitement. But much of his work was for foreigners or provincials; it found somewhat less favour with Parisians, who preferred something a little less agitated.

The *genre pittoresque*, as it was called at the time, or the Rococo taste as we call it, was, in its more exuberant forms, best suited to small items (Pl. 296), although the Italians and the Germans were to adopt it also on a large scale. Meissonier's style was taken up with great success by several important Parisian goldsmiths in the 1730s, notably Thomas Germain, Jacques Roëttiers and Pierre Germain (Pls. 302, 304 and 305), and, because work in silver was so frequently copied by artists working in porcelain and faience, it is often to be seen in that branch of the decorative arts (Pl. 306). Closely related to silver, of course, is the art of the bronze-founder and chaser, and the Rococo phase saw the production of many wonderful mounts of bronze (gilded, on the most sumptuous specimens) that were fitted to all manner of luxury goods, from commodes to exotic porcelains and lacquer-work. Several entrepreneurial shopkeepers in Paris made a speciality of commissioning such bronze-mounted wares for sale to those (mostly ladies) seeking fashionable ornaments for their tasteful rooms. These specialist merchants were called *marchands-merciers* and their role as establishers of fashion was rather important.

Although Rococo was essentially a three-dimensional style, in clever hands it can be rendered successfully in two dimensions, as Pl. 300 demonstrates.

That calmer version of the Rococo manner which appealed to Parisians (and at first it was to private patrons rather than the Crown that the style appealed most) was the invention of Nicolas Pineau, an architect and decorator who usually worked alongside the architect J.-B. Le Roux. It was Pineau who gave the French interior the character it assumed in the 1730s (Pl. 301) and the great change he brought about was noted and widely admired at the time because it adhered to the

forms, which of course often embodied a degree of asymmetry, notably in the ornamental cartouche (see Chapter 10). Juste-Aurèle Meissonier (his father was a French goldsmith from Provence who worked in Turin) came to Paris sometime before 1718 and was so skilful and inventive that he was first appointed goldsmith to

French late Baroque tradition while enveloping this in a haze of fluid ornament of great delicacy and inventiveness. Pineau also designed furniture (Pl. 299) and his style of carved furniture was immensely influential (Pl. 309), although imitations were not always carried out with the delightful grace of which he was such a master. Much of Pineau's mural decoration was published; no less than 60 plates appeared in the fourth volume of Jean Mariette's *Architecture françoise*, while that important book *De la distribution des maisons de plaisance et de la decoration des edifices en general*, which came out in two volumes in 1737–8, is devoted to the style for which Pineau is celebrated. The book deals with houses, relatively small in scale, made for a somewhat informal lifestyle (*maisons de plaisance*), and in a way epitomises the spirit of French Rococo tastes. The author, Jacques-François Blondel, was a member of a family several of whom figure prominently in French architectural history, and was very well informed indeed on architectural matters. In 1743, he set up a school in rooms at the Louvre to train architects, and several of its students became important members of the profession during the second half of the century. Blondel wrote a number

Pl. 298 Dressing-mirror of gilt bronze, probably made for Queen Marie Leszcynska, the wife of Louis XV, in 1726. Engraving from Huquier's collected works of Meissonnier of 1734 and 1750. The mer-babies are treated very much in the manner of Stefano della Bella (see Pl. 171).
Victoria and Albert Museum, London (Mus. no. E.211–1967)

Pl. 299 Designs by Nicolas Pineau for armchairs; about 1730. Note the bow-shape crest-rail and the fluid forms generally. This formula for an armchair [*fauteuil*] was one of the most comfortable ever devised, but its vertical back legs tended to be weak.
Musée des Arts Décoratifs, Paris (Mus. no. A4501)

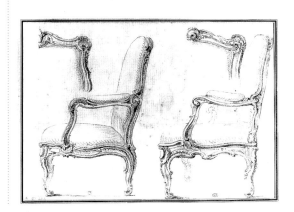

Pl. 300 Design for an embroidered wall-panel believed to be for the small château at Choisy, where Madame de Mailly was to entertain Louis XV; 1743. Naturalistically embroidered honeysuckle trails across the silk ground, while the border was to be executed in green silk with black shadowing, possibly in shallow relief. Artists skilled in designing Rococo ornament participated in the decoration of Choisy – Chevillion, Peyrotte, Slodtz and Mondon, for instance.
Bibliothèque Nationale, Paris

states strained themselves economically, as did several other lesser states which could even less afford such expense, in building vast residences for their rulers with attendant pleasure-pavilions, bath-houses and stables, not to speak of extensive parks beyond. As with Versailles (see Chapter 11), fashion dictated that all these buildings should be decorated and furnished in the French taste.

The Germans, of course, had splendid architects of their own who worked in the German Baroque tradition, more closely affiliated with Italy than with France. Those German artists and craftsmen working in the realm of room decoration and furnishing were also by

of influential treatises on architecture and as a critic of the contemporary scene his judgement, one suspects, may be trusted. Of Pineau, he insisted that he had 'infinite admiration' but, when the Rococo manner had become altogether too extreme and tediously overloaded with meaningless ornament, as happened in the 1750s, he was among those who advocated a return to a more measured style. Parisian Rococo lost its fire in the 1760s, seized up and became well mannered; symmetry was reimposed.

While dealing with matters to do with Rococo taste in Paris, we should draw attention to two pieces of furniture which are of interest. The heavily-carved armchair shown in Pl. 308 was made by a leading Parisian chair-maker in about 1749 for the Duchess of Parma, a French princess – daughter of Louis XV. The general heaviness of the chair and its carving, together with the fact that its (original) upholstery with heavy gold braid applied to silk velvet would make an uncomfortable seat, indicate that this chair was intended for show in a room of state. In total contrast is the elegant but simple chair shown in Pl. 309, also made by a prominent chair-maker; it must date from about 1745, but it has only the most simple carved ornament and relies for its effect on paintwork in white with blue trimming. A chair of this kind would have fitted well into some of the *maisons de plaisance*, perhaps a house in the countryside close to Paris, that Blondel illustrated in his book. Could it conceivably have been made for the same room as the commode shown in Pl. 321?

We turn now to Germany, not yet a single nation but still made up of a huge number of states, most of them small. Only three were of a size and strength to be reckoned as powers on the European scene – Bavaria, Saxony and Brandenburg-Prussia, with Munich, Dresden and Berlin as their respective capitals. These three

Pl. 302 Silver service by Thomas Germain, produced in 1733–4 at the height of the early phase of true Rococo, which lasted until about 1737. Inspired by the example of Meissonnier, the tension with which Germain controls his designs is characteristic of the best French Rococo – exuberant, certainly, but also balanced and never wild. Painting by François Desportes.
Nationalmuseum, Stockholm

and large more familiar with that tradition than that of the French. French talent had therefore to be brought in, when it was a question of producing imitations of the newest French forms. Some French architects of the first rank, like Robert de Cotte and Germain Boffrand, visited German cities in order to advise on projected palaces, while many lesser French architectural talents went to work in Germany, often with happy results. A few French craftsmen also went there, notably carvers of ornament. And several German architects received training in Paris so that when they returned home, they were able to produce delightful buildings in the French spirit (Joseph Effner's Pagodenburg in the park at Nymphenburg is a charming example). The same was probably the case with cabinetmakers, some of

Pl. 303 Centrepiece of silver designed by Juste-Aurèle Meissonnier in the full-blown early Rococo style, made for the Duke of Kingston in 1735. *Victoria and Albert Museum, London (Mus. no. E.262–1967)*

Pl. 304 Design for a water-jug in a collection of designs for silverware, published in Paris in 1748 by Pierre Germain who was probably, but by no means certainly, a relation of Thomas Germain. Many of the designs are by Jacques Roëttiers and maybe others, but Pierre Germain presumably composed some of them. All three silversmiths were among the very top rank of those who worked in the Rococo manner. *Victoria and Albert Museum, London (Mus. no. E 1276–1897)*

Pl. 305 Design from the same suite as Pl. 304, this time for a '*sauciere*' in the form of a seashell. *Victoria and Albert Museum (Mus. no. E.1233–1897)*

whom must have visited Paris while on their obligatory long study-tour as journeymen, and would surely have found a welcome among the many cabinetmakers of German extraction then working in Paris. A man such as Samuel Beyer, who made a pretty little marquetry table for the palace at Ansbach in 1763 which is entirely French in appearance and spirit, must have spent some time in Paris. So numerous were the German cabinet makers who were practising in Paris by the end of the 1750s that a French drawing-master was offering special classes in drawing to German-speaking students in the Parisian furniture trades.

French taste, or information about it, mainly reached Germany and other countries through the medium of prints, however. Original prints from Paris were available in important cities such as Frankfurt, Leipzig, Munich and Augsburg. Copies were also made and sold, principally at Augsburg. And, finally, designers in Germany (notably at Augsburg) were busy producing fresh designs that drew much inspiration from these French prints. Indeed, it was the amalgam of the French idiom with that of the German late-Baroque taste that was to produce almost a new style, and certainly a wonderfully vibrant version of Rococo, which embodied a controlled tension that manages just, but only just, to hold back what would otherwise be totally wild scrollwork (Pl. 311). Handled by masters, South German Rococo is a true delight, and in this style were produced amazing works of art, and not just small in scale. Whole churches, vast entrance halls, great dining rooms and libraries were decorated and furnished in this manner.

The man who did most to spread French taste to the western parts of Germany was François Cuvilliés. Born in what is now Belgium but trained in Paris between 1720 and 1724 (i.e. before the fully-fledged Rococo had evolved), he spent his career in the service of the Elector of Bavaria at Munich, where he was court architect although he also worked elsewhere, on loan as it were. So well had Cuvilliés understood the French manner

Pl. 306 Chamber-candlestick of Vincennes soft-paste porcelain with shell-like handle and rim, painted with purple-red and some gilding to accentuate the wonderfully controlled spiralling of its form; 1753. *Musée National de Céramique, Sèvres*

PI. 307 Chinese vase of green celadon mounted in Paris between 1745 and 1749 with fine bronze mounts in the Rococo manner. Ornamental objects of this kind were usually commissioned by specialist dealers in luxury wares [*marchands-merciers*] and sold from elegant shops in the smartest streets in Paris.
Reproduced by permission of the Trustees of the Wallace Collection, London (Mus. no. F.105)

that he could interpret French prints of architecture and ornament, published after his stay in Paris, as if he had been a Parisian who had never left his native city. He could thus take a French model and add a touch of South German Rococo to the decoration (Pl. 310), so that even Frenchmen seem to have viewed engravings of his work as if they were French rather than German. His engravings constitute the largest body of Rococo designs by one artist; the first series was one of the earliest publications of Rococo designs in a substantial number, and Cuvilliés was as a result immensely influential during the middle decades of the century, not only in Germany.

The ceilings at Bruchsal, dating from the 1750s, certainly owe much to Cuvilliés (Pl. 311) and the way details such as a door-hinge can contribute to the decoration of a whole room is a point made neatly by the example reproduced in Pl. 312.

As we have seen, Augsburg had long been important as a centre where artisans and designers could learn about the latest styles, and this was especially so during the Rococo period. A painter from Munich, Johann Georg Bergmüller, was appointed Director of the Academy at Augsburg in 1730 and numbered among his pupils several artists who were to become outstanding exponents of the Rococo manner. He himself published six suites of proto-Rococo ornament in the style of Claude Gillot (see p. 139) in the late 1720s. His most celebrated pupil was Jeremias Wachsmuth, whose many suites of Rococo ornaments included stunning designs for vases. Franz Xaver Habermann, a prolific designer

of Rococo ornament, trained as a sculptor and travelled in Italy before settling in Augsburg in 1746. His scroll-work is always beautifully controlled yet lively and his furniture of the 1760s is in the German taste, and not at all reminiscent of French work. Johann Michael Hoppenhaupt should also be mentioned; he worked first under Johann August Nahl, who had left Berlin in 1746 and had been trained in Paris and whose spirited version of Rococo was something like that of Cuvilliés and imbued with a certain reticence.

The Italians, of course, could manage Rococo of the German kind but rarely chose to do so (Pl. 317 shows a lively example from Venice); moreover, Rococo of a provincial sort was to be seen all over Central Europe and also established quite a foothold for a while in Portugal. The English, it has to be said, never really mastered the style; it did not particularly suit them and for the most part Rococo ornament sits awkwardly on English artefacts of the time. 'Gothic' and 'Chinese' suited the English better, as we shall see (Chapter 15). Excellent Rococo compositions were produced by Georg Michael Moser, an immigrant from Schaffhausen near Basle in Switzerland who was a chaser of metalwork and taught drawing in London (he taught the young George III, among others), and there were of course others, such as John Linnell, the celebrated cabinetmaker, who could handle it well. But English Rococo tends towards attenuation and openness, along with wayward excrescences, which made it difficult to achieve the tension that is an essential characteristic of good Rococo design.

PI. 308 French armchair originally in the Ducal Palace at Parma, sent from Paris about 1749. Probably made by Nicolas-Quinibert Foliot, one of several distinguished members of a family of chairmakers. This chair retains its original velvet seat decorated with rich silver-gilt galoon and embroidery in gilt thread.
The Hermitage Museum, St Petersburg (Mus. no. 411 Mb.)

PI. 309 Cane-seated and backed chair with minimal carving and with painted decoration. Made by Claude Séné, probably the most renowned of all the mid-18th-century Parisian chair-makers, whose mark it bears. It would have been fitted with a squab that largely hid the gap between the seat and the back-rest, and thus somewhat altered the chair's silhouette.
The Metropolitan Museum of Art, New York; Rogers Fund, 1926 (Mus. no. 26.220.2)

Pl. 312 Bronze hinge of Rococo form on a door in the Residenz at Würzburg.
The Residenz, Wurzburg

Pl. 310 Plate from a suite of engravings by François de Cuvilliés, published between 1738 and 1754. Cuvilliés worked for the Elector of Bavaria and his designs were published in Munich, but several suites also appeared in Paris. This composition for a bed in a niche adheres very closely to the French fashion, but some of the Rococo ornaments seem rather more boisterous than would be acceptable in France at this time.
Victoria and Albert Museum, London (Mus. no. 22.575/2)

Pl. 311 Stucco decoration of a coved ceiling in the Schloss at Bruchsal, dating from the 1750s. The exuberance of the best German Rococo was always tempered by a strong inward tension that, as it were, prevents it flying apart. Centripetal force is a vital ingredient of Rococo.
The Schloss, Bruchsal, near Mainz

Pl. 313 Pattern for a woven silk drawn in about 1734 by Anna Maria Garthwaite, a celebrated designer at Spitalfields, London. Trees and other vegetation growing from an island floating in mid-air were a characteristic motif in European silk design in the first half of the 1730s.
Victoria and Albert Museum, London (Mus. no. 5971–22)

Pl. 314 Bookbinding, probably by A.-M. Padeloup (see Pl. 295), of about 1735. The binder must have taken note of the currently fashionable patterns on silks, and adopted the 'island' formula for his own work.
Courtesy of Sotheby's, London

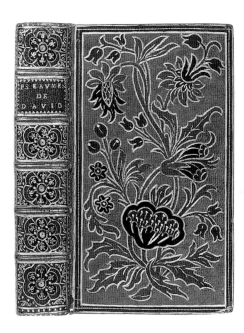

Pl. 315 Silk from the Lyons silk-weaving establishment of Jean Revel, who seems to have been the first to develop a system for shading three-dimensional bodies naturalistically on a loom, a development that had taken place by 1733.
Victoria and Albert Museum, London (Mus. no. T.187–1922)

Pl. 316 Shell ornament is carried to an extreme in this design for a small carriage in which a lady could be pushed around her garden, no doubt paying a special visit to the shell-bedecked grotto that was being built in a secluded glade. Design by Jean-Baptiste Chevillon. Probably about 1740.
Bibliothèque Nationale, Paris

The second quarter of the 18th century saw great changes in the design of figured silks, a field in which the silk-designers at Lyons set the lead by bringing out, every six months, fresh designs that other European silk-weaving cities had perforce to follow. For a while, in the 1740s, English silks woven at Spitalfields were considered, even by the French, to be almost as excellent as their own products because in London at that time a skilful designer, Anna Maria Garthwaite, had established a prominent position for herself. The silk-mercers demanded materials with increasingly naturalistic patterns (usually floral; the weavers of such silks in Spitalfields were referred to as working in 'the flowered silk branch'), and designers were busy during the first third of the century devising means of achieving this. Achieving naturalism of course meant that one had to be able to render light and shade, but within the technical limitations imposed by the weaving loom. In the early 1730s the most advanced naturalistic depiction of flowers was produced by a contour-like system, where areas of different colours abut but do not blend (Pl. 313). The great step forward was the invention of the system of *points-rentrés*, a way of interlocking the colours which avoided producing a hard line along the edges where the colours would otherwise have abutted. The first magical designs produced at Lyons by this method in the mid-1730s are represented by the splendid silk illustrated in Pl. 315 but the Spitalfields designers (with Anna Garthwaite at their head) followed the Lyons lead within a year or so. The English obtained information about new patterns fairly easily, because a number of unscrupulous Lyons designers were in the habit of composing their new patterns every six months and selling copies to foreign rivals, cynically knowing that no one else would outpace their own establishments at Lyons. By the time the rivals had set up their looms to weave the new patterns, the French would have devised something new. In the 18th century, it was not the cut of a silk dress that gave its date away; it was the pattern of its material, which no amount of disguising with trimmings and bows could hide. A woman of fashion was therefore forced to buy new dresses within a year or two, if she wished to remain in the swim.

The pattern shown in Pl. 313 has island-like patches from which trees and enormous flowers incongruously grow: this was the fashionable motif in the early 1730s. It is still present in Pl. 315, which dates from the mid-1730s, although the 'island' is there contained in a shell. A Parisian book-binder has adopted the same general

Pl. 317 An amazing design for a festival gondola in the full-blown Rococo taste, beautifully managed by the Venetian artist Giovanni Battista Piranesi while working in Venice in the 1740s, before returning to Rome, where he was to become a leading exponent of Classicism.
The Pierpont Morgan Library, New York (1966.10.11)

formula on a binding of these very years (Pl. 314), breaking away from the traditional bookbinder's repertoire of repeating patterns or lace-like schemes around a central medallion.

Shell and shell-like forms played an important part in Rococo ornament, as we have seen. This predilection for shells received reinforcement in 1742 through the publication of a book on shell-collecting with a frontispiece by François Boucher, the famous painter of *galanteries*; he depicts shells of many kinds, alongside sponges, coral and a tortoise on a beach being carried ashore by a triton couple. By the mid-1730s, the well-known art-dealer and purveyor of curiosities Gersaint had been making visits to Amsterdam in order to pick up distinctive shells of high quality suitable for amateur collectors – for those who merely liked to have a few stunning specimens lying on their drawing-room table. This liking for shells produced some strange results, such as the garden-carriage shown in Pl. 316 designed in about 1740 by Jean-Baptiste Chevillion, one of the best designers of ornament in this manner, and the gondola by Piranesi in Pl. 317.

Textile designers are required to produce patterns that can be repeated endlessly up the length of a piece of material (Pl. 319). Coloured engravings like that by Gabriel Huquier of the mid-1740s may well have been a source of inspiration for silk-designers at this time (Pl. 318). The Huquier pattern embodies rockwork and shells, as well as exotic flora – and the pattern comes from a collection of designs that were supposed to look as if they were Chinese. Totally implausible designs of Oriental inspiration already had been devised in Europe in the 17th century, on a small scale. A fresh wave of chinoiserie swept over Europe early in the 18th century but the largest wave of all arrived as a ripple in the 1730s, had become substantial by the 1740s and carried on flood-like into the 1770s. Then there was a lull before the last notable wave arrived around 1790 and lasted into the 1820s. The arch-priest of chinoiserie was Jean Pillement, whose airy fantasies evidently delighted his contemporaries (Pl. 320), judging by the number of imitations they spawned. The design of his that we illustrate is of late date but he had been producing compositions in the same vein at least since 1750 when he was working in London. While there he produced a book that was popular with ladies of leisure which gave them ideas for decorating objects of great variety in a 'Chinese' manner. *The Ladies' Amusement*, as it was

Pl. 318 Coloured engraving by Gabriel Huquier from a suite claiming to show Chinese flowers and plants! Published in Paris in 1745.
Bibliothèque Doucet, Paris

Pl. 319 A delightful Spitalfields silk of about 1748–50 undoubtedly designed by Anna Maria Garthwaite (see Pl. 313), with a naturalistic pattern rendered entirely in coloured silks. Such meandering patterns remained in fashion until the 1760s, but were then rendered in a more rigid manner.
Victoria and Albert Museum (Mus.no. T.188–1922)

Pl. 320 Engraving from a suite of six designs for 'Chinese huts' by Jean Pillement. Published in 1770, this is a rather late manifestation of his style which is here seen at its most extreme.
Museum für Kunsthandwerk, Frankfurt am Main (Mus. no. LOZ 2428)

Pl. 321 Front of a commode in the High Rococo style made in 1742 for the bedchamber of Madame de Mailly, at the time a new mistress of Louis XV, in her small château at Choisy (see also Pl. 300). The room was entirely decorated in blue and white. Made by Mathieu Criard and delivered by the *marchand-mercier* Thomas Hebert, the brilliantly executed lacquerwork is thought to be by Etienne-Simon Martin. Note the way the lively Rococo painted ornament plays counterpoint to the silvered-bronze mounts. *Musée du Louvre, Paris (Mus. no. OA 8170)*

Pl. 322 The Mondon manner was eagerly taken up in Germany, notably by Johann Esaias Nilson, as is shown in a composition emblematic of 'Wood and Stone' published at Augsburg in 1752.

Pl. 323 It is often difficult to determine what the scale of a Rococo composition might be, but in reality such seemingly large structures as that shown here were rarely built; this is a fantasy of a kind that much inspired the makers of small-scale objects like porcelain figures and of centrepieces for dining-tables made in various media. Design by Jean Mondon dating from 1736.

called, must have come out in the late 1750s in London; a second edition appeared in 1762. In 1760 he had published, both in London and Paris (how was this managed in the middle of England's seven years' war with France?), a book of designs of fantasy flowers in the Chinese taste that were to be useful for designers 'of silks and *indiennes*' (i.e. printed cottons, which were becoming the rage at that time and were eventually to ruin all but the most resilient of the silk-industries of Europe). Two other French designers played an

Pl. 325 Wall-sconce made of hard-paste porcelain at the royal manufactury at Sèvres in about 1760 to the designs of Jean-Claude Duplessis, who was on the staff of the factory. He was a goldsmith who came to Paris from Turin; he often worked in bronze and made handsome mounts for porcelain, among other things. It is green, white and gilt.

Victoria and Albert Museum, London (Mus. no. 467–1895)

produced to help in the porcelain factories at Meissen and Nymphenberg, where they produced delightful confections that graced mid-century dining tables in fashionable circles in many parts of Europe. And what the porcelain-makers did was soon followed by the makers of faience, although it is virtually impossible to contrive a crisp effect in this medium.

Towards 1750 in France Rococo designs for some reason seem to have got heavier, and the joyful spirit that informed so much early Rococo seems to have spent itself. It was as if those who continued to work in the Rococo manner said to each other, 'Now we must be serious'; for by 1750 quite a few voices had been raised in criticism of the apparent frivolity of the Rococo (Pl. 324).

The marvellous Sèvres porcelain wall-sconce of about 1760 (Pl. 325) displays much the same spirit, although, because it is the work of Jean-Claude Duplessis, who was designer at the Sèvres porcelain factory at this time, it is so accomplished that the relative severity of its central element is skilfully disguised by the delightful freedom of the two flanking branches which are treated asymmetrically. Madame de Pompadour owned several pairs of these candle-holders; this one may have been hers.

Madame de Pompadour, the most important of Louis XV's mistresses who 'reigned' from 1745 until her death in 1764, is today often credited with having played a part in the creation of the Rococo style, but this had already reached its fullest development before she caught the King's eye. Her role was that of a patron with a passion for building and interior decoration who had access to the royal purse and could spend lavishly on luxurious new houses and apartments for entertaining the King. She must have had good taste and, when placing commissions, she could of course indicate her preferences in terms of shape, motifs and colours, but her involvement in the process of design is unlikely to have been greater than that. The example of delightful informality in luxurious surroundings that she set was, however, enormously influential and she encouraged a number of artists working in the Rococo manner, notably François Boucher. But in fact her reign extended well into the period when Classicism was regaining a foothold and many of the buildings made for her, and their contents, were in a well-developed version of the Rococo or even in early forms of unmistakable Classicism (see Chapter 14). It was after all her initiative that lay behind the decision to have the Court Architect Ange-Jacques Gabriel build a small casino for her in the gardens at Versailles in 1762. Although Gabriel, at 64, was already somewhat conservative in his architectural manner, the Petit Trianon, completed in 1768, four years after Madame de Pompadour had died, represented a complete break with the Rococo.

important role in bringing chinoiseries to the fore. The first was Jean-Antoine Fraisse, who issued a suite of 'Chinese' designs in 1735, when he was working for the Duc de Bourbon at Chantilly and was involved with the Duke's porcelain factory there. The other designer who must have handled chinoiserie well was Alexis Peyrotte. His name crops up frequently in the history of the decorative arts at this period. He was appointed designer of furniture to the Crown in 1749 and is known to have provided designs for the chairmaker N.-Q. Foliot (see Pl. 309). His speciality, however, was said to be chinoiserie and Huquier published some designs in this vein by him in the 1730s.

We noted that Rococo was best suited to works on a small scale, but designs like that by Jean Mondon shown in Pl. 323 confused people and were of course not intended to be taken literally – although some people, notably the Portuguese tile-painters, did so. The French never did that, however, but quite substantial architectural fantasies of Rococo scrollwork were produced to go on the dinner table. They might be made with melted sugar or of marzipan, or they could be built on a *papier-mâché* framework. I should like to have included an illustration in a French pastry-cook's manual which indicates the kind of purpose Mondon must have had in mind for his compositions in this genre. As we noted in the previous chapter, German porcelain-makers began to produce figures for this kind of table decoration, and designs inspired by Mondon, executed by Johann Esaias Nilson (Pl. 322) were later

CHAPTER 14

ROME AND PARIS

Pl. 326 The filing-cabinet [*cartonnier*], intended to stand at one end of the accompanying writing-desk, made for Lalive de Jully to designs provided by Le Lorrain in 1756. This group of furniture was praised by the Comte de Caylus and enjoyed much renown. It was seen by many well-informed and interested people at Lalive's house. This photograph was taken when the clock had just been found in another collection and what is actually shown here is a full-size cut-out photograph of the original clock placed on top. The actual clock has since been reunited with the *cartonnier*. The mounts are by Philippe Caffieri. *Musée Condé, Chantilly*

Pl. 327 Design for sepulchral monument by Jean-Laurent Le Geay, perhaps drawn and engraved in the early 1740s while a student at the French Academy in Rome and surely showing the influence of Piranesi, also in Rome at this time. The unhappy girls clutching each other for comfort in the presence of monumental stonework and the spooky figure below epitomise the early Piranesian Classical manner. Le Geay returned to Paris in January 1742; although he made no buildings in France, he was highly praised by his superiors, and Nicolas Cochin later claimed that it was his return to Paris that first prompted the return to good taste in architecture.

Rome has been the site where more remains of Antique Classical civilization are to be seen than anywhere else and has, of course, been so since Classical times. What is more, all the revivals of the Classical manner of building and decoration have first sprung from the fecund soil that its vast assemblage of exemplars provides – exemplars not only of the relics of Antiquity but also of the subsequent Classical styles from the Renaissance and Baroque periods, which in themselves derive from the potent and ever-present Antique model.

As we shall see here, a fresh Classical style now also had its inception in Rome, although its development took place in Paris in the third quarter of the 18th century. Paris had long been the chief centre for the academic study of the Classical manner, so that Classicism's strongest bastion was, in effect, the Academy of Architecture in Paris, whose task was 'to discuss the rules of architecture', which, by implication, could only mean those of Classical architecture. The Academy in Paris was established in 1671 but a French Academy had been founded in Rome in 1666 'to cultivate good taste and the manner of the Ancients', and the most talented young French artists (including architects) were sent to Rome to spend several years studying the Antique culture and its derivatives.

Adherents of the strong French academic tradition found much wrong with Rococo decoration and, already in the 1730s, when the style was in its infancy, criticism was being levelled at those who practised in this manner. The critics spoke of tormented decorations, extravagant contours and how Rococo forms and ornament 'made nonsense of architecture'. The great French writer Voltaire subtly ridiculed the Rococo idiom (in 1733); four years later, the well-informed Jacques-François Blondel (see p. 141), wrote in mockery of 'the ridiculous jumble' of disparate motifs that constituted so much Rococo ornament. In the 1740s several writers demanded a return to the canons of taste that prevailed under Louis XIV – the Golden Age of French Art, as they saw it. More seriously, the Comte de Caylus, an antiquary whose opinions were widely respected and whose advice on matters of taste was therefore eagerly sought by discriminating people, also inveighed against the bad taste in interior decoration at this time and in 1749, in a paper read before no less august an institution than the Academy in Paris, spoke of its meanness and the lack of that nobility inherent in Classical art. Another great salvo was fired in the winter of 1754–5 in two articles written by Nicolas Cochin, a designer at the Menus-Plaisirs. From his vantage-point close to the court and leading figures in the field of architecture and

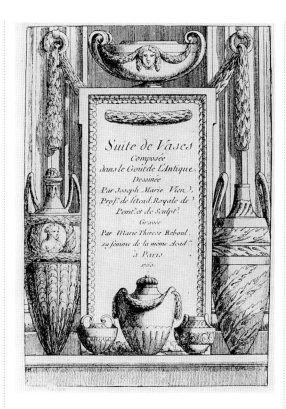

Pl. 328 Title-page to a suite of engraved designs for vases by Joseph-Marie Vien, published in Paris in 1760. The catkin-like tails of the festoons were a much loved motif of the early Neo-Classical designers in the late 1750s. The designing of vases was a sideline for many architects and artists at this period, and numerous suites were published. *From* Suite de Vases composée dans le gout de l'Antique, *1760*

decoration, Cochin could probably see more clearly than most that Rococo decoration had become altogether too undignified and lax; he addressed his criticism primarily at those practising the decorative arts, and expressed the hope that their 'inventiveness' would exhaust itself and that the time when this would come about was fast approaching. He also urged architects to stop feeling they always had to be thinking up something new and recommended they return to the sound principles of building respected in the not so very distant past (i.e. the time of Louis XIV).

The Rococo movement suffered a mortal blow at the hands of Caylus and Cochin but did not, of course, die at once. At first there was a loss of nerve, so that the exuberance of Rococo ornament was reduced and its forms began to stiffen. In Paris Rococo had died away by the 1770s; elsewhere it lingered on. But we must now observe a phenomenon that sometimes (perhaps always) occurs when new styles are introduced. First, an extreme version of the new style is proposed, which provokes a fierce reaction. From this springs a more moderate version, which comes to be widely accepted, although a few expressions of the earlier extreme manner still make an appearance. Finally, everyone falls in with a thoroughly digested version of the moderate style which, sporadically, is taken further so as to border once again on the extreme. In Paris the victory of the style that later came to be called 'Neo-Classicism' had been won by the early 1770s.

Let us now look at what was happening in Rome, because here we find somewhat similar developments in

taste taking place. There, too, much licence was taken in architecture and decoration in the early part of the century, and there too there was a reaction among those of academic inclination against the extravagances being perpetrated in many quarters. Two architects working in the ancient traditions were, however, making their mark in Rome in the 1740s. Nicolo Salvi and Luigi Vanvitelli became business partners in 1744 and were responsible for some buildings that made a strong and favourable impression on many of those who saw them (Salvi's Trevi Fountain was one of them). They advocated, rather as Cochin was to do, a return to a style based on the buildings of Antiquity, to which, however, they added borrowings from the Renaissance and High Baroque. The paths trodden in Rome and in Paris were not identical but they ran more or less parallel.

The young French students at their Academy in Rome in the 1740s saw not only the buildings of Antiquity but also those of later periods, including many which were new. Because it was their profession they were, moreover, alert to novel tendencies in the rendering of Classical idiom, but perhaps the strongest influence on them of all was the intermittent presence in Rome from 1740 of Giovanni Battista Piranesi, a Venetian designer and painter of views. A difficult character, dismissive of much that was going on around him, he nevertheless poured forth ideas and images (in his designs and numerous engravings) that fired the imagination of a great many of his contemporaries, including several of the French students (Pl. 327). His many views of the Holy City and its Classical monuments (the chief subject of Roman views at this period) have a monumentality that is quite unlike that of other contemporary topographical artists, while his early fantasies showing awesome prisons, first published as a suite about 1747 and re-published with two extra plates in 1760, were highly disturbing and unsettling; the sense that the individual blocks of masonry are of enormous weight conjured up an oppressive image that appealed to a surprising number of people.

A French student at the Academy in Rome who took heed of Piranesi's monumental manner and of the general tendency in Rome to return to the strict rules of the Classical tradition, was Louis-Joseph Le Lorrain. In 1749 he returned to Paris, where he was befriended by the Comte de Caylus. The energetic Caylus helped a number of young artists to get important jobs, and Le Lorrain was one of them. By 1754 Le Lorrain was sending a discriminating patron in Sweden some designs for mural decoration in a Classical style which embodied several novel motifs, also some furniture designs which one observer in Paris stated were like nothing anyone had seen before. Caylus played a part in securing Le Lorrain the Swedish commission, and was probably also involved in persuading a prominent diplomat, Ange-Laurent Lalive de Jully, to order some

Pl. 329 Writing-desk, filing-cabinet and ink-well made in Paris by René Dubois about 1765. Believed to have been made for Louis XV, who later gave it to Catherine the Great of Russia. This suite has many of the features of Lalive's furniture (Pl. 326) but is less ponderous and has much more delicate ornaments. It was perhaps designed by Charles De Wailly (see Pl. 345), and is, anyway, an interesting variant of the Lalive formula, carried out with great sensitivity.
Reproduced by permission of the Trustees of the Wallace Collection, London

furniture in the Antique taste from Le Lorrain. All three men were members of the Academy, where they could have met, but also belonged to the circle of artists, intellectuals and patrons of the Arts who met at the regular salons presided over by Madame Geoffrin, a lady who wielded considerable influence. Distinguished foreigners were invited to attend these gatherings, and introductions were made which led to important commissions, the most notable being the decoration and furnishing of a whole suite of rooms in the Palace at Warsaw in the mid-1760s, all in the most modern Parisian taste.

Le Lorrain's designs for furniture for Lalive were drawn in about 1756. Whether those he designed for Sweden were in a similar taste, we cannot be sure, but we know that Lalive's furniture was couched in an uncompromising and extreme form of Classicism because three of the pieces survive (Pl. 326). As our illustration shows, they were massive, almost brutally block-like. They were made of ebony, with gilt-bronze mounts by the celebrated bronze-caster Philippe Caffieri (we are not sure who executed the woodwork). Several commentators of the time saw the likeness of this furniture to that of André-Charles Boulle, the most illustrious of all Louis XIV's cabinetmakers (Pl. 257) but they possessed features that did not figure in Boulle's repertoire – heavy garlands ending in what resemble gigantic catkin-like tails which often thread their way through apertures in friezes, bold Vitruvian scrolls and key-frets, and massive pilasters with plain fluting that flank large areas of ebony enlivened only by a thin stringing of inlaid brass.

Lalive was exceptional at the time in opening his house and art-collection to the interested. Thus, this curious new suite of furniture soon became widely known, and, judging by several contemporary illustrations that show furniture of similar character, a certain number of imitations must have been made. Many people, on the other hand, were put off by the uncompromising nature of Lalive's pieces. It did, however, show the way, quite unmistakably, for those who wished to break with Rococo and re-adopt Classical formality, with its vast repertoire of forms and ornament. The Lalive style, if we may call it that, was promulgated by a large body of engraved designs by an architect of no great talent named Jean-François de Neufforge, the earliest of which probably date from early 1756, which was at about the time Lalive's furniture was being made. At that very time Le Lorrain and Neufforge were working together on a project set up by Caylus describing ancient Greek monuments, so will have had ample opportunity for comparing notes. Neufforge's rather uncouth and monotonous designs were enormously influential in the provinces and abroad. More pleasing, but equally chunky, were the designs published by Jean-Charles Delafosse in 1767, although they must have been drawn rather earlier (Pl. 332). The Lalive manner was carried on into the 1770s in goldsmith's work, often

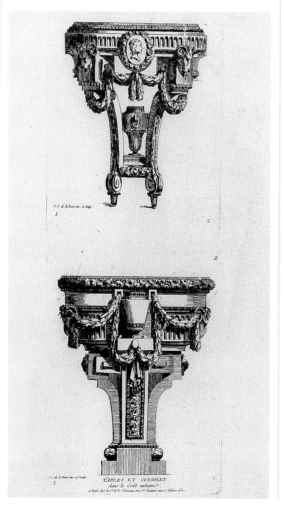

PI. 330 Mural decoration with a bed-niche by François-Dominique Barreau de Chefdeville, who executed several designs for the official residence of the Intendant at Bordeaux, between 1760 and 1765. The similarity in style of this composition with that of Lalive's *cartonnier* (Pl. 326) will be apparent. The bed, placed sideways in the niche, already has many characteristics of Neo-Classical and *Empire* beds around 1800. Barreau had been a pupil at the French Academy in Rome in the 1750s. He designed the room at a new house into which Lalive de Jully moved in 1762, where Le Lorrain's desk and *cartonnier* were to stand.
Archives Nationales (N/III Gironde 37 [pce 36])

PI. 331 Small silver candlestick by the famous Parisian goldsmith François-Thomas Germain (son of the even more celebrated Thomas Germain; see PI. 302); 1762. This piece, in the advanced monumental style, has an elegance springing from this goldsmith's great skill and its small size. One of a pair, it may have belonged to Madame de Pompadour.
Musée Nissim de Camondo, Paris

PI. 332 Designs for console-tables by Jean-Charles Delafosse published in 1771 but drawn earlier, possibly by 1767. They are described as being 'in the Antique taste'.
Victoria and Albert Museum, London (Mus. no. E. 551–1907)

Pl. 333 Mustard-pot of silver with blue glass liner, made in Paris in 1773–4 by a not especially well-known goldsmith who has, however, produced an object of great charm, even though the forms he has used are very much in the Le Lorrain taste. *Victoria and Albert Museum, London (Mus. no. M.173–1914)*

Pl. 334 Engraving after a gouache by P.-A. Baudouin of 1765 showing a bedchamber in a Classical taste that is advanced for its time; the night-table is still in the Rococo taste. This is one of the very first French illustrations of a chair with a medallion back and straight legs standing in a contemporary interior. Baudouin's brother-in-law François Boucher the Younger, who designed furniture in the Neo-Classical manner, may have inclined his taste towards this style.

with happy result, because the smaller scale and light-coloured material reduced the style's ponderous character considerably (Pl. 333).

Most people in Paris were, however, disinclined to have their furniture and other decorative objects couched in the extreme Lalive manner. They therefore at first retained familiar Louis XV forms and added some Classical motifs here and there.

Some points now need to be made about various factors affecting our story that had their origins in Rome in the 1750s and 1760s. A building of enormous influence was the Villa Albani, built to the directions of Cardinal Alessandro Albani, one of the greatest patrons of the 18th century and a celebrated collector of antiquities. The villa was begun in 1746 and work continued through the 1750s. It was an exceptional building with several novel features, but its main interest lay in its exemplary refinement, and its rural setting; it was seen as a modern evocation of an ancient Classical Roman villa – an enormously appealing notion to people at the time.

It is possible that Piranesi had a hand in some of the decoration at the Villa Albani; during the 1760s he was anyway certainly responsible for the decoration of several palaces for his fellow Venetians, the Rezzonico family. Pope Clement XIII (a Rezzonico) had Piranesi design schemes for his own country retreat, Castel Gandolfo, while Cardinal Giambattista Rezzonico had him do much work at the Quirinale, and the Senator Abbondio Rezzonico likewise employed Piranesi in his town palace on the Campidoglio, the very centre of ancient Rome. Piranesi's publication of 1769, *Diverse maniere…*, in which he illustrated some of the items he had designed (Pl. 338), summed up this period of interior decoration. As the book had parallel texts in Italian, French and English, it was internationally influential although this was more often apparent much later – at the end of the century and into the early 19th century. The lion-headed sway-backed figures with paw-like feet (monopodia) shown in our illustration were to become a stock motif of the Empire and Regency styles, as we shall see (Pl. 356). Many of the plates for Piranesi's book, incidentally, were ready by the end of 1767 and it is interesting to note that several of the French students at their Academy in Rome assisted with the decoration of the Rezzonico palaces and must have carried home with them closely observed impressions of their furnishings.

The 1750s also saw the foundation in Naples of the Accademia Ercolanese, which had the task of publishing the finds of the excavations at Herculaneum that were, however, abandoned in 1765 in favour of those at Pompeii. The Academy's publications came slowly – far too slowly to help those seeking to establish a new Classical manner in the third quarter of the century; the latter achieved their aims by other means. There were, for example, many other excavations taking place in Italy

d'*Antiquités...* of the Comte de Caylus's collection of Egyptian, Etruscan, Greek and Gaulish objects which came out in seven volumes in Paris between 1752 and 1767, and Sir William Hamilton's luxurious four-volume publication (paid for by himself) of his first collection of 'Etruscan, Greek and Roman Antiquities' (subsequently sold to the British Museum), which appeared in Naples in 1766–7 with a text by the French antiquarian Pierre-François D'Hancarville and splendid coloured illustrations. Both works were immensely influential, the latter especially because its illustrations in colour soon inspired artists to devise a new sub-style of Neo-Classicism, in the 'Etruscan manner' with a distinctive colour-palette based on that of Greek red-figure ceramics. Indeed, Hamilton stated that he hoped his publication would be of help to designers working with the decorative arts; the chief result of this came to be seen in the pottery of Josiah Wedgwood (see Chapter 15).

We can now resume our study of what was being done in Paris. Having seen something of the boldly outright modernism of Lalive's severe furniture and its derivatives, we can now look at the more cautious approach adopted by most people. Rectangular blocks were all very well for the Classical purist but can offend the eye if unadorned; and, in a room, they can hinder circulation. Rounded forms tend to be more attractive and easier to live with. The architectural pundit J.-F. Blondel advocated a golden mean, a compromise, and suggested that contrasting elements should be combined. So one can have curvaceous sofas amid Classical columns, or a commode with an angular body can have curving legs and floral marquetry. The secretaire in Pl. 340, made in Paris between 1763 and 1767, has such a rectilinear form but its marquetry decoration and the gilt-bronze mounts were added in order to soften the otherwise severe effect. Similar devices were employed by architects to soften the geometric forms of their Classical buildings.

A number of Blondel's contemporaries were at the same time urging people who wished to be in the vanguard of fashion to emulate the taste of the days of Louis XIV. We saw how Lalive's furniture was black, of ebony, and massive, somewhat like that of Boulle (see p. 154 and Pl. 326) but not like it in technique (i.e. not veneered with tortoiseshell and brass marquetry, for instance), but a number of Parisian cabinetmakers now started to produce furniture in the boullework technique to meet the new demand. Some of Boulle's sons, and Etienne Levasseur, who had been trained in the workshop of one of these sons, were in the forefront of this development. Indeed, there was no break in the practice of producing boullework after their father's death because such work was always needing to be repaired, so the craftsmen kept their hand in right on into the time when it was again required for making *new* furniture 'in the Boulle manner'. The practice

Pl. 335 Chair by the distinguished Parisian chair-maker Louis Delanois, about 1770–71 and possibly made for the Pavillon de Louveciennes, the *maison de plaisance* built by Louis XV for his new mistress, Madame du Barry. Delanois was among the very first chair-makers to adopt the 'Louis XVI style', which this form of chair unmistakably epitomizes. In this photograph it still sports its original embroidered silk covers (now in a poor state of repair), which are extremely rare survivals.
Courtesy of Sotheby's Inc., New York

Pl. 336 Wax model of a chair in a particularly rich version of the fully developed Louis XVI taste, designed by Jacques Gondoin, a distinguished designer to the Crown, about 1780. The model was made to show to a client, and has alternative arm treatments and no less than six forms of leg from which to choose. The elaborate drapery greatly changes the silhouette of this chair; such textile embellishment was not so uncommon at the time for expensive chairs to go in rich surroundings.
Private collection, Paris

from the middle of the century onwards, many of them in Rome and its vicinity; some of the finds were published (enough to assist those wanting illustrations of Classical motifs) while newly founded museums and collections housed many of the discoveries, and could be visited by those who could travel. Of this extensive literature, two publications must be mentioned – the *Recueil*

Pl. 337 A jewel-cabinet made for the Comtesse de Provence by J.-H. Riesener, the royal cabinetmaker, in 1785. The plain surfaces of the mahogany carcass are decorated with gilt-bronze mounts of the utmost refinement. The distinguished designer Dugourc may have provided the drawings for this exceptionally fine piece of furniture, but the initial concept may have been Belanger's. The cabinet has been in the royal collection since 1825.
The Royal Collection, Buckingham Palace

Pl. 338 Plate from Piranesi's *Diverse maniere...* of 1769 which had the English title of *Divers manners of ornamenting chimneys and all other parts of houses taken from the Egyptian, Tuscan and Grecian architecture*. The fireplace-surround shown here has a mixture of all three styles. The book contained illustrations of objects designed by Piranesi for members of the Rezzonico family, but also some views of mural decoration in a fashionable Roman coffee-house couched entirely in the Egyptian taste, which inspired many imitations during the rest of the century and into the next (e.g. Pl. 347).

blossomed in the later part of the century and continued far into the next (see Pls. 402 and 416).

Extensive passages of repeated ornament characterize Classical decoration; designers have always been adjured not to deviate far from the traditional forms when they work in this style. Consequently, when Neo-Classicism restricted inventiveness, designers sought new areas in which to demonstrate their ingenuity. One such was the ornamental vase and during the early phases of Neo-Classicism numerous suites of vases were published (Pl. 328). Introducing Classical vases in a design for mural decoration or a building could help to reduce the severity of the composition in many cases.

The seal of royal approval on the new Classicizing tendency was set by the King, Louis XV, when he built a small pavilion at Versailles for his mistress Madame de Pompadour – by no means the first building he had given her but one that was of considerable significance in the history of taste. It was conceived in 1762 by the Royal Architect-in-Chief, Ange-Jacques Gabriel, who was fairly conservative but was of course fully steeped in the Classical tradition. Although he modified the plans slightly before building began, it was nevertheless one of the very first domestic buildings to be couched in a decisively Classical manner in the middle of the century. The Petit Trianon had no Baroque features, and Rococo was totally absent. Standing, as it did, in the park at Versailles, it was seen by many people and many were the buildings it inspired. The interior, decorated after 1767, was even more Neo-Classical in style. All the major rooms are rectangular; there are no rounded corners and only one ceiling is coved. It may well be, incidentally, that Gabriel's design of the Trianon was to some extent influenced by English Neo-Palladian architecture; somewhat similar buildings had been erected in Britain 25 years earlier (p. 174).

The Petit Trianon was completed at the end of the 1760s, by which time Madame de Pompadour was dead

Pl. 339 Design by Bélanger for a jewel-cabinet (now lost) made for Louis XV to give to his grand-daughter-in-law, Marie Antoinette, to hold her trousseau on her marriage in 1770. As she was to be the Dauphin's wife, confronted crowned dolphins adorn the top. The arms of France and of Austria flank the central medallion. Profile portraits of the Dauphin and his wife by the famous sculptor Houdon, cast in bronze and chased by Gouthière, were to grace the apron. The whole piece was apparently covered in red velvet embroidered in relief with gold thread. Two side cabinets may have accompanied this piece. A drawing for one is in Sir John Soane's Museum, London.

Louis XV died in 1774 and was succeeded by his grandson, Two of Louis XVI's brothers became lavish patrons of the Arts, as did the new Queen, Marie Antoinette. Richard Mique was the Queen's architect. The Comte de Provence employed the architect Jean-François Chalgrin, who favoured a rather pared-down version of the current style, while the Comte d'Artois had the more famous François-Joseph Belanger as his architect. The latter had entered the Academy of Architecture in 1764 under the protection of the Comte de Caylus. He never went to Rome but he visited England in 1766, as did Gondoin at about the same time. In 1767 he became Designer to the Menus-Plaisirs (that seminal organization) and Inspector in 1777. Belanger was a key-figure, along with Gondoin, in the development of the Louis XVI style, and the Pavillon de Bagatelle that he built for Artois was greatly admired.

All three patrons, with their architects (Mique, Chalgrin, Belanger) were responsible for creating highy intimate, small apartments where informality and great comfort reigned. Because of France's disastrous

and her place had been taken by Madame du Barry, who thus became its first occupant. For her also was built, in 1771, the Pavillon de Louveciennes where everything was in the most up-to-date form of Classicism, exquisite in every detail. Leading Parisian craftsmen provided the furnishings (Pl. 335) and the building represented, now fully established, the triumph of Neo-Classicism in Paris, which flourished until the Revolution at the end of the 1780s. Behind the scenes in the design process may have been a man who had studied in Rome (where he had met Piranesi) and subsequently visited England and Holland before returning to Paris in 1766. Jacques Gondoin was appointed Designer of Royal Furnishings in 1769 and seems to have played an important role in the formation of the Louis XVI style, that graceful and delicate version of French Neo-Classicism which reigned in the 1770s and 1780s. An example of his work is to be seen in Pl. 336. Far too little is at present known about this interesting man, but it seems inconceivable that he was not involved at Louveciennes.

Pl. 340 Upright secretaire from the celebrated workshop of Jean-François Oeben, an exceptionally skilful German cabinetmaker (one of many) who came to Paris in about 1740 and was given a royal appointment and workshops at the Gobelins manufactory in 1754. This model of desk must have been designed before he died in January 1763; it bears his stamped mark although it was probably made between 1763 and 1767 when J.H. Riesener worked as foreman under Oeben's widow. When Riesener married her and formally took over directorship of the firm he used his own mark and several secretaires of this type bear his stamp. It is an example of an essentially new class of furniture where a lockable writing-leaf, hinged at the bottom, falls forward to form a writing-surface, with pigeon-holes, etc., tucked away behind the leaf when it is closed. There was a double-doored cupboard below, with shelves and (usually) a safe.
The Earl of Rosebery's Collection

financial state at the time, the rooms' smallness was presented as an economy but, so luxurious and costly were the refined furnishings and decorations of these small spaces, that they were in fact nothing of the sort. Be that as it may, many of the manifestations of this phase of French decorative art, created with spontaneity and a very loose adherence to the Classical tenets, are of a refinement that has scarcely ever been equalled, and the rest of Europe again marvelled at what France could produce in the way of superb luxury goods. Many commissions were placed with Parisian purveyors by foreign sovereigns and other patrons, even though such items were unbelievably expensive. The design for a Sèvres porcelain service for Catherine II of Russia is shown in Pl. 344; the cost of the order, which included tea and dinner-services, an elaborate centrepiece, and ornamental vases, came to no less than 245,168 livres, a gigantic sum. However excellent the design and costly the materials, none of these objects would have been as exquisite as they were had it not been for the amazingly skilful workforce that carried out the intentions of their designers. Most of the workforce was French, but a surprising number were of foreign extraction. The most striking example of this phenomenon is the number of German cabinetmakers in France: Oeben was German; he was eventually succeeded as royal cabinetmaker by Riesener, also from Germany, as were Carlin, Weisweiler, Schwerdfeger, Molitor, Evald – all men of the very first rank. Most of them came from the Rhine Valley area, which extends into the Low Countries, whence came Van Risenburgh and Van der Cruse.

It is difficult to exemplify Belanger's taste with a single illustration, because he was so constantly inventive and remained so throughout his long career, but Pl. 339 shows a very important commission that he fulfilled for the King in 1770, a jewel-cabinet for Marie Antoinette, and Belanger has here designed a sumptuous piece of furniture in an ultra-modern taste for the time. It should be contrasted with the jewel-cabinet made for the Comtesse de Provence fifteen years later, which is one of the very finest pieces of French furniture of the period (Pl. 337). While the body of Marie Antoinette's cabinet was faced with richly embroidered crimson velvet (surrounded by gilt-bronze mounts by Gouthière), the body of the Comtesse's cabinet is of mahogany, a wood that does not lend itself to fussy decoration, and it will be seen that the gilt-bronze mounts have been placed on the plain wood with great discrimination, an elegant symmetrical ornament (based on the old grotesque formula) occupying the centre of the main panel while the other embellishments are confined to the edges, thus enframing the largely bare mahogany. It has recently been suggested that Jean-Demosthène Durgourc provided the drawings for the cabinet. He was certainly capable of doing so, as he was a highly distinguished designer who, with his brother-in-law

Pl. 341 Mural decoration with grotesques in the Duc d'Aumont's house designed by P.-A. Pâris, an architect who had made a careful study of the *Logge* of Raphael in Rome before returning to Paris; executed in 1775–6. Some of the panelling is preserved in the Johnson Gallery, Middleburg, Vermont. *Bibliothèque Municipale, Besançon*

Pl. 342 Drawing by Clérisseau executed in Italy before 1767 when he left the country, showing grotesque ornament in the Raphaelesque manner flanked by a narrow panel of *rinceaux* which would have been repeated on the right of the main panel. Included in an album of drawings presented by the artist to Catherine II of Russia. Of the four framed plaques in the main panel, that at the top takes the form of a Greek shield called a 'pelta' while that at the bottom, an 'oval-with-points', became popular in the last two decades of the century. *The Hermitage Museum, St Petersburg*

Pl. 343 Drawing of a small writing-table set with Sèvres porcelain plaques, probably to be made by the distinguished cabinetmaker Martin Carlin to the orders of the Parisian *marchand-mercier* Dominique Daguerre in 1782. The drawing, with several others, may have been shown to the Duke and Duchess of Sachsen-Teschen (she was Marie- Antoinette's sister), who were Governors of the Austrian (formerly Spanish) Netherlands, and resident in Brussels.
Metropolitan Museum of Art, New York; Gift of Raphael Esmerian, 1959 (Mus. no. 59.611.6)

Pl. 344 Three rejected designs for Sèvres porcelain plates intended to fulfil a huge order placed by Catherine II of Russia in 1776–7. All the motifs are of Classical origin and were to be executed in ceramic enamel colours. In the compartments are simulations of antique cameos.
Manufacture Nationale de Sèvres Archives, Sèvres

Belanger, must be counted among the most influential innovating artists of this period. But as Dugourc often assisted Bélanger by working up his designs into finely detailed finished drawings, it is possible that it was Belanger himself who designed this superb object.

A handsome commode by Adam Weisweiler in the Metropolitan Museum, New York (not illustrated here), is faced with panels of Japanese lacquer. It dates from the 1780s. As with the Comtesse de Provence's cabinet, the bronzes are confined to the edges, leaving the panels on the front face free. This time they are not of mahogany but of an especially fine Japanese lacquer cut from imported screens or cabinets and disposed on their new backgrounds with a very sure eye. Commodes had by this time long been a principal item of furniture in the decoration of splendid rooms (commonly standing beneath an associated pier-glass), and the front face provided a conspicuous space for imposing decoration. Commodes were in fact largely for show. Another material that could be framed by bronzes applied to a wooden carcass was porcelain from the royal manufactory at Sèvres. Special plaques were produced for this purpose and such combinations of material were much in favour from the mid-1760s onwards (Pl. 343). Often set into small pieces of very delicate furniture, which were best suited to use by women in their boudoir and other small rooms, such items were mostly sold by specialist dealers in expensive luxury wares for the fashionable market.

Pl. 345 Design for a wall-panel in the private box at the Comédie Française that was decorated for the opera singer Mademoiselle Contat, who created the role of Suzanne in Beaumarchais's (and later Mozart's) *Le Mariage de Figaro* and was the mistress of the Comte d'Artois, one of Louis XVI's brothers (see p. 158). Painted by Charles de Wailly, 1783–5.
Musée des Arts Décoratifs, Paris

Pl. 346 Panel of wallpaper produced in Paris at the celebrated Réveillon wallpaper manufactory; about 1790. Such papers could be assembled vertically with the motifs in various combinations. The patterns thus produced still refer back to the grotesque formula. The colours here are delightful.
Musée du Papier Peints, Rixheim (Mus. no. 985 pp. 1–3)

The business of these *marchands-merciers* had to be backed by extremely large amounts of capital, since the outlay in having the knick-knacks in which they traded made was enormous and could involve co-ordinating the work of several different kinds of skilled craftsmen. As they had their fingers on the fashionable pulse, they felt able to commission items that would find favour among a fashionable clientele and to some extent, therefore, they also guided fashion. The *marchands-merciers* accepted and carried out commissions for luxurious furnishings but also produced stock for their own glamorous shops, which then attracted the casual buyer.

We must now turn again to Rome to look for a moment at the legacy from Raphael's decoration in the

Pl. 347 Drawing of wall decoration in the Villa Borghese in Rome (with alternative treatments on the two halves), inspired by designs published by Piranesi in 1769. This Egyptian Room was designed by the architect Antonio Asprucci about 1778 and was widely admired at the end of the century.
The Getty Research Institute, Resource Collections, Santa Monica

Logge and in the *Loggetta* at the Vatican in 1516–19 (see Chapter 2). Interest in the Raphael originals revived in the 1740s in Rome and Paris, and was given further impetus when the Parisian publisher Jombert included several engravings of the *Logge* decorations in a compendium of 'out of date' designs which he published in 1765. More important was the publication in Rome by G. B. Volpato of the entire decorative scheme of the *Logge* (previous publications had only reproduced parts of it) after drawings by the scholarly architect Pietro Camporesi which had an enormous influence on European designers, who now once again wanted to produce Raphaelesque grotesque-patterns. In the meantime, of course, the originals were still to be seen at the Vatican, and many interested artists were perfectly familiar with them. The British architect James 'Athenian' Stuart, who seems to have spent some years in Rome in the 1740s acting as a guide to the ancient monuments, returned to England and in 1759 decorated the Painted Room at Spencer House, in London, with remarkably faithful painted renderings of the *Logge* decorations, complete with spiralling *rinceaux* on the pilasters flanking panels of grotesques which are weaving their way round plaquettes and roundels in symmetrical patterns (the room survives; see Pl. 374). Stuart's designs do not seem to have inspired many direct imitations, although the notion of painting grotesques on walls was taken up eagerly by other leading British architects. Several Italian decorative painters were brought over to England to execute such embellishment (see Pls. 376, 377 and 380).

Infinitely more fruitful, on the other hand, was the role played by Charles-Louis Clérisseau, who was in Italy from 1749 until 1767. He spent about four years at the French Academy in Rome, during which time he became close friends with Piranesi, who lived nearby. Clérisseau worked as a drawing-master and as a painter of views of the ancient monuments (including fantasy scenes based on an assemblage of actual buildings that do not in fact stand together). He clearly was very familiar with Raphaelesque grotesque ornament as well as with genuine Antique ornament and many studies of such decoration survive from his hand – a large album having been presented to Catherine II of Russia, in which is to be found the drawing reproduced here as Pl. 342. It shows a scheme of mural decoration drawn by Clérisseau in Italy some time before he left that country in 1767, which has all the hallmarks of a mural scheme by Raphael and his assistants – the spiralling *rinceaux* (but with only single, not the paired, stems of the James Stuart versions) flanking a panel of grotesques that incorporate framed plaquettes of circular, rectangular and fanciful forms. It was this formula which was now, from the 1770s onwards, taken up in Paris and elsewhere by a host of architects and artists. As Clérisseau himself wrote in an introductory note to the Russian album, grotesques 'are an inexhaustible source for decorating in a beautiful manner the interiors… of modern buildings'. In mural decoration and the like, grotesques in fact took on the role previously played by Rococo scrollwork.

He came back to Paris in 1768, but then went and worked in England for a couple of years before finally returning to Paris in the early 1770s. There he designed the decoration of a salon in a house occupied for a while by the rich tax-farmer Laurent Grimod de la Reynière, which had grotesque panelling and *rinceaux* pilasters that were probably executed about 1774. Soon after, the architect Pierre-Adrian Pâris decorated a dining room in the house of the influential Duc d'Aumont with grotesques (1775–6; Pl. 341). Pâris (an architect of some importance whose name is not all that well known) had studied the Raphael decorations in Rome. In 1777, Belanger was decorating panels at Bagatelle (the Comte d'Artois's *pavillon* outside Paris) with grotesques in the Clérisseau manner, a formula he may already have tried out in 1769 when Clérisseau had advised on a garden pavilion for the Comte de Lauraguais. Clérisseau urged Belanger to bring back from Rome the young sculptor Nicolas Lhuillier, who brought with him a copy of Piranesi's then new book, *Diverse maniere…* of 1769 (see above, p. 155), which was a revelation to Belanger. But, even more important, he seems to have established firmly, with this work for Lauraguais, the combination of painting and sculpture (in the form of plaster reliefs) in the creation of (grotesque?) ornament on Parisian walls and Belanger himself designed some of the chief advanced examples of the genre in the 1770s and 1780s.

A motif that made its re-appearance at this stage was the velarium, a representation of an awning of the kind suspended in the open air above amphitheatres, garden-sites for banquets and other festivities in Classical times. Pl. 345 shows a semicircular velarium, and a sketchily rendered circular one is in Pl. 346. Such fan-like ornaments were quite often used, tucked into right-angled corners. The motif derives from Antique frescoes and is to be seen in grotesque decoration executed under Raphael's direction at the Vatican and elsewhere.

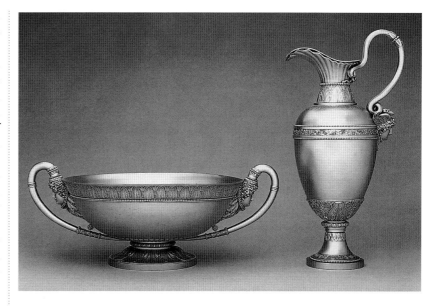

Pl. 348 Ewer and basin of silver made by Henri Auguste, celebrated Parisian goldsmith, in 1789–90. The elegant 'Grecian' design is based on patterns devised by Jean-Guillaume Moitte between 1784 and 1789. Note how ornament is confined to bands and focal points, leaving large areas of plain silver undecorated but, in this case, with a matt surface. Acquired in 1802 in Paris by William Beckford.
The Arthur and Rosalinde Gilbert Silver Collection

Pl. 349 A particularly graceful specimen of the Klismos-type chair, modelled on Greek illustrations on vases, made in Copenhagen about 1800 to the designs of Nicolai Abildgaard, at this time Director of the Danish Royal Academy, then a firm bastion of Neo-Classicism. Abildgaard had spent some years in Rome in the 1770s and was familiar with the main developments in Classical archaeology of his time.
Kunstindustrimuseet, Copenhagen

Pl. 350 Table of the late 1780s, already displaying some of the severity of form that was to become so characteristic of *Empire* furniture after 1800. Probably by the leading Parisian cabinet-maker Adam Weisweiler, with mounts of great refinement, presumably the work of Pierre Gouthière. Veneered with pearwood and maple.
Reproduced by permission of the Trustees of the Wallace Collection, London

Grotesque patterns remained fashionable and very popular until well into the 19th century. A characteristic of many grotesque panels of this phase in the formula's history is the 'oval-with-points' which is shown in Pl. 346 but is also present in the drawing by Clérisseau with which we opened this part of our story (Pl. 342).

It should be added that, in France at this time, grotesques were always called 'arabesques' and have been called that since then. As these patterns have no Arabic features, it seems unnecessary to continue to use the confusing French term for our purposes here. The reader should, however, bear this in mind when reading French texts on the subject.

Rinceaux could of course be used as a horizontal frieze. Such versatility is a most useful quality in an

Pl. 351 Ink and watercolour design by Dugourc, probably of about 1790, no doubt connected with the work he was doing for the Spanish Crown. Although following the Raphaelesque tradition, it will be noted that the outer panels are decorated with Egyptian motifs.
Rijksprentenkabinet, Rijksmuseum, Amsterdam

Pl. 352 Silk design (*mise-en-carte* on squared paper with full-sized pattern ready for setting up on the loom) of about 1770 by the celebrated Lyonnais designer Philippe de Lasalle, whose exceptional skill was widely recognized at the time and won him, and the silk-weaving establishment for which he worked, huge orders not only from the French Court and aristocracy (until the Revolution), but also from foreign monarchs and their courtiers.
Musée des Tissus, Lyons

ornamental pattern (Pls. 329 and 350). Pl. 344 shows one of two multiple designs for some especially grand Sèvres plates of 1776–7 in which various motifs derived from grotesque patterns have been employed, as have sphinxes (popular at this period and, again, in a less delicate form, after 1800; see Pl. 353, and a form of *rinceau*, popular around 1800, consisting of oval rosettes set at an angle running in one direction (see Pl. 391).

Rinceaux and grotesques were of course much used in their homeland, Italy, at this period where, after all, Raphael's versions, as well as many 16th- and 17th-century derivatives were still to be seen, and several publications of the *Logge* decorations first saw the light of day. That the forms received approbation in the highest quarters is demonstrated by the fact that in the 1780s Pope Pius VI completed the building of the vast Museo Pio-Clementino in the Vatican to house the papal antiquities. The new museum was decorated with grotesque mural panels closely imitating those of Raphael nearby, and had a powerful influence on young architects visiting Rome at the end of the century, notably Percier and Fontaine, whose contribution to the history of design is discussed below (p. 166).

Very like some of the mural decorations in the Museo Pio-Clementino, in its composition and general style, is a fine design by Dugourc, which probably dates from about 1790 (Pl. 351) and may have been connected with the extensive work this extremely talented French architect carried out over several decades for the Spanish court. It is of additional interest because it incorporates Egyptian motifs (in the flanking pilasters), a genre of which he had been a proponent in the 1780s and which he continued to employ into the next century. Piranesi had included Egyptian compositions in his *Diverse maniere…* of 1769 and these had never been totally absent since then; but they began to come to the fore in the 1790s, partly due to Dugourc's championing, but also because an Egyptian room had been created in the Villa Borghese in Rome in about 1778, which attracted a lot of attention at the time (Pl. 347). Completed in 1782, it was designed by Antonio Asprucci and painted by T. Conca, who to some extent based his compositions on those in Piranesi's book showing how he had decorated the English Café at the foot of the Spanish Steps in Rome in the 1760s.

Before moving on to consider the last phase of Neo-Classicism, a word should just be said about naturalistic floral decoration, an important part of the Louis XVI style that provided some of the 'contrasts' to Classical features advocated by Blondel (see p. 156). Flowers were to be seen everywhere, and a whole school of flower painters thrived as a result, in the silk-weaving business, in painted mural decoration, carving, embroidery and in subsidiary decoration of every kind.

Whether the so-called *Empire* style should be regarded as a continuation of that of Louis XVI is

Pl. 353 Massive centre-table in the Royal Palace at Madrid, made in Paris in the first years of the 19th century to support a heavy slab made in Spain that is composed of 410 samples of marble and hardstones, mostly of Spanish origin. The six superb sphinxes must be by Pierre Thomire and the overall design was presumably by Dugourc, who was then living in Madrid.
Royal Palace, Madrid

debatable. Many of those who were important in our story – designers as well as skilled craftsmen – worked on under Napoleon, but some new stars were by then to be seen in the artistic firmament. The term *Empire* is used to describe the style in favour during the whole of the Emperor Napoleon's rule, from 1799 (although he only took that title in 1804) until his final defeat in 1815. One might therefore think that 'the Napoleon style' would be a more apt title for it. Today the term *Empire* tends to be used to cover the style favoured in France between 1795 and 1820.

Napoleon, highly successful at first on foreign battlefields, introducer of idealistic reforms that were widely popular at home, founder of France's excellent education system, believed that order should be coupled with strength: this led him to embrace the prevailing nostalgia for Classical Antiquity, and especially that of Imperial Rome. During the Napoleonic period forms tended to be severe, with harsh profiles and unashamedly bombastic ornament, all of which undeniably produced a sense of grandeur reflecting the dominating, dictatorial stance adopted by the regime. The style, however, had its lighter side, notably in furnishings intended for use

Pl. 354 An imposing piece of *Empire* furniture made between 1796 and 1803 (probably closer to the latter date) by the firm of Jacob Frères, which took over the running of the business of Georges Jacob on his retirement. Made entirely for display, it takes the form of a chimneypiece; it may have been intended to stand on the opposite side of a room facing a real chimneypiece of much the same shape. The splendid patinated bronze caryatids support a heavy frieze and marble slab, and the fine mounts are placed with great precision so as to leave exposed a large expanse of the striking amboyna-wood veneer, with which the carcass is faced.. The design must have been supplied by Napoleon's favourite architects, Percier and Fontaine.
Victoria and Albert Museum, London

165

work. David and Jacob certainly made such chairs, as did various craftsmen in England, Italy and Scandinavia. A particularly graceful Danish specimen of about 1800 is shown in Pl. 349. It was a form that was to influence English chairs of the Regency period more than French products, however.

A distinguished piece of *Empire* silver is the dressing-mirror given by Napoleon to his first wife, the Empress Joséphine, in 1805 (Pl. 355). Made by a leading goldsmith, J.-B.-C. Odiot, the beautiful figures supporting the large oval glass were probably modelled after drawings by Pierre-Paule Prud'hon, a painter who can be ranked with David and who provided designs for many of the most important pieces of decorative art during this period.

We must now introduce two men who made an indelible mark on the history of design, Charles Percier and Pierre-François-Léonard Fontaine. Young in the 1780s, they were to become Napoleon's favourite architects, and much of his life with Joséphine, as well as with his second wife Marie, and everything he was doing when in Paris during those fateful years, was lived amid surroundings devised by these brilliant decorators – for that is really what they were. They built very little (and what they did is anyway of no concern to us here) but they decorated and totally transformed the rooms in Napoleon's many residences (both the formal and the

by women, and managed sometimes to contrive elegance and a certain grace by using similar motifs treated with less severity. On the whole, however, *Empire* has a swaggering image very unlike that of the *ancien régime* – the time of Louis XVI.

Yet the roots of *Empire* are to be found in the style evolving in the 1780s in Paris. The famous painter Jacques-Louis David played a significant role in the development of *Empire* taste by including furnishings of advanced Classical form in his paintings depicting Classical stories – for example, his *Brutus with his Dead Sons* and his charming scene of Helen with Paris, both of about 1788. It seems that David had the important furniture-maker Georges Jacob produce actual pieces in such forms for use in his studio, based on his own designs, and it is evident that, even at this early date, David was well informed about the form of Roman furniture, so that what he depicted was 'archaeologically correct' to a remarkably high degree.

A form that fired the imagination of artists in several European countries at this time was that of the Greek *klismos* chair, which could be an object of great elegance, judging by depictions on Greek vases and metal-

Pl. 355 The Empress Joséphine's dressing-mirror, given to her by Napoleon. Made in 1804–5 by the Emperor's goldsmith, Martin-Guillaume Biennais, collaborating with J.-B.-C. Odiot, an equally renowned goldsmith. The supporting figures probably derive from drawings by Prud'hon.
Private collection

Pl. 356 Wash-stand of tripod form with Sèvres porcelain basin and jug. Made for the Empress Joséphine's villa on the edge of Paris about 1802. Of mahogany with gilt-bronze mounts, it sports a ewer and wash-basin of Sèvres porcelain decorated in the fashionable manner. The three large monopodia topped by small sphinxes may seem ridiculous, but the design has grace and cleverly allows the user to lift the jug out with relative ease.
Château de Malmaison, near Paris

very informal ones) as well as most of the chief houses in Paris at the time. Their influence was immense.

Percier and Fontaine's first truly important commission was to create a bedchamber for Madame Récamier, a celebrated beauty who presided over a fashionable salon. The task was given in 1798, seemingly to the architect Louis-Martin Berthault; but he acted here and on subsequent commissions as site-architect for Percier and Fontaine who provided the drawings; in effect, the ideas were theirs. No expense was spared and the room became one of the sights of Paris, accessible to all who were interested, even if they were unacquainted with the owner. Many visitors described the room, some with an accompanying sketch. The next important commission was to rebuild a country retreat that Napoleon had given to his wife Joséphine in 1799. Although they were not permitted, at this early stage in her relationship, entirely to rebuild Malmaison, what they created pleased Joséphine greatly, and set an example in its intimate charm that others could follow. With that, Percier and Fontaine were established as Napoleon's official court architects.

Their *Recueil des Decorations intérieures* contains a large number of illustrations of elaborately decorated rooms designed by them. Other architects and designers had occasionally published views of rooms – Daniel Marot and Thomas Sheraton, for example – but never had so many illustrations of fashionable interiors been assembled in a single volume. The illustrations are meticulously drawn, with great attention shown to

Pl. 357 Terracotta group by the French sculptor Joseph Chinard depicting the wife and son of a French general; about 1808. The day-bed on which she sits contemplating a portrait of her husband (who was probably away on campaign with one of Napoleon's armies) is in the most fashionable taste; the bed and her costume are meant to evoke an image of intimate family life in Imperial Rome. Height 56 cm (22¹/₁₆ in.) Length 70 cm (27⁹/₁₆ in.) Depth 35 cm (13³/₄ in.)
Collection of the J. Paul Getty Museum, Malibu, California

Pl. 358 Page from an anthology of Roman artefacts suitable for adapting, at the hands of imaginative designers, into contemporary furnishings. Drawn by J.-N.-L. Durand and published in a book based on his lectures given at the Ecole Polytechnique in Paris, 1802–5.
Victoria and Albert Museum, London (Mus. no. 65 GN)

Pl. 359 Drawing-table by Jacob-Desmalter of 1811 of particularly elegant form, with veneers of yew-wood burr, gilt-bronze mounts and blued steel legs.
Musée National du Château de Fontainebleau

Pl. 360 Coloured design by Percier of 1789 showing his style at its most chaste. The bed *à l'antique* has a single head-board supported by a sphinx; there are short posts at the foot-end. A *rinceaux* frieze runs along the base, which is supported on lion's-paw feet. The separate tester with curtains, supported by tall posts, stands on a dais in a niche. The whole composition is in shades of grey, with details in black, white and terracotta – an 'Etruscan' colour-scheme.
Private collection, Paris

detail (and now, at last, upholstery is included as a matter of course), and each scene is carefully described; whole sides of rooms are shown in elevation. The entirely linear method of drawing that they favoured, with no shading and concentrating on outlines, was in fashion at the time (it was claimed that one could measure objects from such drawings) and has a certain dry elegance. Presentation volumes with the engravings coloured and shaded by Percier himself, however, show how delightful their interiors could actually be (Pl. 360).

Percier was a brilliant draughtsman and had been taken on as a young man in the drawing-offices of two of the leading and most advanced designers of the day – first by P.-A. Pâris (see Pl. 341) and then by J.-F. Chalgrin, the Comte d'Artois's architect (see p. 158). He studied at the Academy under J.-D. Le Roy, the great authority on Classical Greek buildings and the author of an important book on the subject, which he revised and expanded in 1770. In 1786 Percier went to Rome where he met Fontaine; they became close friends and were inseparable ever after. In Rome they studied the usual monuments but with even closer attention, it would seem, than others were doing, and it is noteworthy that over two-thirds of the drawings they executed at this time concerned Renaissance buildings and ornaments,

not the Antique or, for that matter, the Baroque variants. They also paid much attention to the very recently finished Museo Pio-Clementino (see p. 165) where the colourful grotesque schemes painted on the walls by Simonetti and Camporesi made a strong impression on them. The result of their studies in Rome was a book published in 1798 (in Paris) on the palaces and houses of that city, paying especial attention to the Renaissance heritage but also to the new Museo with its colourful frescoes. A coloured version of the book, dated 1798 and dedicated to 'Madame Bonaparte' (i.e. Joséphine), now at Sir John Soane's Museum, includes a handsome coloured view of the impressive entrance to this new building, with its pair of gigantic Egyptian figures flanking the doorway and a hint of grotesque mural-painting beyond. What is more, the Roman book greatly extended the repertoire of Classical ornament available to designers – and an extremely pretty coloured representation of a panel of grotesque ornament (*arabesques*) said to be found in a private residence must have powerfully inspired those who managed to gain sight of a coloured-up copy of the book.

Like their book on Roman palaces, the *Recueil* came out in serial sections. The first appeared in 1801 with 36 plates and by 1805 the number had reached 54; all 72 had appeared by 1812. So welcome was this book to designers that a third edition appeared in Paris in 1827 and an Italian edition in Venice in 1843. In 1869 it was still being cited as an indispensible mine of information. Of course Percier's book (for the designs were his: Fontaine was the business brains of the partnership) had imitators both in France and abroad, and the style they promulgated spread across the whole of Europe and westernized North America. This dissemination was encouraged by the fact that Napoleon installed members of his family or closest entourage as heads of state and prominent citizens in many European capitals – in Rome, Milan, Florence, Naples, Amsterdam, Madrid, Kassel, Würzburg, Munich and Stockholm. What is more, journals were now beginning to appear that carried reports of developments in the furnishing of elegant houses, supplemented by illustrations, sometimes coloured. This was an international phenomenon; some of the earliest of these journals were published in Weimar (1787) and Leipzig, and a German publisher brought the practice to London. Pierre de la Messangère's *Meubles et Objets de Goût* was a very early Parisian manifestation of this brand of journalistic enterprise, published first in 1802 and appearing into the 1830s.

A character whose opinion on matters of taste was greatly respected during Napoleon's time was Dominique Vivant, Baron Denon, who occupied much the same role as the Comte de Caylus had done under Louis XV. Denon, who, as a young man, had been curator of Mme de Pompadour's collection of medals, later served as a diplomat, first at St Petersburg and then at Naples, where he amassed a distinguished collection of Greek vases that he later sold to Louis XVI (1788). He was protected by the painter J.-L David during the worst period of the Revolution, when his association with the monarchy placed him in considerable danger, but having survived the Revolutionary years, and being a man of great charm, he was soon frequenting Joséphine de Beauharnais's salon, where he met her future husband Napoleon Bonaparte. As an antiquary, he accompanied Napoleon on his successful campaign in Egypt, and recorded not only the battles but also the ancient temples and other monuments. These drawings were transmuted into a massive work with superb colour-plates that, at a stroke, greatly increased people's knowledge of Egyptian art (1802), and in consequence revived interest in France and elsewhere in Egyptian decoration. In 1802 Denon was appointed Director of the Parisian Mint, whence handsome medals were struck to his design recording Napoleon's achievements – which did much to spread the *Empire* style yet further. Vivant Denon was virtually Minister of Art under Napoleon and very little work of any importance on the artistic front was executed in Paris at that time without his approval.

The elegant little table shown in Pl. 359 was made in 1811 by the firm of Jacob, by this time under the direction of one of the two Jacob brothers who came to be known as Jacob-Desmalter. Its trumpet-shaped legs of blued steel contrast well with the reticent gilt-bronze mounts and the burred yew-wood veneer. The Jacob firm was still enormous; in 1807 it employed 370 workmen and its annual output was valued at some 700,000 francs. It had furniture to the value of 500,000 in its stockrooms and could handle very substantial enterprises. It collaborated with the foremost carvers, upholsterers, gilders and bronzeworkers, and could call upon the best designers – including Percier, Prud'hon and Denon – for drawings in connection with a special commission that was deemed to be beyond the capabilities of its own draughtsmen. The quality of its work was invariably of the highest standard. So important did the authorities consider the activities of the firm of Jacob to be, that they were permitted to export furniture from France to England at a time when the two countries were at war. Large sums of money were at stake.

Pl. 361 Section of a French wallpaper of the period 1815–20. This could be joined to pieces of the same pattern to form a frieze in the late *Empire* taste.

The course of Neo-Classicism, after the hiccup of the Le Lorrain-Lalive prelude and the early years of transition, ran from the manner of Gabriel around 1770 with its Corinthian columns and other rich decoration based on the style of the early Roman Empire, to the sobriety of the Republican period at the end of the century, with Doric and Tuscan columns much in evidence and ornaments in general pared down to the minimum; finally, it all ended in the grandiloquent taste of Napoleon, who adopted the full-blown style of late Imperial Rome, not because he liked it particularly, but in order to dominate. Neo-Classicism became tedious to most people and was eventually swamped by the rising tides of Romanticism. It survived merely as one of the many styles from which one could chose during the 19th century, and by no means the chief of them.

CHAPTER 15

LONDON, DUBLIN AND PHILADELPHIA

1720-1820

The three cities mentioned in this chapter-heading were the largest in the English-speaking imperium. Their location, respectively in England, Ireland and on the east coast of America, also neatly emphasises the vast geographical extent of this association of peoples whose roots mostly lay in a British culture that was, effectively, ruled from London. Whatever their political or religious affiliations, discriminating citizens in this enormous Diaspora looked to London for refined consumer goods and information about European fashions. That the Americans gained political independence in the 1770s did not greatly alter matters in this respect; the two nations continued to trade profitably with each other and American tastes long remained in tune with those of the British. To be sure, some American intellectuals enjoyed a heady period of flirtation with French ideas and taste at the end of the century, but the long-established and well-founded link with Britain was far stronger.

Although the distance across the Atlantic was great, it did not take much longer to send goods (and information) to Philadelphia (or Boston, her chief rival for supremacy as the first city in the Thirteen Colonies) than it took for them to reach cities in Britain, such as Norwich, Exeter or Edinburgh – because roads almost everywhere were so bad. So even by 1720 the citizens of Boston could have new London fashions in their shops within three or four months, and one doubts whether their counterparts in the chief provincial cities of England could do much better.

London had expanded enormously during the 17th century, and by 1800 its population bordered on the million mark; it was by far the largest city in Europe and had been so during much of the 18th century. As the capital of Britain it was a major focal point of communications, with the country's largest port at its heart. Seat of Government, the court, and of the unrivalled (by 1750) financial services that the City of London could offer, London also had a skilled workforce, often extremely specialized, whose production of consumer goods, many of them luxury wares, was of great importance to our present survey.

London was itself a major market, and its most refined and demanding customers pushed the producers of luxury wares to greater heights. With the rest of Britain and the largely captive market of the Americas (because of London-imposed trading restrictions), it will be seen that Britain's potential market was huge. Add to this Britain's old trading links in Europe – Portugal and Spain, the Baltic littoral, much of Middle Europe, and parts of the Eastern Mediterranean – and then the massive expansion of intercontinental trade

between London and the Americas and with Asia, and it will be understood how, during the 18th century, London came to enjoy a commanding position in a new global trading system. And influence followed trade, which , in the decorative arts, meant that British goods were widely imitated, sometimes with great sensitivity but sometimes in rather bizarre ways.

All of this of course had repercussions in many parts of the realm. Old industries such as the weaving of woollen and worsted materials in East Anglia took on a new lease of life, and many smaller provincial industries blossomed; some increased enormously – notably the Staffordshire potteries and metalworking in such Midland cities as Sheffield and Birmingham. Production methods were improved, specialization in the workforce was introduced; new forms of goods were devised and greater attention was paid to design. The finish of goods also improved, thus making them more attractive to the potential customer. All these improvements within the fast-expanding industries of Britain excited much interest, not merely amongst industrialists. Travellers, artists and others curious to see these new wonders visited industrial districts, and during the late 18th century the factories of Manchester, Birmingham, Coalbrookdale and Staffordshire were regarded as some of the greatest sights in the land. By 1800 or so, incidentally, even the new factory buildings, often embodying steel-frame construction and other novel features, were a source of considerable interest among architects.

One of the most striking examples of the new industrial thinking is provided by the Staffordshire potteries, which at the beginning of the century were mostly still producing fairly crude wares, in no way rivals to the products of the new porcelain factories of Germany and France. Yet, by the 1780s, Staffordshire had made Britain's single most important contribution to the history of ceramics – the development of creamware. This

Pl. 363 Case for an organ designed by William Kent, probably in the 1730s, showing his fully developed manner, which owes much to Roman decoration of the late Baroque period. Published in 1744 by his disciple John Vardy in a volume devoted to the work 'of Mr. Inigo Jones and Mr. William Kent'.
By courtesy of the Trustees of Sir John Soane's Museum, London

Pl. 364 Mahogany table from Langley Park, Norfolk, probably supplied in the early 1740s when the house was being furnished under the direction of the Norwich architect Matthew Brettingham. Brettingham was at the time working at nearby Holkham Hall, where he was paid for carving seat-furniture and picture-frames, but it seems unlikely that he did more than oversee that kind of work which, however, in the present instance, is of the highest quality.
Courtesy of Christie's Images, London

had a more or less white body under a clear lead glaze; it was indeed creamy white and, by this time, the ware itself had become so refined, and the simple forms in which it was produced so attractive, that creamware was welcomed into the dining-rooms of even the most discriminating people.

The pottery-owner Thomas Weildon was one of those who played an important part in the development of creamware in the middle of the century. In 1754 he was joined by the young Josiah Wedgwood, who carried out endless experiments over more than 20 years to discover how to refine the ware even further, how to achieve a clearer glaze that would not run, and (above all) how to achieve consistency in the materials being used. In 1765 he felt he had been sufficiently successful to offer a creamware tea service to Queen Charlotte, who graciously accepted it and allowed Wedgwood, by this time owner of his own pottery, to use the title of 'Potter to the Queen'. He soon re-named his product 'Queen's Ware'. As he later said, he always believed in aiming for the top; he was an astute businessman as well as a clever potter.

By the 1780s creamware was the chief product of the Staffordshire potteries, with Wedgwood's enterprise definitely in the lead (Pl. 391), although from the 1770s onwards creamware was also being manufactured successfully at Leeds. Enormous quantities were exported to Europe and America, and several rival factories were established abroad to produce imitations. While creamware was successful even among rich people who could afford porcelain, its great appeal was to middle-class markets at home and abroad. It was stylish, robust, had a pleasing finish and was affordable; it truly constituted 'value for money'.

The soundness of British products was what appealed most to middle-class Europeans. If you wanted to be grand and live in great luxury, surrounded by expensive gew-gaws, it was best to look to France. England, on the other hand, was the home of sturdy common sense (e.g. Pl. 368; see also Pl. 386). A fashion journal that first came out in Weimar in the 1780s explained to its readers that English furniture was solid and practical while French was less so, because it was 'more contrived and ostentatious'. It was also said that the backs of French chairs were weak and tended to break. The Weimar journal was widely read in Middle Europe and had a number of imitators, the most important of which was published in Leipzig. All these publications, without exception, reported with approval on English pattern-books and imported consumer goods.

However, the problem with British goods was that insufficient attention was paid to the aesthetic aspects of their design. For example, Britain developed flock wallpaper ahead of other nations and made good profits out of this trade until the French learned how to make it. The French then took advantage of the Seven Years' War

between France and Britain (1756–63, during which period British exports rarely entered France) to consolidate their own wallpaper industry and introduce British know-how, which they acquired by bringing over some workmen from England. By making duty payable on imported British papers, the French furthered their industry's position after the war, but they gained greatest advantage over the British by paying skilled and often independent designers handsomely for new patterns. Wedgwood was to do something similar when he engaged the sculptor John Flaxman to provide designs for Neo-Classical ornament on his pottery (Pl. 385) but this enlightened practice seems to have been a rather exceptional case, whereas in France it was quite common. The fate of English wallpaper also befell English printed cotton. Technically they were ahead of other nations by the middle of the century and were excellent in quality, but the level of design was generally poor, whereas French printed cottons achieved a worldwide reputation for their charm during the last quarter of the 18th century. The names of Réveillon and Jouy are still famed today; they are synonymous with fine wallpapers and fine printed cottons, which were both delightful and of good quality. An English manufacturer or an English village might have been remembered in this way if only more attention had been paid to the matter of truly appealing designs.

France and Britain were almost constantly at war during the 18th century. It was essentially a question of which nation should dominate the western world. The populace of each country no doubt had a loathing for its opponent, but the two nations were well matched and thinking people on both sides of the Channel had considerable respect for each other. Like the rest of Europe, the people of Britain were interested in French taste and fashions, and many cultivated Britons visited Paris often. The flood of British aristocrats crossing to Paris immediately after the end of the Seven Years War had ended in 1763 and their exclusion from all that Paris could offer had at last ceased was a particularly notable manifestation of this British interest; many were the purchases they made during these excursions. But there were likewise many people in France who were curious about English practices, not just in the field of politics and social organization, but also in English manufactures (as we have just noted), architecture and interior decoration. Curiously enough, it was not considered repugnant in some quarters in France to display an interest in what Englishmen had to offer. For example at the court of Versailles, even during the Seven Years War, the royal ballet performed a 'contre-danse [country dance] d'Anglais and d'Anglaises', while, soon after the war, English mahogany furniture was advertised for sale in Paris newspapers. By the 1770s 'anglomania' was widespread in Paris, its most noticeable expression probably being the presence of mahogany furniture in the English taste in many houses. It seems, also, that the work of Robert and James Adam (see p. 178) was sufficiently widely admired in France by 1766 (early in their career, be it noted) for a French publisher to propose bringing out a work on the antiquities of Rome dedicated to these two Scottish architects. This was some years before the Adams had begun to publish illustrations of their own *Works* (1773).

A number of French architects visited England during the 18th century and it is interesting that one of them, Belanger, who came over in 1766 and remained in England for a year, chose England instead of Rome (see p. 158). Gondoin was in England at about the same time, and Clérisseau worked in England for some years in the first half of the 1770s. There were others, but these three played a very significant role in the development of French taste during the Louis XVI period, as we saw in the previous chapter, and what they learned in England must have produced fruit when they were back in Paris. It may well also be the case that Ledoux, one of the greatest innovating architects of this period, paid a visit to England from 1763 to 1765. He never went to Rome, it seems, and some features of his subsequent architecture show signs of a knowledge of what had been going on in England during the 1750s and early 1760s.

And what had been going on? It was something rather peculiar. In the 1720s an influential group,

headed by the Earl of Burlington, adopted a form of Classicism that had been fashionable in Northern Italy in the 1560s. It was particularly the work of Palladio they admired (see p. 35), and his treatise on architecture (1570) became the bible of this 'Neo-Palladian' movement. Formidable sanction had been given to their selection of Palladio as their deity by the fact that England's first great post-Gothic architect, Inigo Jones,

Pl. 366 A 'chest-on-chest' of walnut made in Philadelphia between 1760 and 1780. The English origins of this design are obvious.
Courtesy of Israel Sack Inc., New York

active in the 1620s and 1630s, had followed the teachings of the same great Italian master. Nevertheless, it was very much a case of England going her own way, because the rest of Europe was at this point about to plunge itself into the delights of Rococo, with its dancing rhythms and not infrequent excesses. The new English Classicism, and there was no doubt that is what it was, appeared measured, serene, chunky, and sometimes a little chilly. A great many imitations of 16th-century Italian villas erected long before in the sun-baked countryside near Venice now made their appearance on rainswept English hillsides.

While Palladio had shown elevations and plans of buildings in his treatise, he had given no indication as to how he envisaged the rooms should be furnished – and we are still unclear as to how they originally looked. Fortunately, Burlington had employed a painter, William Kent, to help with the decoration of the houses in which he was interested. This was in 1719. In the early 1720s Kent painted a ceiling at Kensington Palace with grotesques, and was to paint something similar at Rousham in Oxfordshire about 1740. Neither ceiling had anything to do with Berainesque grotesques; they were a harking-back to 16th-century Roman models. Kent had spent ten years in Rome before Burlington brought him back and he will have missed much of the impact of the arrival in the London print-shops of Berain's engravings. An early assignment given to him was to edit a book for Burlington on the designs of Inigo Jones; this appeared in 1727 and gave further impetus to Neo-Palladianism at the very moment when Rococo was about to burst forth on the Continent. Kent subsequently turned more and more to designing interior decoration and soon adopted a decidedly heavy form of Classicism with bold Baroque overtones that was magnificent in the large (Pl. 362) and could have much charm when executed in small. He brought to the design of furniture a knowledge of the late 16th-century Italian style in that field, but more that of Florence (which he knew well) than of Venice (which he did not see) (see Pl. 363). It was when Kent was in Rome that Giovanni Giardini's designs for furniture were published (1714; see Pl. 224), and decoration like that shown in Pls. 211 and 221 was to be seen everywhere. So here once again we have Rome powerfully influencing decoration in countries far to the north – countries that were now beginning to play important roles on the world scene.

Pl. 362 shows Kent's proposals of 1725 for decoration of the saloon at Houghton for Britain's first Prime Minister, Sir Robert Walpole. The bold pediments over door-cases and the chimneypiece, the cushion mouldings of bay-leaves, the frequent use of festoons, and the chesty terminal figures are already characteristic of his manner, a more fully developed expression of which is shown in Pl. 363. The Kent style permeated English design during the second quarter of the 18th century;

the superb table shown in Pl. 364 characterizes it at one remove from Kent but with some features he used – the scallop-shell, key-fret and lion's paws. John Vardy, who had been Kent's pupil, served up the Kentian manner in a lighter version towards the middle of the century (Pl. 365). The robust cabinet-form of the organ to be seen in Pl. 368 is a late expression of the Kentian formula produced in the 1760s. It follows that adopted by English cabinetmakers for the bureau-bookcase, a form that came from Holland to England (p. 129) but was now perceived all over Europe as being characteristically English. Indeed, in many cities on the Continent, especially in Germany and Scandinavia, cabinetmakers liked to be able to call themselves 'English cabinetmakers', or at least to describe the furniture of this class that they imitated as 'English writing desks'.

We have surveyed the genesis and evolution of Rococo in France (Chapter 13), but Rococo did not really suit the English, as we have also noted. Nevertheless, there were several designers active in England between 1730 and 1765 who handled Rococo extremely well. Matthias Lock was the first to do so with real success, and to publish some of his designs afterwards (Pl. 367), and the furniture-maker John Linnell also managed the style delightfully. Thomas Chippendale, who is often thought of chiefly as a Rococo designer, performed that task unevenly, often marrying it – as did other English designers at the time – to motifs in the Chinese or Gothic styles (Pl. 371), both of which were rendered with much fantasy and scant attention to what

Pl. 367 A magnificent engraved composition for a cartouche by Matthias Lock, dated 1746 but probably drawn some years earlier. The design was reissued in 1768 by the well-known printseller Robert Sayer, showing that such Rococo patterns still had validity in London at that late date. The vase perched on the wildly swirling protuberance to the right, the vigour of which should surely have sent it spinning, is characteristic of the incongruous nature of much English Rococo, even at the hand of a master of the idiom. The Metropolitan Museum of Art, New York; The Elisha Whittelsey Collection, The Elisha Whittelsey Fund, 1953 (Mus. no. 53.638.45)

Chinese and Gothic ornaments were really like. But the results appealed greatly to people of the time, who had romantic ideas about the Far East and the Middle Ages, in roughly equal measure.

In a way Rococo ornament was used in England very much in the manner that Blondel, over in Paris, was

advocating for French interiors, namely by providing contrasting effects to soften a Classical room (see p. 156). Many English schemes of decoration that are essentially Classical in their Neo-Palladian guise have interspersed ornament that is dancing and light-hearted, thereby softening the sober forms of Antiquity. Indeed, it was as a relaxer of Classical rigidity that Rococo played an important part in Britain during the middle decades of the 18th century, enabling decorative artists to adopt flowing lines for much of what they created at this period (Pl. 365).

Most Chinese ornament of the period was a highly inaccurate rendering of real Chinese motifs (for which reason it is best to call it *chinoiserie*); but a book of patterns of real Chinese artefacts drawn in China by the young architect William Chambers and published in 1757 both in London and in Paris (while the British were at war with France) provided accurate information on the subject for the interested. It was not,

Pl. 368 A plate from Thomas Malton's treatise on perspective drawing, published in 1775 but clearly based on drawings executed at least a decade earlier, when he had run a cabinet business in the Strand. The open-backed chair at bottom right is of the mid-century Chippendale type. The upholstered arm-chair is of French form but English making. The organ is in the style of about 1760, as is the large bookcase above, which has a mixture of Classical and Gothic detailing.
By courtesy of the Trustees of Sir John Soane's Museum, London

however, until late in the century, when Chinese bamboo chairs were imitated on quite a large scale, that Chambers's work on China finally bore significant fruit in the decorative arts. Nor were original Gothic designs rendered with accuracy to any great extent, although Horace Walpole had important features of rooms in his villa at Twickenham, Strawberry Hill, created in the 1750s and 1760s more or less faithfully in the image of tombs, ceilings and screens at Westminster Abbey and at Canterbury and Rouen Cathedrals. Mostly, however, Gothic patterns of any great degree of elaboration tended to be a mixture of Gothic styles, often of widely differing dates. A large number of pattern-books for what were essentially playful Gothic and Chinese designs made their appearance in England during the middle decades of the century; Matthew Darly's *New Book of Chinese, Gothic and Modern Chairs* of 1751 is a good example of the genre ('modern' meant Rococo), and many of Jean

Pl. 370 A handsome carved mahogany pier-table made in Philadelphia about 1770. It shows how well the best makers in the chief East Coast cities could follow a London fashion – usually with emphasis on a certain feature (here, the exceptionally vigorous curve high up the leg), thus making the imitation subtly different from the original London model.
The Metropolitan Museum of Art, New York; Kennedy Fund, 1918 (Mus. no. 18.110.27)

Pl. 371 Design for a 'Chinese Sopha', published in the 1754 edition of Chippendale's *Director*. A typical Rococo sofa has here been provided with a canopy that has an amusing chinoiserie tester. Intended to furnish a lady's boudoir, the curtains could be lowered if she decided to take a siesta on this immensely fashionable and very expensive piece of furniture.
Victoria and Albert Museum, London

Pillement's lively chinoiserie designs were published in London in the 1750s (see p. 147).

If 18th-century English imitations of the Gothic style were a product of Romanticism, so also at first were those in the style of Ancient Greece; but, unlike the former, which only became a respectable subject for scholarly study in the 1840s, the latter was being studied with immense seriousness by a few people in England in the 1750s. The future architect James Stuart, later to be called 'Athenian' Stuart, together with his friend Nicholas Revett, had been studying the ancient monuments in Rome in the late 1740s. They issued *Proposals for publishing an Accurate Description of the Antiquities of Athens* in 1748 and managed thereby to persuade some rich Englishmen in Rome to finance a study-tour to that city, which they reached in 1751. They returned to England in 1755 with numerous drawings of ancient Athenian buildings and their decoration, many of which they worked up into a celebrated book on the subject, the first volume of which was published in 1762. By this time, of course, the drawings had been available in London for some years to those interested. Stuart was also of course well versed in Roman antiquities and, soon after his return to London, was therefore able to set himself up as the leading Neo-Classical pundit (see p. 162).

Stuart was made a member of the Society of Dilettanti, a London dining-club of rich young Englishmen whose chief qualification for membership was that they had travelled to Italy; nevertheless, many of them were genuinely interested in Classical studies. They sponsored the publication of Stuart and Revett's book, and several members gave Stuart commissions for decorating rooms in their own houses. By 1757 Stuart was designing furniture in a pioneering 'Neo-Classical' style, and a year later he erected a Doric (i.e. Grecian) temple in the park at Hagley. These were the very years during which Le Lorrain was designing furniture for La Live de Jully in Paris (see Pl. 326). Whether the two men met in Rome is not known but they could have done, as their stays in that city overlapped by a year or so. However, there could be many other reasons for their styles at this time having similarities.

Stuart was responsible for designing the first important integrated Neo-Classical ensemble in England, when he carried out decoration in the principal rooms at Spencer House in London, beginning in 1759. Lord Spencer was a Dilettante and the Society took a keen interest in the progress of the work, commenting and even, it seems, giving its sanction to schemes suggested by Stuart who, what is more, used quite a number of Greek motifs that he was about to publish in his celebrated work.

Nevertheless, the decoration Stuart executed at Spencer House was by no means all inspired by Greek models. At least as much is of Roman inspiration, culled from his own observations while in the city in the 1740s, and from the early published works of Piranesi (see p. 155) and earlier antiquaries such as Montfaucon (1719) and Desgodetz (1682). As for many others before and since, a major source of inspiration for Stuart's decoration at this time, however, were the *Logge* of Raphael at the Vatican (1515–19). As was pointed out in Chapter 14 (p. 162), Stuart's *rinceaux* patterns on the walls of

PI. 372 The back-plate of the movement of an elaborate astronomical and musical clock of about 1760, showing Rococo engraving with a Chinese pavilion amid scrollwork 'peopled' by exotic birds. Made by Henry Jenkins. *The British Museum, London*

PI. 373 Gothic is mixed with Rococo scrolls in this design of 1754 by John Linnell, an important furniture-maker who had great facility with the pencil. This is not one of his happiest compositions (he had here to encompass an awkwardly shaped fireplace-opening), but it makes the point well. *Canadian Centre for Architecture, Montreal/Collection Centre Canadien d'Architecture, Montréal*

the Painted Room at Spencer House derive directly from the *Logge* – more literally than many of the French derivations of this period. The French developed their own versions where each scrolling vine has a single stem (see PI. 342), whereas Stuart's have paired stems, as do Raphael's original paintings (PI. 374).

Stuart provided designers in Britain and elsewhere (his *Antiquities of Athens* was sold widely abroad) with a fresh stock of motifs, the most notable of which was the anthemion – a honeysuckle-like palmette within a frame that is roughly oval with a pointed top (see PI. 375, top). He also designed a Classical tripod that was executed in bronze, copies of which several members of the Society of Dilettanti commissioned and placed in prominent positions in their houses, almost as a sign of their membership. It was first made in the early 1760s by a celebrated bronze-founder named Anderson, who died in 1767. His moulds were probably acquired by the famous metalworking entrepreneur Matthew Boulton (see below, p. 185) who made further copies in the 1770s. Stuart was later to design silver for Boulton, and both Boulton and Wedgwood (two giants of British business acumen in industry at this time) deferred to him in matters of design.

However, by the mid-1760s Stuart was almost entirely overshadowed by the energetic and extremely ambitious young Scottish architect Robert Adam, who had established himself in London on his return from Rome in 1758. It was not until the early 1760s that Adam achieved undoubted success in his profession; but by then he had secured commissions from the Lords Harewood and Scarsdale, the Earl of Coventry and the Duke of Northumberland. After that his business flourished dramatically, until about 1780 when he in turn began to be eclipsed by James Wyatt who, however, worked very much in the later Adam style throughout his own career.

Adam set his stamp on the appearance of whole buildings, together with their interiors and their furnishings. He controlled the design of every feature although he tended to employ contractors who had worked with him before and on whom he could rely to produce results that would fit in with his overall schemes. In this he was most effective and his close attention to detail is made abundantly clear in the handsome publication, *The Works in Architecture of Robert and James Adam*, which came out in instalments from 1773, with a first volume of five appearing in 1778 and a second in 1779. It shows furnishings as well as whole buildings.

When in Rome in the 1750s, Robert Adam had engaged Clérisseau (see p. 162) as a teacher and later as a draughtsman. When Clérisseau came to England from Paris in the early 1770s he seems to have worked in Adam's drawing-office for a while. The cross-fertilization of ideas, patterns and ways of handling specific motifs that these and other presumed interactions betoken at this period must have been enormous.

PI. 374 A bay of the Painted Room at Spencer House, above dado level; designed by James 'Athenian' Stuart in 1759. He was responsible for the decoration and furnishing of the principal rooms on the *piano nobile*, some of which he couched in a Grecian manner. But the principal source of inspiration for the painted panels and pilasters shown here was Raphael's Vatican *Logge*. Indeed, the pilasters are an almost literal reference to these icons of Renaissance Classical ornament, even down to the paired vine-stems.

William Chambers was likewise a first-rate architect and his treatise 'on the Decorative Part' of architecture, which came out already in 1759, was of seminal importance in the rejuvenation of Classicism. It provided many new motifs that other designers could copy. Chambers also designed furniture and ornaments such as clocks and candelabra. In 1759 he designed a chair for the President of the Society of Arts, which has straight legs that are clearly based on a Classical form. The form

is very like that of the legs on a French writing-desk in the Wallace Collection (Pl. 329), which may have been designed by Charles De Wailly, who had become friendly with Chambers in Rome. Perhaps there was a link over the inception of these two pieces of furniture. Another excellent designer of furniture was John Linnell. He taught design at the St Martin's Lane Academy, the principal centre in London of propagation for the Rococo style in the second quarter of the century, but later learned also how to manage the Classical manner extremely well. Often, he cleverly combined the two styles in a particularly happy amalgam.

The most famous English furniture-designer of all time must, however, be Thomas Chippendale. His chair designs were especially influential, and were imitated throughout Europe and the American colonies (Pl. 382). The English openwork chair-back, so different from the standard mid-century French models, continued to develop in the hands of London chairmakers over the next fifty years. Their designs were summed up in a number of pattern-books. Those of Ince & Mayhew (1759–62), Robert Manwaring (1765 and 1766), George Hepplewhite (1788, which embodied the Adam taste in middle-class form) and Thomas Sheraton (1793 and 1802) trace the evolution admirably (Pls. 381 and 383).

Both in London and Paris, pattern-books of all kinds were published in parts, usually in gatherings of about six sheets (called *cahiers* in France), which could subsequently be bound together in single volumes. Quite a number of English books with illustrations of patterns also came out in French editions at this period (Chippendale's *Director* was one of them) or had parallel texts in French like Adam's *Works*. No doubt it was hoped that these French editions would find a market in France, but the main reason for producing versions in French was of course that the language was readily understood by all educated people at the time and could therefore reach out to such people throughout the western world. English pattern-books of all kinds were sold by print-sellers on the Continent and in America. Sometimes they were plagiarized by foreign publishers; a German version of Sheraton's *The Cabinet-Maker and Upholsterer's Drawing Book* of 1791–3 appeared in 1794 in Leipzig, and two editions of Thomas Shearer's *The Cabinet-Maker's London Book of Prices*, published in London in about 1788, came out in Philadelphia in 1794 and again in 1796 with a slightly different title (showing that it was evidently useful there). In the last quarter of the century, incidentally, Britain became the chief exporter of prints of a technical nature, having gained supremacy over Venice in this business. Indeed, a number of young Italians from the Veneto came to London in the late 1780s and went to work in the immigrant designer-publisher Bartolozzi's studio and no doubt others came and worked elsewhere.

Pl. 377 Part of the Drawing Room ceiling at Moor Park, Hertfordshire, with painted decoration (within an essentially Neo-Palladian framework) by Cipriani; about 1765. The architect was probably Leoni.

Pl. 378 An exceptionally fine English cabinet, in the Neo-Classical manner, of mahogany inlaid most skilfully with engraved brass 'grotesque' ornaments; 1760–70. This piece was probably designed by an architect, but Robert Adam seems unlikely to have been responsible. William Chambers seems a more likely candidate; he might well have had the assistance of an artist like Cipriani, or of one of the French architects who visited London in the 1760s – Bélanger or Gondoin, for instance, both of whom handled this kind of ornament well on their return to Paris, or, just possibly, Le Geay, who was in London in 1766 and was well acquainted with Chambers. *Courtesy of the Pelham Galleries, London*

The adoption of mahogany for the making of fashionable furniture in London became general in the 1730s, soon largely replacing walnut which had been in vogue for half a century or more. Because it was dense and strong, mahogany allowed furniture-makers to include slender members in their designs – for instance, for chair-backs (Pl. 381) and for the glazing-bars of glass-fronted cabinets (Pl. 368). Parisians adopted mahogany for furniture eagerly in the 1770s, an aspect of the *anglomanie* that swept through the French capital at that time, and had been receiving the occasional ship-

ment of mahogany furniture from England in the late 1760s. The robust character of much furniture made of this timber appealed not only to the British, as the splendid card-table shown in Pl. 386 illustrates. The clean lines of most English furniture of the later decades of the 18th century were often imitated abroad, not only in America but also on the Continent.

We now need to look briefly at glass and silver, and ceramics. The general introduction of lead oxide as a constituent of English glass (see p. 133) made the metal very heavy. When excise-duty was levied on English glass by weight, in 1745–6, it obviously became desirable to make glassware lighter, and this particularly affected the design of drinking-glasses. Bowls were made small, stems became more slender. Embellishment was increasingly provided by decoration applied after the glass itself was made – by gilding, enamelling and engraving. Later in the century (about 1760) the cutting of glass to produce multiple facets, particularly on the slender columnar stems, which by this time had become the commonest form, was introduced. Decoration could also be embedded inside such stems, and often took the form of spirals; one or more elongated and spiralling bubbles became popular, as did white spirals produced by including rods of white glass within the molten metal and, in both types, twisting them (Pl. 387). These two forms came in around in 1745 and

became something of an American speciality (an early example is shown in Pl. 388) and, once machinery was applied to the process early in the 19th century, it became the way glassware was generally made; this technique could be used for very complicated forms.

Silverware in England at this period followed closely the main developments in taste, and English Neo-Classical silver must be counted as one of the country's great achievements (Pl. 389). At least two major architects, Robert Adam and James Wyatt, provided designs for silver (Pl. 390), and the sculptor John Flaxman did the same for items in a Classical vein bearing distinguished figural ornament (Pl. 394). As elsewhere and at other periods, silverware set the patterns for other trades, notably, at this time, in the field of ceramics.

The production of large numbers of identical items leads easily to standardization in the manufacturing process, especially when it comes to measurements where two or more components have to be assembled. An early example of this was in the making of chairs that had seats and back-rests covered with Turkeywork, a knotted-pile fabric woven on a loom, produced in great quantity in Norwich during the last decades of the 17th century. The panels were woven to a standard size (they had a border) to fit the wooden chair-frames that

Pl. 379 Design for the painted chimney-board to go into the fireplace-opening in the Etruscan Dressing Room at Osterley Park. Dated 1777, it was published in Adam's *Works*.
By courtesy of the Trustees of Sir John Soane's Museum, London

Pl. 380 Design for the window-wall of a splendid room by Michelangelo Pergolese, dated 1784, showing the Adam manner continuing. Pergolesi was probably encouraged to come to England by Adam and decorated interiors for him including the Long Gallery at Syon Park in 1768. He made a speciality of composing 'grotesque' (arabesque) ornament and may well have helped Adam form his own style in this genre.
Victoria and Albert Museum, London (Mus. no. E 1617–1907)

1755, respectively. Faceted cut-glass stems were produced from about 1760. Although London was the main centre of production, Newcastle produced fine glass, much of it for export to the Continent, while Bristol and Stourbridge added their production to the considerable flow of glass coming from British glasshouses during this period. The West Country wares were no doubt shipped in great quantity to America. After 1780 much cut-glass was made in Ireland, where the making of moulded glass was also undertaken with success. The making of moulded glass, however,

were made elsewhere. Practices of this kind had become far more widespread by the second half of the 18th century; for example silversmiths could purchase standard forms like finials and feet cast in silver and then fit to their own products; much silverware of the middling sort was made in this way at this period, especially in London.

The production of 'Sheffield plate' was another important factor in the spread of British design at the time. Produced by fusing films of silver to both sides of copper sheet by a rolling process, this ware was at first

Pl. 381 Three chairs made in Philadelphia between 1785 and 1800 with backs in the style promulgated by Hepplewhite's pattern-book of 1788, of which fresh editions appeared in 1789 and 1794. Unlike fashionable London chairmakers, those working in the provinces tended to fit stretchers between the legs of their productions; only a chairmaker who was very sure of his capabilities risked making a chair without this strengthening. *Philadelphia Museum of Art (Mus. no. 27–10–2, 31–34–61 and 6–66–1); respectively given by Mrs Charles Wolcott Henry, the Bequest of Elizabeth Gilkson Purves in Memory of G. Colesbury Purves, and given by Miss Eliza Royal Finckel*

Pl. 382 A German chair imitating closely the Chippendale style. Elegant yet sturdy, this form soon spawned many imitations in Germany. Made for the Schloss at Wörlitz, near Dessau, some time after 1766; the architect F. W. von Erdmansdorff was responsible for this building and probably had a hand in this chair's appearance. *Private collection*

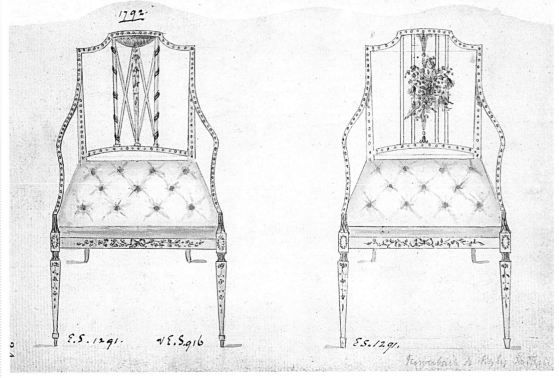

Pl. 383 Two chairs from a manuscript order-book kept in the office of the Lancaster firm of Gillows in the late 18th century. This page is dated 1792 and shows chairs in the style made familiar to a wide public by Thomas Sheraton's published patterns of 1793 (republished in 1794 and 1801). The Gillow versions shown here were of painted and varnished beechwood, and had buttoned loose squabs on their caned seats.
The Westminster City Archives, London

Pl. 384 An elegant London-made armchair in the French style; from the 1780s. A set of chairs from Heythrop Hall in the Wallace Collection are of closely similar design; they were made in Paris (perhaps by J. B. Tilliard) and gilded in England shortly before 1788. Until this period English upholstered chairs did not have a gap between the seat and the chair-back.
Victoria and Albert Museum, London (Mus. no. W.42–1946)

Pl. 385 Blue and white jasperware vase, impressed 'Wedgwood 1786', presented to the British Museum by Josiah Wedgwood himself in that year. The model was prepared for him by John Flaxman and is based on an original Greek vase in the Museum.
The British Museum, London

Pl. 386 A sturdy mahogany card-table of plain outline and pleasing proportions, made in the English taste in 1788 by the Quaker cabinetmaker David Evans, who was one of the leading citizens of Philadelphia. The gilt-brass handles were obtained from Birmingham.
Philadelphia Museum of Art (Mus. no. 50–2104–1)

Pl. 387 Characteristic English drinking glasses of the third quarter of the 18th century, with twist-decorated stems. In addition, their bowls are decorated with enamel painting, probably executed in the Beilby workshops at Newcastle. The small wine-glass is dated 1764; the larger pair date from about 1770.
Victoria and Albert Museum, London (Mus. nos C.21–1936 and C.626 and 627–1936)

Pl. 388 Covered bowl of pressed glass believed to have been made at the glasshouse of Henry William Stiegel at Mannheim, Pennsylvania, between 1772 and 1774. The American glasshouses were in the forefront of developments leading to the industrialization of glassmaking by pressing the metal into moulds. *The Corning Museum of Glass (Mus. no. 55.4.69)*

Pl. 389 Silver tureen made by the firm of Matthew Boulton and John Fothergill at Soho, outside Birmingham, bearing the new Birmingham assay-office's mark for the year 1776–7. James 'Athenian' Stuart sometimes supplied Boulton with designs for silver; the *rinceaux* pattern round the body is one that he favoured (see Pl. 374). *Courtesy of the Assay Office, Birmingham*

success derived to a large extent from constant experimentation with different metals and their alloys, and with the improvement of the tools that were required to work them. So important was this last factor that, certainly by 1785, it was forbidden to export from the area a whole range of specialized tools, and each firm guarded the secrets of its own processes most jealously.

Matthew Boulton and his family and partners informed themselves about everything that could affect the manufacturing of metal objects and their sale. Their notebooks are full of observations of technical and other matters relative to their purposes drawn from both foreign and British publications. They were always alert to the potential of new materials, such as ceramic cameos from Wedgwood's factory, *papier-mâché*, tortoiseshell and mother-of-pearl. When they did find a material that suited their business, such as Derbyshire feldspar (which

used for making small items, such as buttons. From about 1760, however, it began to be used extensively in the copying of models in silverware but at about a third of the cost. 'Sheffield plate' became highly popular wherever British goods were shipped and of course once again provided information about British metalware shapes and was widely copied.

One of the chief manufacturers of this ware was Matthew Boulton, who established a factory near Birmingham in 1762. A man of enormous energy, great imagination, skilful in business matters and indefatigable in his search to improve his trade's techniques, Boulton's career epitomizes the amazing success enjoyed by the metalworking trades in the so-called Black Country in and around Birmingham and Manchester, as they poured out millions of objects of great variety for consumption in every known country of the world. This

Pl. 390 Silver hot-water jug on stand equipped with a water-heater, designed by James Wyatt. It bears the mark of the London silversmith, John Robins, and the 1779 London hallmark. There is evidence, however, which suggests that this model was originally made by Boulton & Fothergill at Birmingham and sent by them to London for hallmarking before Birmingham had an assay-office for the hallmarking of silver of its own (see Pl. 389). Robins, who is best known for small wares, may at first have received such jugs from Boulton's for hallmarking and presumably continued to do so even after the Birmingham office had opened. *Courtesy of Messrs. Asprey Ltd, London*

Pl. 391 Creamware tureen enamelled with a blue border pattern and gold. Stamped 'Wedgwood and Bentley, Etruria'; about 1771. It is easy to see here why these elegant products were so popular, even in highly discriminating circles.
Victoria and Albert Museum, London (Mus. no. C.972A–1929)

Pl. 393 The Closet chimneypiece in the Egyptian manner at Thomas Hope's London residence in Duchess Street, as illustrated in his publication on the house of 1807.
Victoria and Albert Museum, London

Pl. 392 Silver tea-pot by Paul Revere, of Boston, Massachusetts, of 1789. Although Revere is famous for the part he played in the fight for American independence, he began to produce silver in the most fashionable English taste again as soon as the War of Independence was over.
Museum of Fine Arts, Boston; Bequest of Mrs Pauline Revere Thayer

they turned on a lathe and mounted with ormoulu to produce ornamental vases), they had to ensure that the source of supply was guaranteed and the quality remained consistent. Boulton was so aware of what was happening in his own field in France and Germany that, for instance, he arranged for some special plates used in the wire-drawing process to be smuggled out of France from Lyons; he also engaged several German and French workmen with special skills, notably in the field of gilding, after having received reports on their talents from people he trusted. He treated his workforce most carefully and at one point insisted that it had cost him 'no small trouble and expense' to assemble such a group of 'work folks as we have now in our Manufactory'.

Boulton's business was by no means confined to producing Sheffield plate, as must be evident from the above. He made inexpensive jewellery and 'toys' (small knick-knacks), as well as sword-hilts, snuff-boxes and shoe-buckles (of the latter he said that he wanted to supply 'all the great City's in Europe' with them). He also made silverware, once he had persuaded Parliament to establish a separate assay-office for the marking of silver at Birmingham (Pl. 389). Also for the luxury market, he produced ornaments of ormolu to go on the mantelshelf or some similar prominent position, and he provided lacquered panels of tinplate colour-printed to imitate marquetry, which cabinetmakers could apply directly to their wares instead of the real thing – apparently with some success. In order to keep abreast of fashion, Boulton also frequented the theatre in London and Birmingham, went to clubs and coffee-houses, attended parties and consulted retailers and generally talked to anyone who might be able to throw light on what new fad was coming next. His ambitions were unlimited and his success enormous. There were certainly other enterprising manufacturers in Birmingham and Manchester, but none have left their mark in quite the way Boulton has done. In his zeal he is often bracketed with Wedgwood – the man who said that he wanted to become 'Vase Maker-General to the Universe', and almost became it.

Pl. 394 A particularly graceful cup in the Grecian taste designed by Flaxman for Queen Charlotte. Made by Paul Storr in 1811–12.
The Royal Collection

Pl. 395 Armchair from Windsor Castle designed by James Wyatt about 1805, when he was carrying out extensive changes to the Castle in a Neo-Gothic style. The general shape of this chair is typical of late 18th-century English seat-furniture and here has a few superficial Gothic trimmings added.
Victoria and Albert Museum, London (Mus. no. W.151–1978)

Pl. 396 Silver-gilt cup made by a London goldsmith in 1806–7 to a design by Jean-Jacques Boileau which has broad bands of tooled mat surfaces separated by raised and cast ornament in the manner he had adopted from Jean-Guillaume Moitte (see Pl. 348).
The Arthur and Rosalinde Gilbert Silver Collection

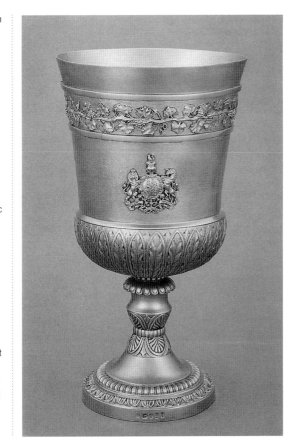

A building that had a profound influence on British taste in architecture and the decorative arts was Carlton House, London, residence of the Prince of Wales (later George IV). It was the work of Henry Holland, architect of many pleasing buildings that owed much to contemporary French inspiration. Carlton House was

Pl. 397 Fruit-stand made by Paul Storr, London, 1810–11, for the future Duke of Wellington. The body and its supports are in the Percier and Fontaine manner but the heavy cast ornament on the base is a fore-runner of the 1820s revival of interest in early 18th-century Baroque decoration.
Victoria and Albert Museum, London, displayed at Apsley House (Mus. no. WM.325–1948)

conceived in 1783 and largely finished by 1787. The interior of this important building was largely decorated by Frenchmen and furnished with a good deal of French furniture. The project was managed by Englishmen but several members of the immediate supporting cast, including Holland's assistant, were French. The result was that the interior was a fairly pure expression of grand Parisian taste of the 1780s. Sheraton (see p. 180) illustrated its Chinese Drawing Room in his *Cabinet-Maker and Upholsterer's Drawing Book* of 1793, and many of the patterns for furnishings that he published were in an anglicized version of 1780s Parisian taste, which drew heavily on what was to be seen in the Prince's splendid mansion. Sheraton's pattern-book was probably more influential than any other furniture book of the 18th century, reaching out across the whole of Europe and over to America, and leaving its mark on the work of furniture-makers in cities all over these territories.

Among the French artists who were employed at Carlton House in the 1780s were several exceptionally skilful decorative painters, familiar with the latest ideas for mural decoration including, of course, grotesque ornament and the painted imitation of wood, stone and bronze. The subtlety with which they achieved this was to bear fruit in Britain well into the 19th century. One of the most accomplished of these painters was Jean-Jacques Boileau, who went on to work for the Maecenas

Pl. 398 Cabinet by George Bullock of Liverpool and London, about 1817; of larchwood with panels of ebony inlaid with brass ornament and with fine brass mounts. Made for the Fourth Duke of Atholl.
Fitzwilliam Museum, University of Cambridge

William Beckford at Fonthill 'Abbey' in the late 1790s. He was also a designer of some talent and designed distinctive silverware (see Pl. 396).

The Prince of Wales ruled Great Britain as Regent from 1811 until 1820, when he became King but, in the Arts, the 'Regency Period' is usually reckoned to have begun in 1800 and we shall adopt this dating for our purposes. The Regency style to a large extent echoes that of the *Empire* taste in France. There was the same bombast in official and representational buildings and their decoration, but domestic Regency, as with domestic *Empire*, produced settings and furnishings of much charm. The decorative arts of the period as a result often display elegance of line and simplicity in ornament. To this Classical purity were often added naturalistically-rendered flowers in garlands, bands, sprays or skimpy festoons – a tendency that increased towards the 1820s (Pls. 396 and 401). At this late date that style also often acquired a blowsiness, even a coarseness, which had not been present earlier. However, as in France, the English late 18th-century manner in all the 'luxury arts' continued into the next period, but because English late 18th-century products tended to be more robust than their French counterparts, the loss in delicacy and exquisite finish of the highest class of such luxury wares in the Regency period is less obvious than in that of the contemporary *Empire*.

During the Regency, the Sheraton style, with all that it entailed, remained in great favour in Britain as well as abroad. Sheraton's first publication was followed by two more in 1803 and 1804–7 (the last uncompleted at his death in 1807). Staffordshire and Leeds creamware continued to pour out in great quantity from the potteries, as did a robust 'bone-china', equally well suited to middle-class consumption, leaving a certain amount of fine true porcelain for the rich to use. Glassware, carpeting, wallpaper, worsted upholstery materials, Sheffield plate, lighting appliances and much else also swelled the lists of products flooding the country and leaving it for abroad.

An important figure in the establishment of a rather severe form of Regency Classicism – the Grecian manner – was Thomas Hope, member of a rich Scots-Dutch banking dynasty. Between 1787 and 1795 he had travelled extensively in Greece, Sicily, Spain, Egypt, Turkey and Syria, as well as in mainland Italy. Already in the 1790s he was patronising Flaxman, whom he had met in Rome while the latter was on a study-tour partly financed by Josiah Wedgwood (see Pl. 385). In Rome he and Flaxman had both met Percier, the young Frenchman who was to become Napoleon's architect, and both Englishmen were greatly impressed by Percier's passion for Roman Classicism. Hope adopted a style based on that of Percier's illustrations to his *Recueil des decorations interieures* (see p. 168) for the decoration of his London house (Pl. 393) and, later, for his country villa, The Deepdene in Surrey. Hope had opened his London house to respectable visitors in 1804 as a lesson in taste and, in 1807, published his *Household Furniture and Interior Decoration Executed from Designs by Thomas Hope* (note here the reference to interior decoration that was also included in Percier's title) which embodied a markedly propagandist element in seeking to improve standards through educating artists and designers. A small illustrated work by Hope in which fashionable people are represented dressed in the Grecian manner, seen in rooms containing furnishings in his London house, appeared in 1812 with engravings by Henry Moses, who became an important disseminator of the Hope manner. He had engraved a book by Hope on Classical costume in 1809 and brought out an expanded version of the 1812 publication in 1823. He later worked for Schinkel in Berlin on the latter's influential book of patterns for decorative artists and manufacturers entitled *Vorbilder...*, the publication of which began in 1821 and lasted until 1837 (Pl. 403).

Hope acquired Sir William Hamilton's second collection of Greek vases (see p. 156); the first was already in the British Museum) and arranged them in several small rooms specially designed to receive them. He had also acquired some good Egyptian antiquities on his travels and we can see some of them displayed in a closet on a chimneypiece designed by him in an Egyptian manner (Pl. 393). Denon's celebrated work of 1802 on the monuments of Egypt (see p. 169), which was published both in England and France in the same year, was a primary source for Hope's Egyptian style and he

Pl. 399 Cabinet made for the Gratz family of Philadelphia in about 1810–20, probably by Joseph Barry, a cabinetmaker of that city who had emigrated from London and employed a number of European journeymen. He may have acquired the marquetry panels of brass and ebony on a visit that he paid to London in 1819. In any case the design is presumably influenced by the work of George Bullock, who had died the year before.
Philadelphia Museum of Art; Gift of Simon Gratz in memory of Caroline S. Gratz (Mus. no. 25–76–1)

will also have had the benefit of his own visits to many of the same sites to further fire his imagination. What is more, he will certainly have seen, when in Rome, the impressive Egyptian-style entrance to the Museo Pio-Clementino and Asprucci's work in the Egyptian manner at the Villa Borghese. The Egyptian taste spread quickly in Regency England, spurred on by Hope's publication and, in 1808, by the appearance of George Smith's *Designs for Household Furniture* which included Egyptian designs as well as Gothic, Chinese and, of course, Grecian.

By the first decade of the century the Gothic taste was beginning to appeal more widely in Britain. Here James Wyatt became a prime mover in the 1790s, during which time he was, amongst other things, restoring Salisbury Cathedral and building that vast Gothic folly, Fonthill Abbey, for William Beckford. Wyatt was also invited to carry out work at Windsor Castle for George III; a chair dating from this time is shown in Pl. 395. It will be seen that the Gothic element is here simply grafted on to what is essentially a Sheraton-type chair.

A masterly expression of the Grecian taste is the elegant silver cup made for Queen Charlotte by the notable London goldsmith Paul Storr in 1812–13, to the design of John Flaxman (Pl. 394), who was able to conjure up a Classical air even with products that had no precise Antique equivalent. Storr received most of the principal commissions for silverware at this period (see Pl. 397). He became one of the chief exponents of the early Baroque Revival, producing many fine pieces in a Neo-Louis XIV manner.

Mention should be made of Benjamin Latrobe, who had trained under the British architect S. P. Cockerell in the 1780s and worked on his own in London from 1790. In 1796 he emigrated to America, where he designed the elegant Bank of Pennsylvania in Philadelphia in the Grecian manner (1798–1801), no doubt with a certain amount of its furnishings. He certainly designed furniture for the Capitol in Washington and for the White House in the same city around 1809. His presence at the very centre of the American political scene presumably affected American taste considerably at this time.

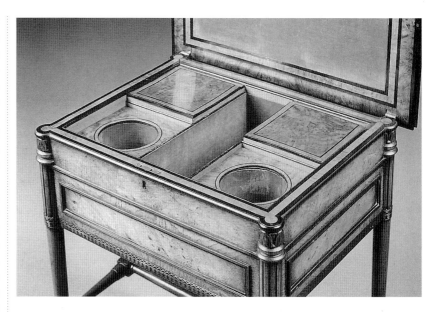

Pl. 400 The interior of a tea-poy exquisitely made of oak, partly ebonized, and inlaid with brass marquetry. Probably from a suite of furniture seemingly supplied by George Bullock in about 1815 for the use of the Portuguese ambassador to London.
Courtesy of Christie's Images, London

Pl. 401 Satinwood dressing-table of considerable distinction in the 'post Sheraton' style of about 1815–25. It has Sheffield-plate handles that cannot be later than the 1830s. The doors of the superstructure open to reveal three mirrors: a circular one in the middle and rectangular ones behind each door. The naturalistic flowers are of great delicacy.
Courtesy of Christie's Images, London

A rather heavier style comes in during the second decade of the century. This found expression in a most handsome manner in the workshops of George Bullock, who died in 1818. Established at first in Liverpool, he set up business in London around 1813 and became the leading innovative maker of furniture in Britain for the next five years (Pl. 398). He was a sculptor by trade and his furniture commonly has bold sculptural features, notably in the fine brass mounts. Bullock also made great use of marquetry both in woods and in brass, and sometimes sought inspiration from English flora for the leaf or plant patterns that he used. Bullock's wares were often illustrated in that informative fashion journal, *The Repository of the Arts*, which was brought out by the enterprising publisher from Leipzig, Rudolf Ackermann, between 1809 and 1828. In its heyday, the journal had a circulation of about 2,000 copies, many of which will have been handed round to reach a far wider readership. What would seem to be a piece of furniture

strongly influenced by the work of George Bullock is the Philadelphia-made cabinet shown in Pl. 399.

The last plate of this chapter (Pl. 402) shows the Golden Drawing Room at Carlton House in 1819, in the state it was in after the architect John Nash had contributed to its decoration after about 1814. The Classicism is now heavy and the furniture is massive. The frame of the huge mirror set at the back of the sofa-alcove is in the Neo-Rococo taste. We treat that manner in the next chapter.

Pl. 402 Illustration from Pyne's *Royal Residences* of 1819, showing a mirror-backed sofa-alcove in the Golden Drawing Room at Carlton House after the alterations carried out by John Nash from about 1814. Note the boulle-work marquetry tables of rosewood, tortoiseshell and ormoulu in a Neo-Louis XIV style, and the Neo-Rococo character of the mirror-frame.
By courtesy of the Trustees of Sir John Soane's Museum, London

CHAPTER 16

EUROPE

Pl. 403 Plate from *Vorbilder für Fabrikanten und Handwerker* [Patterns for manufacturers and artisans], of the kind that were distributed free of charge to public libraries, schools of drawing and artists of merit in Prussia in the 1820s and 1830s. This plate shows designs for cups and candlesticks; it was drawn by Schinkel and engraved by Henry Moses, who had worked for Thomas Hope in London and was among the several celebrated foreign draughtsmen and engravers who worked on the *Vorbilder* illustrations. *Kupferstichkabinett, Berlin (Mus. no. KK B. 2060. 1 b)*

Pl. 404 Upright secretaire of splendid design by Karl Friedrich Schinkel of 1826. The finely judged proportions set this elegant piece of furniture apart from thousands of others of the same general format. The veneers are also superb. *Schloss Charlottenhof, Potsdam*

In all the previous chapters we have focused on the role played by individual cities in the development of style in the decorative arts. For the period 1820 to 1870 we could certainly have concentrated separately on Paris and London because they are the two principal cities featuring in this part of our narrative. However, they now become so closely inter-linked that they can well be treated together. What is more, so many other cities in France and Britain contributed to the total production of decorative arts in these two countries – Limoges, Birmingham, Lille, Stoke on Trent, Châlons, Newcastle, Lyons and Edinburgh, for example – that it is no longer satisfactory to look solely at what was going on in the two capitals. In addition we now have to consider Germany, not yet a politically united nation, still a gathering of states, but each aware of its German-ness, and each with its own centre where innovative creations could make their appearance. So this last chapter is devoted to a survey of developments in our field of interest throughout Europe, but principally in France, Britain and Germany.

Another reason for treating the development of the handful of styles that swept across Europe during the first half of the century as a European phenomenon rather than national manifestations is that each country took up the successive styles at more or less the same

time, as we shall see. This was largely because so many of the principal characters involved travelled abroad in order to see for themselves what was going on among their neighbours. Indeed, the number of temporary displacements among leading artists and pundits during the last century is a phenomenon that strikes one continually as one studies the period. Some stayed for a short while, others actually worked abroad for a number of years – sometimes in order to gain experience, sometimes because their skills were so celebrated and highly valued that they had been invited to join the staff of a foreign firm as a designer, consultant or specialist in a certain technique. An important new reason for visiting each other's country was to see what was being shown at the trade fairs that proliferated throughout the century, where every effort was made by the parent nation to excel and show its products in the best possible light. What is more, a number of French artists, some of them of the first rank, went to England to avoid difficulties arising from the revolutions of 1830 and 1848, while the important German design-theoretician Gottfried Semper was forced to leave Dresden because he had taken part in the revolution of 1849 in Saxony. He fled to Paris and then moved on to London – to the enormous benefit of design education and practice in England. All this, coupled with the increasing number of pattern-books that were being produced – and now also journals devoted, or largely devoted, to matters of design – meant that those who wished to know were so much better informed about what was new than had been possible before.

Let us first turn our attention to Germany, which now begins to play an important role in our story. Germany was to become a unified state in 1871, its chief centre being Berlin, capital of the Prussian state that dominated the new political entity. The first important move towards union had been the establishment of customs unions which simplified the movement of goods and people across political frontiers; this was achieved between 1819 and 1831 and was organized chiefly by Prussia. That efficient nation had already established a first-rate educational system and had an army that was second to none in effectiveness. Prussia had been awarded additional territory by the Treaty of Vienna after Napoleon's final defeat in 1815 and was to annexe the rich states of Holstein and Schleswig by defeating the Danes in 1864. Its triumphant army then turned on Austria, which suffered humiliation in 1866, a traumatic experience that France was also to undergo four years later. At the Treaty of Versailles in 1871 the formation of the German Empire was proclaimed. All this could of course only have been achieved by Prussia and her neighbours having greatly improved internal communications within Germany (the whole of Europe was acquiring railway stystems by the middle of the century when, incidentally, the telegraph was also spreading its tentacles across the world); moreover, Prussia's fast-expanding industries were able to back her war-effort while at the same time producing goods for domestic consumption and a certain number of luxury goods for export as well – notably porcelain and glass.

It was a Prussian Treasury official, Peter Beuth, who in 1819 was appointed Director of a newly-founded royal committee of enquiry into the state of the decorative arts in that realm. In 1821 Beuth established the *Gewerbeverein*, an association for the promotion of the decorative arts. The *Verein* was no mere club for craftsmen; anyone interested in the decorative arts could join and many influential people were members including Baron von Stein, the statesman who had done so much to reform and liberalise the Prussian state, and Karl Freidrich Schinkel, a personal friend of Beuth's, who was the most important German architect of the first half of the 19th century (d. 1841). A technical high-school (college would be a more appropriate title in English) was founded in the same year and, by 1835, Beuth had set up twenty more colleges in other Prussian cities to promote good design in the decorative arts.

Coupled with the establishment of first-rate technical education, Beuth and Schinkel began to publish engravings of what they considered were good designs as exemplars for craftsmen to follow or adapt to their

purposes. At first, in 1821, these prints were issued (free of charge: the state paid) singly, but soon they were gathered into portfolios under the title *Vorbilder für Fabrikanten und Handwerker* (Patterns for manufacturers and craftsmen; see Pl. 403). It is interesting to note that in 1824 Beuth authorised the purchase of two printing-presses from Edinburgh and, from London, a machine for facilitating the engraving of large plates – because Britain at this period excelled in the production of industrial machinery – in order to improve the quality of the engravings in future issues of *Vorbilder* and, incidentally, Beuth immediately had a copy made of the engraving-machine so that two were soon available to increase production.

Beuth and Schinkel visited England in 1826 and stayed for three and a half months. They had visited Paris on the way, spending three weeks there, chiefly in order to see the recent installations in the Louvre in case that would provide helpful pointers about the design of museum buildings, as Schinkel had been commissioned to build a major museum in Berlin. Beuth had been in England several times before and was fascinated by its industrial development and manufactories. But so was Schinkel and, although he records in his sketchbook details of conventional buildings and views of cities, his main interest focused on industrial buildings and details of construction. The two men looked at bridges, gas-works, engineering workshops, spinning-mills, tunnels, dockyards and railway installations. They also paid careful attention to new industrial processes with a view to introducing some of them to factories in Prussia. Both men were energetic and effective (when Schinkel died in 1841, it was probably from over-work) and no doubt their visit to Britain was of fundamental importance to the reforming of industry and design in Prussia, although it is not easy to point to direct sources of inspiration.

The results of these ambitious efforts were demonstrated for all to see at an all-Germany Exhibition of Trade and Industry that was held in Berlin in 1844 (three years after Schinkel's death). There had been exhibitions at various places in Germany throughout the 1840s, echoing the French practice of holding exhibitions of her own industrial products, the first of which was mounted in Paris in 1819.

Schinkel's architectural work in Berlin was mostly in the Neo-Classical taste although his early preference was for the Gothic manner. But so gigantic was his stature as architect/designer that the dominant style throughout Germany until the middle of the century was Classicism in the Schinkel manner. Schinkel had studied architecture under David Gilly in Berlin at the end of the 18th century and began to be associated with his son, the talented Frederick Gilly, for whom he worked on the latter's return from a prolonged visit to England. Schinkel greatly admired Gilly's work and

Pl. 405 Viennese silver coffee percolator of 1821, made by J. Kern. An example of the extreme simplicity of form adopted in some Viennese workshops at this time.
Private collection

Pl. 406 Viennese bookbinding; about 1820? By Ferdinand Hofer. Although the corner-ornament is a hangover from the Rococo, the plain geometric pattern in the centre is of uncompromising plainness to the point of abstraction. Red leather with blind tooling, partly gilded. *Österreichisches Nationalbibliothek, Vienna [Cat. No. 263]*

Pl. 407 Bentwood armchair from the Thonet factory in Vienna – a model shown at the Great Exhibition in London in 1851. Stained beechwood elements were bent into shape while being steamed and held in position until cool and set. In the furniture field the development of forms suitable for manufacture by the thousands in this technique was by far the most important technical development of the 19th century. Thonet's chair-designs were in a sense a minimalistic abstraction of fashionable chair-design of the period. *Thonet factory, Bistritz, near Bratislava*

Biedermeier style, the German variant of late Neo-Classicism, the result was of unusual elegance (Pl. 404). Another pupil of Gilly's was Leo von Klenze, who in 1816 became Court Architect to the King of Bavaria, whose seat was at Munich. Von Klenze had also studied under Percier and Fontaine in Paris and was a highly competent architect and designer. In the early 1830s he composed fine mural decoration in the Munich Residenz, some of it based on wall decoration discovered at Pompeii, a model that Schinkel and many others also found suitable for their purposes from the 1790s onwards.

England and France had been at war with each other, on and off, since the Middle Ages but hostilities between them ended with the defeat of Napoleon in 1815 and they have been at peace since. Indeed they joined forces in 1854 and declared war on Russia in the so-called Crimean War, and have been on the same side during two World Wars in the present century. In what follows it will be seen that the cross-fertilization of ideas is a constant feature of the relation between the two countries.

With Napoleon gone, the French royal family and other *émigrés* could return to France and start to pick up the pieces left by the Imperial debâcle. The royal family moved into the palaces that Napoleon had vacated and gradually re-furnished and re-decorated them, at first in a late *Empire* manner. The exceptionally stylish bed in this style, made for the Duchesse de Berry, a lady of many talents including that of contriving delightful surroundings for herself, was delivered to her apartment in the Tuileries, Paris, in 1823–4 (Pl. 408). Although its form is plain and it thereby echoes the earlier *Empire* manner, it is richly decorated with subtle but elaborate marquetry all over its burr-elm surface, which is inlaid with ash. This dense ornament would have been more evident when the bed was new. Moreover, its severe outline would have been greatly softened by the intricate bed hangings with which it was originally surrounded. During the reigns of Louis XVIII (1815–24) and Charles X (1824–1836) light-coloured woods were much in favour for cabinet-work in France. The late *Empire* style soon became heavier and more loaded with ornament that was denser. This density of ornament combined with rather heavier forms becomes more obvious about 1830, as the richly draped curtains with their heavy rods and tie-backs shown in Pl. 412 demonstrate. A similar development took place in England and in Germany.

Three important pattern-books of ornament emphasizing the Classical tradition made their appearance in the 1830s and 1840s. A book on Classical ornament of all periods came out in Berlin between 1831 and 1843. It was by Wilhelm Zahn and was greatly admired by the leading London decorator Nicholas Morel. C. E. von Bötticher's book of ornament of 1834 also made its

took over Gilly's unfinished projects when the latter died prematurely in 1800. Schinkel, in his early days, designed furnishings in Gilly's manner, a rather heavy variant of Louis XVI. His manner became less heavy but even when he was designing everyday objects in the

appearance, as did the Frenchmen Clerget and Martal's universal encyclopedia of Antique ornament of about 1840. Moreover Beuth's *Vorbilder*, now bound as a volume, was also available by 1830, with an expanded edition making its appearance in 1837. Compendia that sought to be all-embracing were a new feature at this time. Durand's surveys had been among the very first (Pl. 358); hitherto assembled designs for specific classes of object had been the norm.

Right through the middle decades of the century, a taste for plain forms made an appearance here and there although this phenomenon does not square with our normal perception of this period. In the work of the potter Francois-Paul Utzschneider, who was working around 1840 and made elegant stoneware vessels of

Pl. 408 The Duchesse de Berry's bed, made in Paris by Félix Rémond for the refurbishment of her apartment in the Pavillon de Marsan at the Tuileries in 1824. Of a superb elm burrwood veneer, its looks rely on the elegance of its simple form, but it is in fact richly decorated with ashwood marquetry inlay, which must have been much lighter when new. Once installed in its alcove, the bed was further decorated with magnificent silk hangings from Lyons.
Mobilier National, Paris
(Inv. no. GME 6633)

uncompromisingly stark outline and most reticent decoration, his creations received high critical acclaim but the public wanted something altogether richer, and his business did not prosper. Altogether more successful was the Minton factory in England. The handsome jug shown in Pl. 410 is of 'Parian ware', a type of white porcelain with a rather granular finish much used by the firms Copeland, Wedgwood and Minton for small marble-like figures. It dates from 1852. Minton's was one of the foremost English potteries and had been habitually sensitive to the matter of good design, which made it famous and profitable. In 1849 they took on as Art Director a Frenchman named Léon Arnoux who was the son of a succesful French potter and had studied engineering in Paris. Presumably he had a hand in the designing of this plain but stylish vessel. Functional simplicity also often took a Classical form. Two distinguished examples of this may be seen at the Thorvaldsen Museum in Copenhagen (Pl. 409). These showcases were designed by M. G. Bindesbøll in the years 1845–7 and are handsome examples of this class of virtually unadorned furniture. They undoubtedly inspired Danish furniture-designers in the 1950s.

The *Empire* and Regency styles made frequent use of flowers, rendered naturalistically, as secondary decora-

tion in a Classical framework. Flowers become more of a feature in the second quarter of the century, and they spread all over carpets, wallpapers and textiles. The main style at this stage, however, was still a Classical one, although it was fast being overtaken by the Neo-Rococo style in which flowers and vegetal forms played an even more important part (Pls. 415, 417 and 419).

In later decades Classicism continued to survive as just one of a handful of styles to which a designer might turn when faced with a new project.

A curious late manifestation of the Classical style to which attention should be drawn is one that was called *Néo-Grec* by the French. It was apparently worked up at the École des Beaux-Arts in Paris as a style for the century. A characteristic example is shown in Pl. 411, which is from the celebrated Parisian metal-working establishment of Ferdinand Barbedienne. The basic forms are conventional but a seemingly perverse streak causes the designer to add some gawky detail, in this case 'handles' that reach out sideways with their stiff supports like something on an oil-rig. It is a somewhat Mannerist idiom. This piece was shown at the 1855 Universal Exhibition in Paris and again in London in 1862, when it was actually pin-pointed as 'a good example of that peculiar development of the Greek style which has distinguished the ornamental designs of France for the last few years, called Néo-Grec'. The style settled down in the 1860s to providing fairly conventional motifs with stiff metal or metal-like forms reminiscent of those which were favoured for a while in mid-16th-century Antwerp (see Chapter 5). The 'metalwork' often had 'engraved' surface-ornament of a hard, linear form based on the Classical palmette (Pl. 413); this form of decoration was taken up all over Europe, not least in Britain, and is still to be seen on the façades of endless terraces of 1870 and 1880s houses.

We must now return to the 1820s and mention a curious phase of late Neo-Classicism which principally affected Vienna. Classicism is based on rather simple geometrical forms adorned with relatively uncomplicated decoration. It takes skill to handle well and a fine sense of proportion is needed in designing both the chief members and their decoration; but its forms are essentially plain. A number of artefacts of an astonishing plainness were made in Vienna around 1820. They relied for their undoubted elegance on carefully designed forms, helped out with minimal ornament. The coffee-percolator of 1821 shown in Pl. 405 could well have stood on a Parisian breakfast-tray in 1930 without anyone thinking it was an antique. The book-cover illustrated in Pl. 406 must also be a manifestation of this minimalism. Several London bookbinders must have been aware of this development as they adopted for their own covers surprisingly similar geometrical patterns embodying a central diamond-shaped component. A group of German binders had settled in London at

Pl. 409 Showcases in Thorvaldsen's Museum, Copenhagen, designed by Michael Gottlob Bindesbøll between 1845 and 1847. As architect of that curious building, Egyptian outside and Pompeian within (see the ceiling, here), he designed the requisite cases and adopted a severely simple idiom that would detract minimally from the objects displayed within.
Thorvaldsen's Museum, Copenhagen

Pl. 410 A green Parian ware jug of Classical form, made by Minton & Co., acquired in 1852 (when new) by the South Kensington Museum. Minton's had a very high reputation for the design of their pottery.
Victoria and Albert Museum, London (successor of the South Kensington Museum) (Mus. no. 3858–1852)

the end of the 18th century and probably maintained links with their former compatriots. These minimalist exercises went far beyond the simplicity of Biedermeier artefacts in general.

Perhaps the most important expression of minimalism in the 19th century, one that was to have a profound effect on furniture design in our own century, is the range of bentwood furniture made by Michael Thonet of Vienna. A specimen shown at the Great International Exhibition held in London in 1851 is shown in Pl. 407. Made with members of beechwood, steamed and bent to the desired shape and then held in position in a jig until the shape had cooled and set, the ingenious assembling of such pre-formed members could produce a light but extremely robust and resilient structure. The form of the first characteristic Thonet chairs of about 1850 was based on the common mid-century balloon-back chair; the Thonet version followed that outline and braced it skilfully with secondary members attached with screws to the main frame, mostly tangentially. Although several chair-makers in Europe and America had experimented with bentwood, Thonet's spare forms of the 1850s and 1860s were unmistakable and enjoyed enormous commercial success as inexpensive chairs suitable for restaurants and village halls that

Pl. 411 Incense-burner by the firm of Barbedienne, highly succesful metalworkers who became fashionable in the 1850s. This piece, exhibited at the Paris Exhibition of 1855, and again in London in 1862, is in the *Néo-Grec* style, which may be distinguished by the presence of seemingly awkward excrescences (e.g. the handles on this otherwise conventional vase or bottle) or of what look like heavy metalwork objects like those above the door in Pl. 413. Much use is made of fan-like motifs, sometimes in the form of palmettes as here on the stand, between the feet, or in incised crow's-feet, like those on the tie-backs of the curtains in Pl. 413. *Néo-Grec* was a Mannerist form of Classicism, and was vaguely disturbing and uncouth.
Victoria and Albert Museum, London (Mus. no. 2707–1856)

Pl. 412 Design for 'continued' window curtains of 1830, from a collection of *Draperies* by a celebrated Parisian upholsterer, augmented by his successors Osmond and Dezon. Note the heavily gilded Classicized decoration of the pole and tie-backs.
The Samuel J. Dornsife Collection

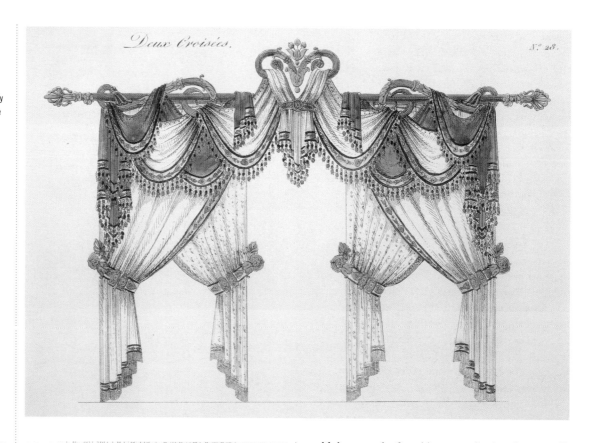

Pl. 413 Parisian upholsterer's design for a portière fronting paired doors, dressed in the *Néo-Grec* taste. Shown at the 1867 Paris Exhibition. The Mannerist character of this style is well demonstrated by this gawky composition, notably in the dagger-like tongues of the tie-backs and in the heavy yoke-like 'metal' bar at the top.
Victoria and Albert Museum, London. From Le Montieur de l'Ameublement, *Paris 1867 (Library press mark PP46D)*

could, however, be found in very polite interiors as well. The formula was the brilliant invention of a German who worked at Boppard on the Rhine. He showed prototype models at exhibitions at Koblenz in 1841 and at Mainz the next year. Prince Metternich was impressed by these early products and persuaded Thonet to move to Vienna, which he did in 1842. In Vienna he worked alongside one of the most prominent Viennese cabinet-makers, Carl Leistler, a man who was to win first prize for his furniture against all comers at the London Exhibition of 1851. Together they furnished the Palais Liechtenstein. In 1849 he set up his own factory. After expanding rapidly and introducing much new machinery, the Thonet establishment grew to become one of the great success-stories of the mid-19th century. By 1904 no less than seven other factories had been set up in various parts of the Austro-Hungarian empire, in places close to extensive beechwoods. Huge quantities of furniture made with this technique were exported all over the civilized world. Rival factories were built once Thonet's patent had expired in 1856. Nevertheless, by 1903 the firm had been able to run off no less than 45 million copies of a model first put on the market in 1859. That is no mean achievement by any standard.

A word should here be said about the mechanisation of industries like furniture-making in the 19th century. At first machines carried out, rather more quickly, work that had previously been done by hand. But the extent of mechanisation before 1870 was a good deal less than we often suppose. It was, moreover, a long time before machines that could carry out entirely new processes were introduced and little thought was given, before the end of the century, to taking advantage of machine-made materials in the design of furniture. Luxury goods of all classes continued on the whole to be made in the traditional manner, by hand, recourse being made to machinery only where repeated ornament was involved. So it is not true to say that it was the introduction of machinery that in itself led to so much poor design in the middle of the last century. Machines are neutral and the most that can be said is that the ease with which decorative features could be reproduced by machinery often resulted in the over-loading of arte-facts with ornament. That so much applied art of this period – 1820 to 1870 – is richly decorated stems, on the other hand, more from a reaction to what people felt was the bleakness of Neo-Classicism. It suggested poverty to people who, as a whole, were enjoying the highest standard of living that Mankind had ever known. Few saw any virtue in plainness. They revelled in richness of ornament and colour, and they ransacked the repertoire of motifs in every conceivable style (including Tahitian and Siberian) in order to decorate the wares that were pouring out of workshops and fac-tories in ever increasing numbers.

A word should also be said about the high quality of the best luxury products of the middle decades of the 19th century. The accomplishment during that period in terms of hand-craftsmanship of firms in London, Paris and the chief German cities that served a discrim-inating upper-class clientèle has never been equalled. A

PI. 414 Portière in the Louis Quatorze taste, although labelled 'Louis Quinze' in the pattern-book containing this imposing illustration, which came out in Paris in 1839. *The Samuel J. Dornsife Collection. From La Pinsonnière*, Recueil des Draperies

PI. 415 Chandelier in a Neo-Baroque style with luxuriant acanthus ornament, fitted with 'Sinumbra' oil-lamps. Made by Messrs Perry & Co. about 1830. *Victoria and Albert Museum, London (Mus. no. E. 2011–1952)*

cabinet in the Victoria and Albert Museum made by the Parisian firm of Fourdinous for the London Exhibition of 1867 is of an exquisiteness and a finesse that is quite amazing, and was carried through right into parts that the eye could not normally see. The finest products of the 18th century are often far more pleasing to 20th-century eyes, but when it comes to perfection of finish, such elegant wares could not match the best that the 19th century could produce. And this was not achieved with the aid of machinery; only with improved hand-working tools!

The most prolific of the many styles that came into favour during the second quarter of the century was that of the Neo-Rococo, usually called *Louis Quinze* or

Pl. 416 One of four pier-cupboards faced with boullework marquetry panels of brass and silver on red tortoiseshell, with ebony framing and gilt-bronze mounts. Ordered from Alexandre-Louis Bellangé, one of the best cabinetmakers in Paris, who specialized in this type of work, by the Duc d'Orléans for his dining room at the Tuileries in 1840. Heavy drapery, like that shown in Pl. 414, was supplied to complement these sumptuous objects.
Mobilier National, Paris (Inv. no. 13623/1)

Pl. 417 Drawing dated 1832 by David Roberts, RA, in pencil and watercolour, for an illustration to Bulwer Lytton's *The Pilgrims of the Rhine* (1834). The frame resembles the form taken by the backs of 'balloon back' chairs so typical of the mid 19th century.
Courtesy of Christie's Images, London

at the head of a nation that had defeated Napoleon, felt that the mantle of royal tradition had passed to them and that they must now uphold the image of courtly splendour, firmly in control of the nation and proud of its achievements not only on the battle-field but in world trade, banking and industry. An astute German prince, visiting England, actually stated that the nobility of that time was growing ever more like that of the time of Louis XIV. This élite employed two members of the Wyatt dynasty of architects, Benjamin Dean Wyatt and his cousin Sir Jeffrey Wyatville, to create palatial settings for their grandiose way of life, in the 1820s and early 1830s. Sometimes they used actual antique French panelling, and a good deal of the superb furniture placed at strategic points in their sumptuous new rooms was also old and French. The Wyatt manner was one of exceptional richness, with much use of gilding and the presence almost everywhere of dense foliate ornament (Pl. 415). In order to produce huge schemes of elaborate ornament on ceilings and walls, *papier-mâché* and a new form of composition were used increasingly; these were much less expensive than wood, but even then, such schemes were very costly.

In the meantime, Napoleonic France may very well have been defeated but, to the returning royal and aristocratic *émigrées* seeking to establish themselves once again in their native land, *their* France had not been defeated at all. Their monarchy had been restored and the royal places were once again filled with the sort of people who had been there before that regrettable Napoleonic episode. The new king, Louis XVIII, the former Comte de Provence, who had done so much for art in France before the Revolution (see Chapter 14), restored the chief palaces to something like their former glory as soon as he could. Amongst other things he retrieved pieces of Boulle furniture (see p. 156) from wherever they had ended up after the turmoil of revolution and war and placed them in the grand rooms at the Tuileries. Although England had not suffered a revolution and there had been no consequent displacement of furnishings, this in other respects is very much like what was being done in the English royal palaces; in both countries there was an impetus to produce new pieces of furniture of French late-Baroque form, decorated in the Boulle technique, a practice that was carried on right into the 1840s under Louis-Philippe (1830–48), the former Duc d'Orléans (Pl. 416). He was much interested in historical matters, as was his son Ferdinand-Philippe, the new Duc d'Orléans, whose apartments, like those of his sister the Princesse Marie, were particularly tastefully furnished. The Orléans family had long enjoyed a reputation for being discerning in matters of the Arts and Louis-Philippe maintained this tradition and had made sure that his children received first-rate tutoring in these matters. The fashionable painter Ary Scheffer was appointed to this task,

Louis XV. However, it often shaded imperceptibly into Neo-Baroque and especially the Baroque of Louis XIV's time, so we can treat it here as a single style. The dispersal of French works of art after the Revolution provided an opportunity for a few English collectors to acquire French 18th-century decorative art of the very highest quality. The wish to acquire and surround oneself with the art of Louis XIV and XV, and a way of life which had been swept away in France by its Revolution, was a notion shared by a handful of members of the upper aristocracy in England, led by King George IV – the erstwhile Prince of Wales, builder of Carlton House and the Marine Pavilion at Brighton. This narrow élite,

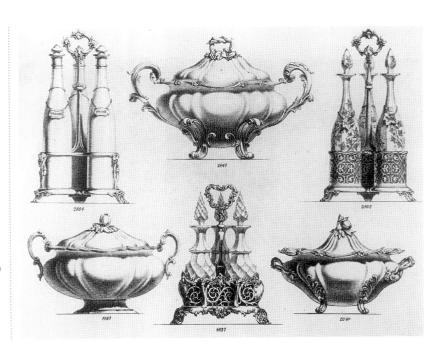

PI. 418 Page from a catalogue of Elkington's electroplated wares issued in Birmingham in 1847. The items are all basically in the Neo-Rococo style. It was in that year that the final technical difficulty in producing silverware by this process was overcome and this catalogue therefore represents a period of triumph for the firm, whose products quickly became celebrated.

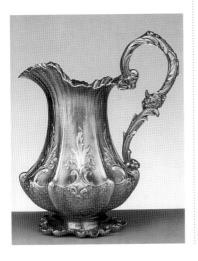

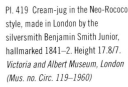

PI. 419 Cream-jug in the Neo-Rococo style, made in London by the silversmith Benjamin Smith Junior, hallmarked 1841–2. Height 17.8/7. *Victoria and Albert Museum, London (Mus. no. Circ. 119–1960)*

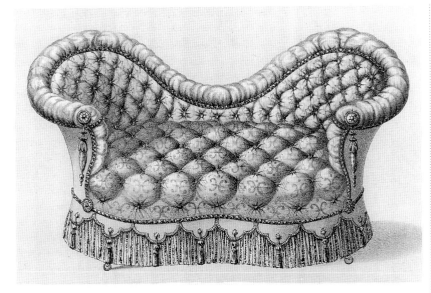

PI. 420 The epitome of comfortable mid-century seating is this brilliantly stuffed and buttoned Parisian sofa of 1864. It was published in a magazine which had the apt sub-title *Journal du Confort*, published by A. Sanguineti. The art of the upholsterer between 1845 and 1890 has never been surpassed in its finish and excellence – whatever may be thought of the aesthetic result. The form *has* to be called Neo-Rococo. Note the deep fringe with its lambrequin.
Victoria and Albert Museum, London. From Le Moniteur de l'Ameublement, *1864 (Library press mark PP46D)*

able, looked rich and was in the main perceived as a feminine taste suitable for drawing-rooms, boudoirs and other rooms that were regarded as the province of women. Women enjoying comfortable circumstances at this time were beginning to be seen more widely as the presiding genius of their own home, who provided a civilized haven within the rough and essentially male world outside. On the other hand, dining-rooms, halls and staircases were regarded as masculine spaces within the home, where a Classical style was more appropriate – or where a Renaissance manner would do very well instead, after the middle of the century. So Neo-Rococo was to be found smothering the general run of products from porcelain factories as well as much domestic silver (PI. 419) and a great deal of furniture – not to speak of carpeting and wallpapers. The frame shown in PI. 417 is the epitome of Neo-Rococo ornament.

The splendidly stuffed sofa shown in PI. 420 is essentially a Neo-Rococo creation and represents, in an extreme form, the type of upholstered seat-furniture that was popular right through to the 1880s – the style that enlightened reformers began to find so objectionable already in the late 1860s on account of its dust-collecting stuffiness and its association with airless rooms made suffocatingly dark by heavy window-drapery and a plethora of small tables covered with knick-knacks. However, handled deftly, it was a style that could have its charms.

The fruitful links between England and France at this period in the decorative arts are well exemplified by the Birmingham firm of Elkington, which had developed the technique of electro-plating, a galvanic process which the firm patented in 1840. It involved plating with silver objects made of a relatively inexpensive alloy. The result proved more durable than Sheffield

and one of the Duke's brothers was taught to draw by Eugène Lami, that painter of delightful scenes of social life among the Parisian upper classes in the 1830s and 1840s. Lami subsequently became an adviser to the royal family and designed a number of interiors in the royal palaces, which influenced taste considerably among the many people who saw these rooms.

The palatial style favoured by the royal courts in London and Paris was closer to that of Louis XIV than that of Louis XV but no clear-cut distinction was made between the two styles. However, it was the Neo-Rococo/Louis XV version that appealed especially to the middle classes and in consequence became the dominant international style among commercial manufacturers during the second quarter of the century. It was a style that entered most homes, because it was comfort-

Pl. 421 Armchair from Windsor Castle designed by the young Augustus Welby Pugin in 1827 when he was about 15 and was acting as draughtsman to the royal purveyors of furnishings, Messrs Morel & Seddon.
By courtesy of Messrs. Temple Williams, London

Pl. 422 Bookbinding in the *style cathédrale* by Joseph Thouvenin; Paris, about 1830. The brothers Thouvenin were among the first to adopt this kind of decoration, which won them a gold medal at the Paris Exhibition of 1823. The covers are printed from a single plate.
Courtesy of Sotheby's, London

Pl. 423 The Duchesse de Berry's Gothic casket of Sèvres porcelain set in gilt bronze mounts. Commissioned in October 1829 by this lively young princess of Italian origin who had a considerable influence on Parisian fashion at this time. Her ordering of this piece may have played an important part in shifting the production at Sèvres away from yet further repetitions of Neo-Classical forms into experimenting with something new. The design was by the factory's *ornemaniste* Charles-François Leloy.
Private collection

plate and was to revolutionize the production of acceptable imitations of silver-ware for middle-class use and was, incidentally, much used for producing items in the Neo-Rococo taste (Pl. 418). The possibilities of this process were speedily recognised by an astute Parisian goldsmith named Charles-Henri Christofle, who managed to buy, for 500,000 francs, the patent from Elkington in 1842. Two years later Christofle was awarded the gold medal at the Paris Exhibition for his work with the galvanic plating of objects with silver or gold. The French royal family were among his clientèle; Louis Philippe himself visited Christofle's works and made him a chevalier of the Legion d'Honneur. Although the firm suffered a set-back during the Revolution of 1848 which un-seated Louis-Philippe, Christofle was soon back on an even keel and the jury of the Paris Exhibition in 1849, in presenting him with another gold

medal, mentioned in their citation Christofle's workshop which, they said, was 'modelled on the finest establishments in England'. By 1858 he was employing between 1,200 and 1,300 people. As this incident shows, the French have always been better than the English at rewarding excellence in the field of design and at cosseting designers in all kinds of ways.

Neo-Classicism had run out of steam in the decorative arts by 1840 or so, but Classicism still made its appearance here and there right through to the end of the century, and there was a revival of the Louis XVI taste in the 1860s which took the place of the Neo-Baroque and Neo-Rococo (i.e. Louis XIV and XV) styles. Neo-Louis XV, essentially a middle-class taste, was at its height generally in France and England during the 1830s and 1840s, but had in turn begun to lose momentum by the early 1850s. Nevertheless, it was the principal European style on display at the great Exhibition of 1851 and remained popular with commercial manufacturers until about 1870. Among other styles on offer by 1830, the two most important were Gothic and Renaissance. Both were of course 'historic' styles so that, with Classical and Baroque and Rococo being available as well, it now becomes legitimate to speak of Historicism being the prevailing taste of the last two thirds of the century. If one adds exotic styles like Turkish, Indian, Chinese and Japanese to the list, it is proper to speak of the period as being Eclectic; indeed, individual objects were sometimes created with two styles combined. The Germans lumped the whole range of available styles under one title, *Historismus*, which is less of a mouthful than Historicism. But, whatever you call it, it was not derived from a single style but from all styles, not just of the past but from all parts of the world. No style was seen generally as being superior to the other although each had its protagonists. When, in 1836, a competition was held for the design of the New Palace of Westminster (the building comprising the House of Commons and the House of Lords, towered over by Big Ben), it was stipulated that the only styles permitted were Gothic or Elizabethan (i.e. the English Renaissance); architects who favoured the Classical manner objected fiercely because they felt that the latter was the only suitable style for a public building that was not a church. The cause of Classicism was dealt a serious blow when Gothic won the Westminster competition.

Historismus affected all the countries of Europe, and the United States of America as well. People in general felt proud that now artists and their clients could choose from the styles of every Nation and every Age, when faced with designing, making or buying an art object. But there were critics as well. A German commentator on the contemporary scene in 1863 summed up the situation neatly. 'The creative spirit does not make progress by constantly looking backwards', he said.

Pl. 424 Silver-gilt and enamelled casket presented by the Princess Hélène of Mecklenburg to her husband, the Duc d'Orléans, shortly after their marriage in 1837. Made by Fossin et Fils. This charming object may seem 'playful' but its Gothic is a great deal more plausible than that of most earlier exercises in that vein. The lady reclining on the lid may represent the Duchess herself. Height 165 cm (65 in.) Length 185 cm (72³/₄ in.)
Hessisches Landesmuseum, Darmstadt

What one borrowed from the past should invariably be blended with a contribution from one's own times, was the intelligent mid-century view. Merely making an exact copy was not the way forward, and 'progress' in this, as in all matters, was what people at the time admired above all else.

Let us now take a brief look at the use, between 1820 and 1870, of the Gothic style in the decorative arts. We saw something of English flirtation with the style in the middle of the 18th century (Pls. 368 and 373) and noted that a passionately serious if still rather dilettante anti-quarian approach to Gothic was adopted by Horace Walpole and his friends, which found an echo in Germany in the small *Gotische Haus* built for the Duke of Anhalt-Dessau at Wörlitz in the 1770s. A German encyclopedia of 1787 shows that whether one should erect a Gothic or a Grecian ruin in one's newly land-scaped 'English Park' was a very real question for princely Germans of a Romantic persuasion at the end of the century. It was not a dilemma that would have seemed strange to English noblemen faced with the same problem. Both anyway had a handful of pattern-books they could consult when it came to furnishing their ruins. Whichever style the princely German's ruin assumed, there were available by 1800 pattern-books of furnishings in the 'Antique or Gothic manner' pub-lished at Augsburg – in which the majority of the designs were in the Gothic taste. But it has to be remembered that Gothic at this time was still regarded throughout Europe as more of an alternative style and a contrast to Neo-Classicism than as an exercise in archaeology. It was also at this early stage a manner favoured largely by the aristocracy and landed gentry.

Pleasing furniture was made in this Romantic Gothic manner here and there in Germany from 1800, and rather more frequently in England, while the French took up the style slightly later, although a very smart study with fancily coloured Gothic panelling was made for a Parisian lady in 1801 by an architect named Coffinet; this was something of a false start, however. All three nations were, nevertheless, producing Gothic items in a Romantic vein by the 1820s (Pl. 422) and this continued into the 1830s (Pl. 424).

Books with illustrations of Gothic architecture and furnishings began to make their appearance in some quantity in the 1820s and 1830s. Auguste-Charles Pugin, a French refugee who had settled in England, attended the Royal Academy Schools in 1792 and even-tually worked as a draughtsman under the celebrated Regency architect John Nash. He specialised in the Gothic style and produced a publication on *Specimens of Gothic Architecture* in 1821–3. Ten years later he bought out a book on Gothic ornaments. Moreover, in the mid 1820s he had been invited by Rudolf Ackermann (an immigrant German publisher) to provide illustrations for his journal *The Repository of Arts* (see p. 191); these he published as a volume in 1827 and they proved immensely helpful to those wanting to make Romantic Gothic furniture and furnishings. The German archi-tect Carl Alexander von Heideloff, who is best known for having restored a number of important Medieval buildings in Germany during the 1830s, brought out a series of pattern-books between 1832 and 1837 contain-ing many designs for Neo-Gothic furniture. The jour-nal 'for Cabinet-makers and Upholsterers' published at Mainz by Wilhelm Kimbel must also have been a useful publication for Germans in the 1830s and 1840s, as pre-sumably also was the 'Magazine for Friends of Good Taste', which was first brought out in the early 1830s by a man named Wittich. Then there were Friedrich Wilhelm Merker's pattern-books of 1830–43 coming from Leipzig, which show how Biedermeier is replaced by Gothic increasingly from 1834. Heideloff knew a lot about Gothic but the other German publications, which all came out in parts over a period of years, contained only very fanciful designs in the Gothic taste.

Some rather more accurate representations of Gothic decoration and furnishings were beginning to appear in England at about this time. Earliest, but not particularly well known, are the works of L. N. Cottingham, whose *Ornamental Metal Worker's Directory* of 1823 records design in iron of the early 1820s and includes many Gothic patterns, as does his work of 1824 on Gothic Ornaments. Much more famous, and decidedly influen-tial abroad as well as in Britain, was Henry Shaw's

PI. 425 Walnut table of about 1855, after a design by A. W. N. Pugin, made (probably by Gillows) for the drawing-room at Uphill Manor, Weston-super-Mare, as a wedding present from Thomas Knyfton to his second wife upon their marriage. The first tables of this form, dating from 1847, are still in the House of Lords in the New Palace of Westminster. The revealed construction of its square underframe is characteristic of Pugin's style.
Courtesy of Messrs Jonathan Harris, London

PI. 426 Armchair of ebony designed by John Pollard Seddon, about 1865. Here you see a successful attempt to make a graceful form of Gothic, suitable for drawing-rooms (the front casters indicate that the chair was intended to be moved about, by lifting it at the back), in a reaction against the monolithic character of furniture in the Pugin manner. One of Seddon's later pupils was C. F. Voysey, who became an important designer in the 1880s and 1890s.
By courtesy of H. Blairman & Sons Ltd, London

Specimens of Ancient Furniture of 1836 which illustrated many items of Gothic and Elizabethan furniture and metalwork, some of which were copied in Asselineau's *Objets du Moyen Age et de la Renaissance*, published in Paris four years later. Complementing Shaw's book was Joseph Nash's *The Mansions of England in The Olden Times* of 1839–49, illustrated with highly evocative scenes of the interiors of such buildings that were a potent source of inspiration for the romantically minded.

The antiquarian Alexandre du Sommerard created a series of romantic Mediaeval interiors in the 1820s in his house in Paris, which was to become the Musée du Cluny, and his son published the collection in five splendid volumes between 1836 and 1846 under the title (in French) *The Arts of the Middle Ages*, which was extremely influential on the Continent, but less so in Britain where several similar collections already existed – notably Walter Scott's at Abbotsford (Roxburghshire) and Sir Samuel Rush Meyrick's in Wales.

By 1820, there was interest both in France and Germany in what the English were making of the Gothic style. Some chairs of a rather dotty Gothic form were made by Jacob-Desmalter (see p. 169) for the Comtesse d'Osmont's Gothic study in her house in Paris at some point between 1817 and 1820 which seem to reflect a knowledge of English Romantic Gothic furniture. The Osmont family had strong Anglo-Irish links (with the Ormonds) and a connection may well have existed at this level as well. Jacob Desmalter himself spent some while in England after having sold his celebrated Parisian furniture-making business to his son in 1825; he worked for a while on the re-decoration of Windsor Castle for George IV. No less an artist than Delacroix came to England in order to study romantic interiors at this time, and he was not the only French artist to do so.

Two French caskets in Gothic styles show rather well the contrast between playful Gothic and a late Romantic Gothic that shows signs of having been influenced by archaeology. Both were made for foreign princesses who married members of the French royal family and therefore resided in Paris. They both exerted influence on the course of French art by the manner in which they lived and had their apartments in the royal palaces furnished. The earlier casket of the two was produced in 1829 for the much-loved Duchesse de Berry, who was Italian (Pl. 423), while that produced eight years later was commissioned by a German princess as a wedding present for her husband the Duc d'Orléans, son of Louis-Philippe (Pl. 424). The earlier casket is a plain box of an essentially Classical form that has been heavily decorated on the surface with elaborate and light-hearted 'Gothic' scrollwork, and has a skyline that bristles with pinnacles, turrets and crockets (Pl. 423). The later casket is not only a delightful object but has well-integrated Gothic decoration that has a plausible ring about it even if specialists in real Gothic might find fault with some of the details (Pl. 424).

At this point we can introduce Auguste-Charles Pugin's son Augustus Welby Northmore Pugin. He had undoubtedly assisted his father with the 1827 publication of *Gothic Furniture* (already mentioned, p. 203) and, at the early age of fifteen, when he was working as a draughtsman for the royal cabinet-makers Morel & Seddon, was providing designs for Gothic furniture to be installed at Windsor Castle (1827; Pl. 421) of which

PI. 427 Drawing of a chimneypiece by Richard Bridgens for the Library at Aston Hall, a Jacobean house near Birmingham; dated 1819. This is an early manifestation of the Neo-Elizabethan style, although it is meant to look as if couched in the Jacobean manner of a decade or two after the end of Queen Elizabeth's reign. Bridgens later published many designs in this manner.
The Watt Family Archive, courtesy of Birmingham Museums and Art Gallery

PI. 428 Silver ewer and basin in the Renaissance style made by the Parisian goldsmiths Mention & Wagner in 1835. Carl Wagner reintroduced into Parisian goldsmithery the decoration of silver plate in the niello technique – in which the bold strapwork pattern on this basin is rendered – and was one of the first to produce work in the Neo-Renaissance manner. The figure forming the handle may have been modelled by the sculptor and antiquary Adolphe-Victor Geoffroy-Déchaume.
Private collection

he later insisted that he was somewhat less than proud. George IV, incidentally, had sent Nicholas Morel to Paris in 1826 to study Parisian fashions in preparation for the huge programme of work – with which the young Pugin was to assist him. Presumably Jacob Desmalter's presence at Windsor (see p. 169) had made the need for such a visit imperative. Pugin converted to Catholicism in 1835, by which time he was convinced that Gothic was the only acceptable Christian style, a point of view that he prosecuted with vigour until his death in 1852. Augustus Welby's book on *Gothic Furniture of the 15th Century* was published by Ackermann in 1835.

Three more books by him came out the next year, two on metalwork and one on timber construction. Through these works was established the vocabulary of Pugin's form of Gothic, which is usually referred to as 'Gothic Revival'. His were no dry copies of Mediaeval motifs; they were based on a profound knowledge of Medieval practice yet his version breathed a life of their own, in their own right. Pugin's work was influential on the Continent, notably in Germany. His style in the various decorative arts was to be seen gathered together by anyone who was able to visit London and take in the Great Exhibition of 1851. He designed the Mediaeval Court, generally thought to be one of the best features of the exhibition, where he had assembled many works of art which he personally had designed. It was a showcase of the Gothic Revival.

In the years 1838–48 Count Alois Arco, a Bavarian nobleman, converted the small castle of Anif near Salzburg into a summer residence and modelled it on

the new style then being put forward in England – a country that he visited several times during this period. He brought back a number of English publications from his visit and these undoubtedly included some of Pugin's recent works. It is anyway clear that Pugin's message was appreciated at Anif – as it also was at Stolzenfels, near Koblenz on the Rhine north of Cologne, where the Crown-Prince Friedrich Wilhelm of Prussia had built an entirely new edifice in the Gothic style, from 1836, which was to contain several strongly Puginesque items of furniture. The designs for Stolzenfels were vetted by Schinkel who was himself, as we noted, greatly fascinated by the Gothic taste (p. 194). Pugin's teaching was also heeded by a German designer working in Leipzig. Georg Gottlob Ungewitter had trained as an architect at Kassel and at Munich but practised at Hamburg and then at Leipzig. He was very much involved with intellectual circles in Germany and was in contact with the great French Medieval scholar, antiquarian and designer Eugène Viollet-le-Duc (see below). Ungewitter produced an elegant volume of designs for Gothic furniture in 1851 which show Pugin's influence with its emphasis on revealed construction; the book appeared in English translation in 1858. Between 1856 and 1861 he brought out a 'Gothic Pattern-book' which contained no less then 216 plates with illustrations of metalwork, stained glass, alphabets and so forth, all based on Medieval specimens.

Eugène Viollet-le-Duc was the son of the Keeper of the French royal residences under Louis-Philippe, and he had an apartment in the Tuileries. His career was dominated by the restoration of Gothic buildings, of which he became the most important practitioner. His chief claim on our attention lies in the fact that he was a most learned archaeologist and an energetic publisher of accurate information, especially about Medieval architecture and furnishing, which greatly increased the knowledge of Gothic structures and ornament. His dictionary of architecture in ten volumes, which appeared between 1858 and 1872, is an indispensable work for those working in the Gothic style; this was complemented by his dictionary on the decorative arts which came out (also in parts) at the same time. Like Schinkel, he was extremely interested in iron construction and in this respect he was a pioneer of Modernism. But his own Gothic designs lacked the robust quality one admires in the work of Pugin. His contribution, and it was enormous, was as a theoretician and archaeologist.

The so-called 'Gothic Revival' style, of which A. W. N. Pugin was the arch-priest, had a relatively short life; it ceased to produce anything very original after the late 1860s. The work of Charles Bevan and of Bruce Talbert, who published a book on Gothic forms applied to furniture in 1867, was fresh but after that Reformed Gothic became less rigorous as taste veered away from the severe forms of the 14th and early 15th centuries and moved towards the so-called Perpendicular Style of the late 15th and early 16th centuries. The new and lighter style of the 1860s was undoubtedly easier to live with in a domestic setting (Pl. 426).

A striking feature of much mid-century work in the decorative arts was its colourfulness, which was especially evident on works in the Gothic manner. Polychromy had a long history back to Percier and his pupils in Paris early in the century, but it was prevalent in the late 1850s and through into the early 1870s. Reformers like William Morris and Philip Webb were advocating strong colours for decorative art objects in the 1850s, and this was picked up by commercial manufacturers in the 1860s. The colourful nature of much work by that highly original artist, William Burges, derives partly from his study of the contents of Medieval church treasuries but also from French inspiration. In terms of colourfulness the French products were by and large even richer than those of this country, but they tended to be a good deal less robust in their polychrome lineaments.

Neo-Gothic has loomed large in the English imagination since Pugin's time, but by far the most important style in Europe from the 1840s to the 1880s was that of the Renaissance revival. This had a number of distinctive forms. There was Italian Renaissance of several periods, there was Northern Renaissance and French, there was a Mannerist variant and there was Renaissance Exoticism (moresques, etc., Pl. 433) The main point, however, is that the Renaissance taste in all its various forms was predominant in Europe during the middle fifty years of the century.

Once again the English started early. Neo-Renaissance sprang from much the same interest in our historical background as Gothic Revival; so it ought not to surprise us to find a sketch of an Elizabethan chimneypiece among the designs of Richard Bridgens which is dated 1819 (Pl. 427). Bridgens published a book of patterns of furnishings some time before 1833, now apparently lost, but an 1838 edition of which contained 27 Elizabethan examples, 25 Grecian and 7 Gothic. He had been associated with George Bullock, a cabinetmaker, sculptor and entrepreneur of Liverpool (see p. 191) who worked at Walter Scott's romantic house at Abbotsford as well as on the furnishing of an Elizabethan mansion in Birmingham; he died in 1818. A later example of the Elizabethan Renaissance style is a superbly colourful wallpaper in the Dining Room at Charlecote in Warwickshire (Pl. 429) which was supplied in 1837 by Thomas Willement, a designer and manufacturer who had drawn some of the plates in Henry Shaw's book on *Details of Elizabethan Architecture*, the first parts of which came out in 1834 (see p. 204).

In Paris a much richer form of Renaissance Revival was taking place around 1833–5. A huge stained-glass window was painted by the Sèvres porcelain factory

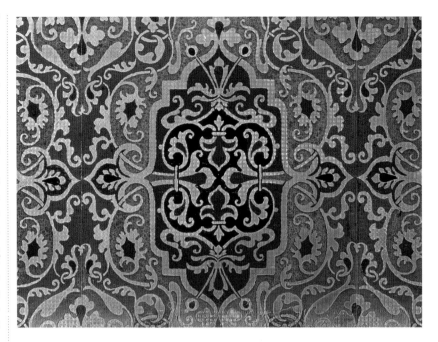

Pl. 429 Wallpaper in a Renaissance style in the dining room at Charlecote Park, Warwickshire, provided by Thomas Willement in 1837. It forms part of an integrated scheme of decoration in a new 'Elizabethan' wing added in the 1830s to this house, which has an association with Shakespeare. Willement was the presiding genius behind the interior work.
Country Life photograph

Pl. 430 French wallpaper of 1840–45 in the Northern or Netherlandish Renaissance manner (inspired by C. Floris or H. Vredeman de Vries). Manufactured by Riottot & Pacon.

(where a studio for glass-painting had been active for some years) that was to go into a window in the Pavillon d'Horloge at the Louvre, a central position in French public consciousness, if ever there was one. It was commissioned by the brilliant director of the factory, Alexandre Brongiart, in August 1832 and drawings had been provided by April 1833 by the extremely capable designer Aimé Chenavard. The design is in the then so-called 'Style Troubadour' but it was officially called a 'vitrail de la Renaissance', a Renaissance stained-glass panel. Chenavard was an enthusiastic exponent of the Renaissance manner and his two publications of the mid-1830s on interior decoration and on ornament helped spread the Renaissance style in France most effectively. He was also intimately involved with the production of the avant-garde art journal *L'Artiste,* in which he consciously set out to teach his pupils how to marry Art with Industry.

A young German jeweller who had learned his trade at Beuth's *Gewerbeschule* in Berlin came to Paris in 1829 and was soon established with his own business in association with the Parisian lapidary Augustin Mention. Carl Wagner quickly became famous for having introduced the revived technique of niello ornament, which he had learned in Berlin, a process with which his name was usually associated although he was immensely skilful in many other processes like enamelling and working with precious stones. He was one of the chief pioneers of the Renaissance Revival in Paris and the ewer and basin shown in Pl. 428 are evidence of this. For very special commissions he would often seek the help of a sculptor and it is possible that the female figure on the handle of the ewer was the product of such collaboration. A number of ewers and basins of this general kind

were made in one or other of the Renaissance styles right into the 1870s, chiefly for showing at one of the many exhibitions of that period. The bronze-caster and chaser Antoine Vechte worked for Wagner early in his career; after the Revolution of 1848 Vechte moved to London, where he in turn executed many remarkable exhibition pieces in the Renaissance manner. The name of Henri de Triqueti must also be mentioned in this context. A brilliant sculptor with a passionate interest in Italian Renaissance bronzes who had received no formal training in any academy but travelled all over Europe looking at as many specimens as he could, Triqueti was responsible for many monumental works including a magnificent bronze vase in the Italian High Renaissance style, made in 1844, a copy of which was apparently purchased by an English collector. Triqueti made several such vases; each took five months to produce. The

Pl. 431 An extremely well-made and compact lady's bureau in the Renaissance style, from the manufactory of Adam and Stephan Barth of Würzburg of 1851, shown at the Great Exhibition in London. Of walnut inlaid with ebony, rosewood, ivory, brass and copper, and with bronze mounts.
Germanisches Nationalmuseum, Nürnberg

Pl. 432 Cabinet in the Henri II style of the French Renaissance made by Alexandre-Georges Fourdinois, a prominent Parisian cabinetmaker, who exhibited it at the Paris Exhibition of 1855 where it was bought by the South Kensington Museum in London. The quality of the carving in relief (of several depths) impressed critics at the time. During the 1960s it served as office-furniture at the Victoria and Albert Museum (successor to the South Kensington Museum) and it was only in the 1970s that its significance was once again recognized; thus do tastes change!
Victoria and Albert Museum, London (Mus. no. 2692–1956)

great revival of bronze-casting and chasing at this period, notably in France, produced much fine work; it was by no means all on a monumental scale and many were the exquisite small decorative bronzes produced at this time.

Among the many artistic giants on the French scene, one had a particularly high reputation internationally – François Froment-Meurice, a virtuoso jeweller who developed a luxuriously rich and somewhat overloaded manner that won him many medals at important exhibitions of the time and the admiration of writers such as Balzac, Theophile Gautier and Victor Hugo. The peak of achievement in mounted hardstone is magnificently represented here by another Neo-Renaissance standing-cup, this time of 1855, by the celebrated maker Jean Morel (Pl. 438). It was made for the son of Thomas Hope, the Regency architect and connoisseur whose contribution to the decorative arts was noted in Chapter 15. This cup was designed by Louis Sévin, who collaborated with most of the great jeweller–goldsmiths of the time including Froment-Meurice. During the Revolution of 1848 Sévin and Morel moved to London and designed a number of pieces that Morel exhibited at the Great Exhibition of 1851. The presence in London of artists of this stature (and there were others, like Vechte who stayed until 1861) must have stimulated British designers and craftsmen in many ways.

Parisian cabinetmakers at this time explored the work of their 16th-century predecessors. At first they borrowed Renaissance features and applied them to pieces of furniture of a kind that had not existed in the 16th century, and moreover they tended to make them of woods that had not been available at that period either. Later, however, they learned how to make what looked very like pieces of that time. Pl. 432 is an example of this but the high quality of its workmanship makes it unmistakably a product of the mid-19th century and it is indeed by one of the very best cabinet-makers of all time, Alexandre-Georges Fourdinois.

A survey of Kimbel's furnishing magazine, published in Mainz, shows that Renaissance designs make their appearance in its pages in 1838–9. In 1839 a German critic of the cultural scene explained how one could swap styles at will. 'If one has tired of Grecian, one can take up the Renaissance style for a change, or one may occasionally switch to Byzantine, and then one can turn to Rococo. 'But,' he added, 'that way Art does not flourish: it goes under.' Germans, like every one else, were still experimenting with the wide choice that *Historismus* offered the designer. Everything suddenly seemed possible, in the 1840s, and it has to be said that many of the results of the freedom that this offered the designer were monstrous.

The French seem always to have taken more seriously the matter of training designers than have the English, at least until the beginning of the present century. This

PL. 433 Book-cover printed from a single plate with moresque ornament in the early 16th-century Venetian manner (see Pl. 51) on a book of Bible stories edited by Henry Cole, working under the *nom-de-plume* Felix Summerly. London, 1844. *Victoria and Albert Museum, London (Library press mark 60 x 126, Forster Bequest)*

PL. 434 Binding on an 1845 edition of Mozart's *The Magic Flute*, printed from a single plate by the Hanoverian Court Binder, Johann Jakob Selenka. A highly eclectic design of formal character with geometrical Gothic elements, and Classicized foliage amid compartments that owe much to the Baroque, it is actually typical of a whole range of 1840s patterns that are difficult to label. *Private collection*

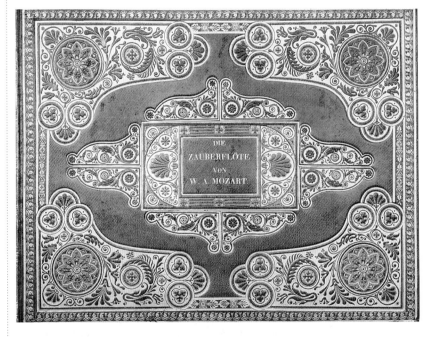

has paid France heavy dividends and, even if French design was not in every case better than that of other nations, the English generally felt that their own efforts were inferior. Back in 1814, John Stafford, a leading upholsterer in Bath, published a book of designs 'for Interior Decorations' which carried a lengthy preface in which he alluded to the superiority of French taste and bemoaned the lack of design education in his own country. It became widely felt in England that something now really had to be done. There was soon also a powerful political reason for trying to improve design in

Britain: the severe economic crisis of the late 1830s and early 1840s which hit industry badly and threatened Britain with the loss of her share of world markets. Enlightened people in England had been aware of the need to establish schools for designers since the middle of the 18th century but effective steps were only really taken in 1837 when a Government School of Design was set up in London. In the meantime, of course, the efficient and well-organized Prussian network of technical colleges (*Gewerbeschule*) was fully established and producing first-rate designers (like Carl Wagner who, we saw, became a leading jeweller in Paris) and it has perhaps not been fully stressed before what a strong influence the German example had on design-education in England during the 1840s and 1850s. Albert, who became Queen Victoria's consort in 1840, was a Prince of Saxe-Coburg and Gotha, and took a keen interest in art-education. He appointed a German artist, Ludwig Gruner, as his artistic adviser. Gruner eventually produced an ambitious and handsomely produced compendium of *Specimens of Ornamental Art* (1850) which had been commissioned by the Government School of Design. That institution had for a while been run by William Dyce (1838–43), who had been sent by the School, in 1837, to visit schools of design in Prussia, Bavaria, Saxony and France and report on what he found. Prince Albert's personal taste favoured the Renaissance style which became that of the establishment and of the School of Design in the 1840s.

A close friend of the Prince's was Henry Cole, who for a while adopted the *nom de plume* of Felix Summerly. Cole was interested in antiquarian matters and designed items including a book-cover decorated with moresques (Pl. 433), like those being used in Venice early in the 16th century (see Chapter 3; note the Renaissance connection again). Cole was later involved, working closely with the Prince, in the preparations for the Great Exhibition of 1851. What made that exhibition of 1851 different from its many predecessors in France and Germany was that it was to be open to all nations and, in spite of many initial set-backs, it was a triumphant success: it made a profit and vast numbers of people came to see it – many of them from abroad.

Unfortunately, what became apparent was the poverty of European design in 1851. Some years later the great German pundit Jakob von Falke actually wrote that, at this epoque-making exhibition, 'there, before the eyes of everyone who could or wanted to see, our wretchedness lay exposed'. The French came out of it rather better than others but the gold medal for a piece of furniture was won by Carl Leistler, the chief cabinet-maker in Vienna – for a magnificent bed in the Renaissance manner, be it noted. England, however, came out of it badly (one strange exception is shown in Pl. 435) although many people were greatly impressed by the building in which the exhibition was housed, the so-called Crystal Palace, because it was made entirely of glass mounted on a steel framework like a huge greenhouse. It was designed by the Duke of Devonshire's former head gardener, Joseph Paxton, who became an architect.

But the message went home in Britain, and enormous efforts were thereafter made to improve British design. As has so often happened, there is nothing like a severe set-back to make the English pull themselves together and the next London Exhibition, that of 1862, demonstrated this in an unmistakable manner, and the excellence of many new British products was recognized widely. It was truly a case of national rejuvenation, as British designers became more professional, although once again it has to be admitted that a number of foreigners helped the process forward very considerably.

The most important of these was Gottfried Semper from Dresden, who was in England between 1850 and 1855. He was engaged by Cole to teach at the School of Design and became friendly with Prince Albert. Like the Prince, he was a strong proponent of the Renaissance manner. He was the most distinguished foreign designer in England at the time and was much concerned with the problems posed by industrialism in the field of design, as a result of which he wrote a book on style – *Der Stil*, which appeared in 1860–63. Semper reinforced the view that slavish copying of historical models should never be the aim; on the contrary, he insisted that while 'old tree-trunks carry the life-force and the nourishment that make the creation of something new possible', it needs to be recognized that 'only new input enables one to produce something new'.

Another German pundit, writing at the end of the century, insisted that it was not until the middle of the century that a style was developed that was truly 'of our Times', and *that* style 'bore the stamp of the Renaissance but was not an apeing of that style'. An excellent early example of a German designer achieving this aim is shown in Pl. 431. Of very different character, but nevertheless serving to show how well good designers after 1851 managed to create high-class works of decorative art in the spirit of the Renaissance that yet had something fresh about them, are the objects shown in Pls. 432 and 438.

Europe's designers did not all want to be confined to working in the Renaissance styles, however, even though there were several of these. They wanted to know about all styles of ornament and their needs were handsomely satisfied by two important works – Owen Jones's *Grammar of Ornament* and Albert-Charles-Auguste Racinet's *L'Ornement Polychrome*. Both were in colour. Owen Jones's work, first published in 1856, was a repertoire of international importance that also appeared in both French and German editions and was reprinted many times. A novel feature of his selection of patterns was the liberal inclusion of designs from exotic cultures

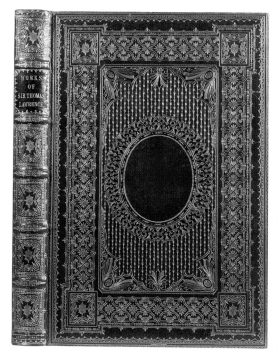

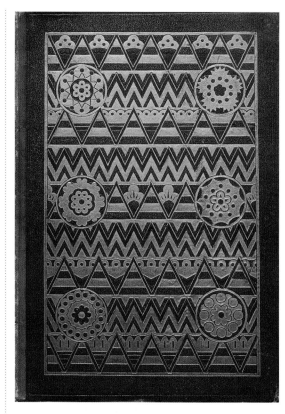

Pl. 435 English mid-century bookbinding at its most elaborate and made for the Great Exhibition of 1851, where it was remarked upon for its excellence. It speaks highly of the state of bookbinding at this time that a little-known binder, A. Tarrant of Holborn, could produce such fine work – but workmanship in many crafts had never reached such high standards as it did in respectable workshops in the middle decades of the last century, in all the great cities of Europe.
J. Paul Getty, KBE, Worsley Library

Pl. 436 Cover of W. Eden Nesfield's *Specimens of Mediaeval Architecture*, London, 1862, an archaeological pattern-book for architects. This was a special cover, the striking pattern of which relies entirely on geometric forms in several colours.
Courtesy of Haslam & Whiteway Ltd, London

Pl. 437 Design for an ecclesiastical book-cover with ornamental metalwork and, presumably, inset gems on the border and clasps. The design of 1865 comes from Messrs Hart and Son, London, manufacturers of ecclesiastical metalwork who worked for such designers as J. P. Seddon and William Burges. Its geometrical motifs have a Mediaeval air but there is a hint of *Néo-Grec* as well.
Victoria and Albert Museum, London (Mus. no. 4597)

which a great many people suddenly found to be immensely attractive. Racinet's no less important book was in a sense a complement to Jones's in that the author took care not to duplicate what Jones had published; it came out in 1869 and again in 1885–87, greatly enlarged. It had fine chromolithographic illustrations. Such colourful assemblages of patterns were a novelty of the mid-19th century.

Owen Jones maintained that 'all ornament should be based on geometrical construction' and it is not surprising, in a century that had witnessed such amazing achievements in industry and engineering, and had enshrined its best mid-century products in a 'crystal palace' of glass and steel, that a liking for mechanistic forms should have made its appearance. Some scholars, indeed, have pointed out that there is an unmistakable geometric ingredient in much design in the decorative arts of the period. Justification for such an assertion is rather neatly provided by four bookbindings (Pls. 434–7). It would be an exaggeration to call what they demonstrate a separate style because these manifestations of geometrical form are far too disparate. But geometrical and mechanical features are found here and there in all the styles we have been considering in the present chapter – not least, surprisingly, in Neo-Gothic. The vaguely Neo-Baroque cover on a book printed in Hanover in 1845 (Pl. 434) embodies plain circles around its formal yet scrolling vegetation. The severe lines of the cover of 1865 shown in Pl. 437 incorporates features of the kind used by the engineer even though its antecedents lie in the Middle Ages. And there can be no mistaking the geometrical character of the binding on a copy of Eden Nesfield's book of 1863 (Pl. 437). But a

style that depends greatly on geometrical forms, and strange linear quirkinesses like those on the 1851 cover illustrated in Pl. 436, was that late flowering of Classicism, *Néo-Grec* (see Pls. 411 and 413), a style that came to the fore in the 1860s.

Other more important developments took place in the 1860s, however, with the arrival on the scene of William Morris and his associates, but they were really the advance-guard responsible for even more important developments after 1870 which have been well charted by others, notably by Nikolaus Pevsner. They can now take over as I bring my story to an end.

INDEX